Legal and Ethical Retributivism

A Restorative Analysis

Halil Cesur

Routledge
Taylor & Francis Group
LONDON AND NEW YORK

First published 2026
by Routledge
4 Park Square, Milton Park, Abingdon, Oxon OX14 4RN

and by Routledge
605 Third Avenue, New York, NY 10158

Routledge is an imprint of the Taylor & Francis Group, an informa business

British Library Cataloguing-in-Publication Data
A catalogue record for this book is available from the British Library

Library of Congress Cataloging-in-Publication Data
Names: Cesur, Halil author
Title: Legal and ethical retributivism: a restorative analysis / Halil Cesur.
Description: Abingdon, Oxon [UK]; New York, NY: Routledge, 2025. |
Series: Routledge research in legal philosophy |
Includes bibliographical references and index.
Identifiers: LCCN 2025008006 | ISBN 9781032914060 hardback |
ISBN 9781032914107 paperback | ISBN 9781003563150 ebook
Subjects: LCSH: Lex talionis | Punishment–Philosophy |
Retribution | Legal ethics
Classification: LCC K5103 .C47 2025 |
DDC 364.601–dc23/eng/20250306
LC record available at https://lccn.loc.gov/2025008006

ISBN: 978-1-032-91406-0 (hbk)
ISBN: 978-1-032-91410-7 (pbk)
ISBN: 978-1-003-56315-0 (ebk)

DOI: 10.4324/9781003563150

Typeset in Galliard
by Deanta Global Publishing Services, Chennai, India

Legal and Ethical Retributivism

This book explores a foundational philosophical tension in contemporary retributivism, revealing ambiguities in its approach to punishment between two conflicting conceptions of restoration: legal justice and ethical love. Through an analysis of the three parties involved in a crime – the victim, the offender and the state – it argues that neo-retributivism has not sufficiently incorporated the ethical face of punishment into its theoretical framework. The pull of legal justice is often so strong that the voice of ethical love is silenced; neo-retributivism is at an impasse. To navigate this, the book engages with contemporary critical criminal justice scholarship, introducing the ideal of loving justice while highlighting an unresolved tension between penal reformism and abolitionism.

The book will be of interest to academicians and researchers working in the areas of philosophy of punishment, criminal law theory, criminal justice, restorative justice, philosophy of law, political philosophy and Hegel scholarship.

Halil Cesur, Assistant Professor, Istanbul Medeniyet University, Istanbul, Turkey.

Routledge Research in Legal Philosophy

Cosmopolitanism, State Sovereignty and International Law and Politics
A Theory
Jorge E. Núñez

Human Dignity, Judicial Reasoning, and the Law
Comparative Perspectives on a Key Constitutional Concept
Edited by Brett G. Scharffs, Andrea Pin, and Dmytro Vovk

Act and Omission in Criminal Law
Autonomy, Morality and Applications to Euthanasia
Roni Rosenberg

Metaethical Issues in Contemporary Legal Philosophy
A Constitutivist Approach
Edited by Stefano Bertea and Jorge Silva Sampaio

Purely Formal Legal Theory
Deontic Networks
Ottavio Quirico

Judges, Decision Making and Empathy
Insights from the Bench
Mateusz Stępień and Ewa Wilczek-Rużyczka

The Illegality Defence in Law
A Constitutional and Human Rights Perspective
Edit Deutch

Legal and Ethical Retributivism
A Restorative Analysis
Halil Cesur

For more information about this series, please visit:
https://www.routledge.com/Routledge-Research-in-Legal-Philosophy/book-series/RRLP

Contents

Acknowledgements

As I drafted these lines, a dark thought crossed my mind – that expressions of gratitude might at times be less about humility and more about bolstering a book's credibility. For a moment, I briefly toyed with the idea of omitting an acknowledgement section altogether, believing that silence might carry a certain integrity of its own. But I quickly abandoned the thought, reminding myself that recognising kindness is a virtue in itself. And so, I now offer what is indispensable to the author but, perhaps, rather tiresome for the reader: my list of acknowledgements.

First and foremost, I express my deepest gratitude to my supervisors, Alan Norrie and Henrique Carvalho, who have always been by my side with their invaluable guidance during and after my PhD. I found my way under their intellectual shelter. I also thank my friends Rıdvan Türk, Hüseyin Varol and Hakan Dönmez for their endless patience in enduring the raw thoughts that burst forth from my mind. I am grateful to Stephen Connelly, Laura Lammasniemi, John Snape, Andrew Botterell, Scott Veitch and David Hayes for taking the time to read some parts of this book and providing helpful comments. Thanks, too, to my colleagues Brihan, James and Paula, as well as Mike Hill and Mike Harvey, for their friendship, helpful conversations and support. I am also grateful to Vahdet İşsevenler, Haşim Özpolat, Abdulkadir Çadak, Erdem Kurtoğlu and Enes Kara for sharing their thoughts on some parts of this book. I am indebted to my PhD jury members, Nicola Lacey and Amanda Wilson, who meticulously reviewed my work, provided excellent feedback and encouraged its publication as a book. Finally, I extend my sincere thanks to the two reviewers at Routledge, whose interventions helped make this book clearer and stronger.

This book was made possible by the full scholarship granted by the Republic of Türkiye Ministry of National Education.

Introduction

1. Setting out the problem: a snapshot of current debates

Retributivism is a theory of punishment around which a voluminous literature has accumulated since the classical works of Kant and Hegel. It has transformed, particularly for the last five decades, from its traditional traits to a more nuanced and comprehensive, neo-classical set of theories.[1] During what has been a period of significant revival, retributive theory has taken many guises, moving beyond the ideas of desert, payback and moral debt towards more intricate principles involving legal vindication, reform and mutual recognition.[2] The result is a debate both within and outside the retributive camp, especially around the question of how it should be understood and framed in light of its underlying features and values. Here there is substantial divergence around the common core.

While some think that retributivism is basically a theory based upon the principle that we punish offenders just because they deserve it,[3] others view it as a more complex and multifaceted theory that can also embrace the ideas of reform, restoration and reconciliation.[4] Yet others seek to place it squarely within the scope of political theory, with a complaint that punishment is

1 Herbert Morris, 'Persons and punishment' (1968) 52 (4) *The Monist* 475; Jeffrie G Murphy, *Retribution, Justice, and Therapy: Essays in the Philosophy of Law* (Springer Science & Business Media 1979); Jean Hampton, 'A new theory of retribution' in CW Morris, RG Frey and G Postema (eds), *Liability and Responsibility: Essays in Law and Morals* (Cambridge University Press 1991) pp.377–414; Andrew Von Hirsch, *Censure and Sanctions* (Oxford University Press 2003); Antony Duff, *Punishment, Communication, and Community* (Oxford University Press 2001).

2 Martin R Gardner, 'The renaissance of retribution-An examination of doing justice' (1976) *Wisconsin Law Review* 781pp 781–815; Matt Matravers, 'Is Twenty-first century punishment post-desert?' in Michael Tonry (ed), *Retributivism Has a Past Has it a Future* (Oxford University Press2011) pp.30–45.

3 Michael S Moore, *Placing Blame: A Theory of the Criminal Law* (Oxford University Press 2010).

4 Jean Hampton, 'Correcting harms versus righting wrongs: The goal of retribution' (1992) 39 *UCLA Law Review* 1659–1702; Antony Duff, 'Restoration and retribution' in Julian V Roberts Andreas von Hirsch, Anthony E Bottoms, Kent Roach and Mara Schiff (eds), *Restorative*

DOI: 10.4324/9781003563150-1

over-moralised in recent decades.[5] Against this, it is argued that political theory does not have to be the essential part of an overall moral framework, emphasising that the justification of punishment is at bottom a moral question.[6] There are also many other versions of retributivism that have complicated an already crowded field.[7] Thus, with constantly changing forms, retributivism exhibits itself as a complex penal theory that cannot easily be encapsulated in a few themes.

Nevertheless, there seem to be two notable emerging threads in recent penal literature in relation to neo-classical (revised) retributivism. These push the theory, which is essentially a moral and political hybrid, in its two different, component, directions. The first is what is called the 'political turn', in which the analogy between interpersonal moral blame and penal justice is rejected in favour of a political or public account of punishment.[8] This is a theoretical move, seeking to replace the moral conception of law and retribution, which has dominated the criminal law field for about five decades. The second is the ongoing debate around whether retributivism is in compliance with restorative justice in terms of providing reform, reparation and reconciliation. A particular focus seems to be on the question of whether legal punishment is inherently punitive.[9] This is a move which pushes the ethical implications of retributive theory.

The 'political turn' approach takes punishment primarily as an exercise of public authority, stressing that any normative enquiry about punishment should start with the question of the legitimacy of state coercion. In cases of public wrongdoing, what matters is the state's reaffirmation of a civil order or free collective life, in which human beings live together as equal agents. Punishment in this sense should, therefore, be placed and developed within a

Justice and Criminal Justice: Competing or Reconcilable Paradigms (Bloomsbury Publishing 2003) pp.43–60.

5 George P. Fletcher, 'Political theory and criminal law' (2006) 25/1 *Criminal Justice Ethics* 18; Alan Brudner, *Punishment and Freedom* (Oxford University Press 2009); Vincent Chiao, *Criminal Law in the Age of the Administrative State* (Oxford University Press 2018); Malcolm Thorburn, 'Punishment and public authority' in Magnus Ulväng and Petter Asp Antje du Bois-Pedain (eds), *Criminal Law and the Authority of the State* (Hart Publishing2017); Guyora Binder, 'Punishment theory: Moral or political?' (2002) 5 *Buffalo Criminal Law Review* 321.

6 Moore, *Placing Blame: A Theory of the Criminal Law*.

7 Mitchell N. Berman, 'Two kinds of retributivism' (2010) University of Texas Law, Public Law Research Paper No. 171. http://dx.doi.org/10.2139/ssrn.1592546; David Hayes, *Confronting Penal Excess: Retribution and the Politics of Penal Minimalism* (Bloomsbury Publishing, 2019); D. Husak, 'Holistic retributivism' (2000) 88 *California Law Review* 991.

8 Christoph Burchard, Vincent Chiao, Rocío Lorca and Javier Wilenmann (eds), *The Political Turn in Criminal Law Scholarship* (Hart 2024).

9 Gerry Johnstone, *Restorative Justice Ideas, Values, Debates* (Routledge 2013); A von Hirsch, JV Roberts, AE Bottoms, K Roach and M Schiff (eds), *Restorative Justice and Criminal Justice: Competing or Reconcilable Paradigms* (Bloomsbury Publishing 2003); J. Armstrong, 'Rethinking the restorative–retributive dichotomy: Is reconciliation possible?' (3 July 2014) 17(3) *Contemporary Justice Review* 362–374.

political framework in which a certain kind of order is constituted and sustained. Much of the literature in this field rejects retributivism on the ground that it does not capture the essence of punishment as a political institution.[10]

A related and yet independent approach, which broadly parallels the political conception of punishment, proposes to view state sanction as a form of 'public quarantine'.[11] Taking its starting point from Derk Pereboom's famous free will scepticism, this model of punishment maintains that offenders are not morally responsible for their actions in the basic desert sense.[12] Yet we can justify punishment by appealing to the right to self-protection and the prevention of harm to others. On this approach, we should identify and take action on the social determinants of crime and prioritise prevention and social justice in a way that reintegrates offenders back into society.[13]

In this book, I share the thought that the realms of criminal justice and social justice should be brought closer together. However, I raise serious questions about the readily accepted division between moral and political accounts of punishment, as I think the divide between the two positions has been created with some sort of distortion and caricature of the moral account. For one thing, the moral account does not view political theory as being detached from punishment. By contrast, for moral retributivists, such as Duff, the sort of moral retributivism they advocate is precisely designed 'to sustain the polity's civil order by dealing suitably with wrongs that violate or threaten that order'.[14] Likewise, Moore claims that retributivism is a legal theory of justice that creates 'an obligation to set up institutions'.[15] For him, why and how the state ought to be responsible for punishing its citizens is a necessary question to be answered 'in terms of a complete justification of a retributive theory of punishment'.[16] In turn, as construed by its own proponents, moral retributivism connects with political theories of punishment.

On the other hand, the division between the two positions is more porous than may be perceived, especially when both are understood in light of the idea of 'political morality'. While the moralistic account presents the moral

10 Peter Ramsay, 'The responsible subject as citizen: Criminal law, democracy and the welfare state' (2006) 69(1) *The Modern Law Review* 29–58; V Chiao, 'What is the Criminal Law for?' (2016) 35(2) *Law and Philosophy* 137–163; Thorburn, 'Punishment and public authority'.

11 GD Caruso, *Rejecting Retributivism: Free Will, Punishment, and Criminal Justice* (Cambridge University Press, 2021)

12 D Pereboom, *Free Will Scepticism and Criminal Punishment The Future of Punishment* (Oxford University Press 2013); D Pereboom, *Wrongdoing and the Moral Emotions* (Oxford University Press 2021).

13 Caruso, *Rejecting Retributivism: Free Will, Punishment, and Criminal Justice*

14 R Antony Duff, 'Criminal law and the constitution of civil order' (2020) 70 *University of Toronto Law Journal* 4–26.

15 Michael S Moore, 'The moral worth of retribution' in Ferdinand Schoeman (ed), *Responsibility, Character, and the Emotions: New Essays in Moral Psychology* (Cambridge University Press 1987) pp.179–219.

16 Moore, 'The moral worth of retribution' p.216.

dimension of punishment in formal and political terms, the political account constructs punishment's public face in moral terms. 'Desert' in the moralistic account, for example, is relevant to punishment only insofar as it concerns wrongs that are legally prohibited by the political authority and applied in accordance with the conditions of both criminal culpability and legal protocols of sentencing. Similarly, the principles of morality in the political account pose constraints on what a political authority can rightfully do, and they provide essentially moral conditions for excusing or limiting punishment. Understood this way, I argue that they are both a kind of political morality. Certainly, the emphasis on political theory in the moral account cannot be seen as strong as in the political account. Nonetheless, the difference between the two is a matter of degree rather than of kind. Both defend a version of ***politically moralist*** retributivism, which associates state punishment with justice despite their different normative emphasises. If I am right, and if the political turn has not done away with the need to think ethically about the justification of punishment, this brings us to the second main thread which involves the claim that retributive theory is insufficiently ethical in its approach.

The second thread in relation to the debates around retributivism is concerned with the connection between restoration and punishment. For those who take punishment as aiming at healing and reconciliation, the idea of retribution has much in parallel with the fundamental tenets of restorative justice.[17] Such proponents argue that, unlike the common way of seeing it (namely, meeting pain with the infliction of further pain), retributivism can provide a mode of punishment that repairs the harms done to the relationships wrought by criminal violation.[18] In their view, retributive punishment is not a simple suffering but rather a peculiar type of suffering that involves the burden of making moral reparation for what has been done.[19] One may consider the imposition of penal suffering as just and fair, but this is not to mean that we should aim to make offenders suffer just for suffering's own sake. Rather, the suffering retributive punishment includes should be of a meaningful sort. That meaning is restoration, reconciliation and healing.[20]

Some proponents of this view characterise punishment as a form of apology, followed by a moral obligation made by offenders to repair harm and make

17 Hampton, 'Correcting harms versus righting wrongs: The goal of retribution'; Stephen P Garvey, 'Restorative justice, punishment, and atonement' (2003) 1 *Utah Law Review* 303; Antony Duff, 'Retrieving retributivism' in Mark D White (ed), *Retributivism: Essays on Theory and Policy* (Oxford University Press 2011) pp.3–24; Christopher Bennett, *The Apology Ritual: A Philosophical Theory of Punishment* (Cambridge University Press 2008)

18 Duff, *Punishment, Communication, and Community* p.30.

19 Garvey, 'Restorative Justice, Punishment, and Atonement' p.316.

20 Antony Duff, 'Responsibility, restoration and retribution' in Michael Tonry (ed), *Retributivism Has a Past: Has it a Future?* (Oxford University Press 2011) p.63–85.

attempts for reconciliation.[21] Others present it in a less morally loaded fashion, by regarding it as a hard treatment that is oriented towards the restoration of rights infringed or threatened by criminal violation.[22] Some define punishment as a form of ***punitive restoration***,[23] while others consider it as a species of ***non-punitive retribution***.[24] Accordingly, there is somehow a great deal of theoretical ambiguity surrounding the notions of retribution and restoration. Despite the conceptual vagueness, however, what is clear within this camp of retributivism is that retributive punishment can be understood as running in conformity with restoration.

In response to what might be called a 'progressive' conception of retributive punishment, there has been resistance that state sanctions cannot be seen as restorative of relationships. On this view, retributivism justifies a punitive status quo that fails to meet the needs of those affected by crime and has nothing to with the idea of restoration.[25] I do not deny the idea that retributivism fails to provide a substantial form of restoration for those who are involved in crime. But I aim to challenge the criticism that retributivism lacks a restorative dimension. Retributivism can indeed be restorative, but the central issue is the nature of the restoration it brings about.

2. Between legal and ethical retributivism: a theoretical impasse

In this regard, I identify two kinds of restoration within retributive thinking. If we are to understand what lies at the core of retributive theory, these two restorative forms need to be brought out in detail: the legal and the ethical.

'Legal restoration' is provided by a legalist approach to retributivism which addresses normative harm, the sort of harm that disrupts the formal mode and patterns of life governed by law. On this view, punishment does not simply inflict deserved suffering on offenders but also restores damaged formal relationships within a political society and reaffirms the authority of the state as a sovereign organisation of power. In other words, punishment in this form is concerned with upholding legitimate public order that is infringed by crime. Drawing on the idea of 'legal justice', I will expound the legalist approach by reference to Hegel's well-known theory of punishment, where at stake is the vindication of free citizenship, the rule of law and the normative regime of rights: 'legal retributivism'.

21 See for example: Bennett, *The Apology Ritual: A Philosophical Theory of Punishment*; Duff, *Punishment, Communication, and Community*.
22 See: Morris, 'Persons and Punishment'.
23 Thom Brooks, 'Punitive restoration and restorative justice' (2017) 36 *Criminal Justice Ethics* 122.
24 Hampton, 'Correcting harms versus righting wrongs: The goal of retribution' p.1685.
25 See for example: M Wright, 'Is it time to question the concept of punishment?' in L Walgrave (ed), *Repositioning Restorative Justice* (Willan 2012) 3–23.

In legal retributivism, the commitment to justice as a value keeping the equilibrium in the world drives one to see punishment as morally good or politically justified, in concert with what is taken to be the core of the retributive view. Crime breaks the balance in the world; punishment restabilises it. It does so by righting the wrongful conduct. Behind this formulation lies the premise that society is naturally balanced – that there is a status quo which is essentially something we wish to maintain, preserve or restore. Retributivism in this form is often explained by the ideas of desert, payback or any other principle that identifies a correspondence between crime and punishment. What underpins its ethos is the precept that justice requires punishment in cases of law violations. It provides an orthodox model of penal justice that extends from Kant and Hegel to contemporary retributivist scholars.

By direct contrast to the legalistic paradigm, there is also what I call 'ethical restoration'. Ethical restoration is provided by a moral-relational approach to retributivism which addresses ethical harm, the sort of harm that damages the intersubjective bonds of shared social life governed by love and solidarity. Punishment in this sense is produced from bottom to top, restoring the ethico-social union within which human beings relate to each other. It creates a retributive kind of suffering for offenders, which originates from an internal – psychological – source through the moral operation of offenders' conscience and which urges them to remake the world they share with others. The aim of punishment, or better, of retributive suffering here is to identify the injuries offenders create alongside the prior injuries that cause crime to arise and then to produce a 'healing' intervention for all stakeholders. I will explain this model of punishment by reference to the idea of 'loving ethics' and call it 'ethical retributivism'.

In this approach, I seek to investigate a moral realm where punishment means more than merely imposing upon someone a deserved deprivation at a politico-legal level. Moving beyond the logic of law that is largely shaped by the idea of desert and formal justice, punishment from this approach is more about whether or how perpetrators undertake suffering after having changed their moral standing in relation to others when they wrong their fellow beings. According to ethical retributivism, a painful moral experience befalls the offender, and so punishment still holds a retributive character. But this sort of retribution is understood within the moral world of the offender as the rightful 'boomerang' effect of behaviour that damages the relationship between them and others. Ethical punishment, in other words, is not the punitive sanction of a legal authority that exacts justice. Instead, it is a moral and psychological form of suffering that is triggered by a broken relationship and seeks to modify the offender.

This conception of punishment is intersubjective, having mainly to do with how criminal violation sets in motion the painful process of how the offender sees themselves and how they relate that self to the world. It is an ethical experience marked by moral disintegration and self-destruction in the face of crime. Punishment, from this approach, is the moral suffering caused by a loss of unity with the world. It is the deprivation of a compact unified world, composed of an interconnected web of structure in which one's life is intimately intertwined with the lives of others. I take the sense of deprivation felt by the offender as a sort of grief at their separation from others. Once undertaken, unlike its legalistic form, punishment in this form moves the offender to repair and reconstruct the relationships that have been injured by criminal violation. It may or may not be followed by forgiveness, but it sets the scene for a substantial form of reconciliation between the offender and their fellow beings. In Chapter 3, I will develop this conception of punishment by reference to Hegel's early writings.

The question is then whether these two kinds of restoration are achievable within retributive thinking. Put it differently, it is worth exploring whether retributivism can have both 'legal' and 'ethical' faces.[26] This is the central question of this book that I will be engaging from beginning to end, in particular in the context of recent neo-classical retributive theories. Addressing this question, I will first make a diagnosis: neo-classical retributivism has not sufficiently incorporated the ethical face of punishment into its theoretical framework. The pull of legal retributivism is often so strong that the voice of ethical retributivism is silenced. There is, therefore, a theoretical impasse in these theories, an impasse created by the conflict between the legalist and ethical approaches or between what I call 'loving ethics' and 'legal justice'.

My diagnosis will focus on Jeffrie Murphy's intellectual biography, illustrating his unique position as a philosopher who embodies the core ideals of neo-classical retributivism while attempting to reconcile his commitment to legal justice with a notion of loving ethics. Early in his career, Murphy argues that retributivism is the only theory of punishment that genuinely respects rational agency and autonomy, though he notes its lack of attention to socio-political constraints that limit individual choice and freedom. In fact, his recognition of retributivism's flaws and fractures reflects, in a way distinct from my own approach to his theory of punishment, an implicit acknowledgement of an impasse. He describes retributivism as 'a theory built on tension – tension between justice and utility, tension between ideal states and actual states, tension between righteousness and humility'.[27] In Chapter 1, I will explore what I call 'Murphy's ambivalence' as a deadlock between legal justice and ethical love, where the former demands strict adherence to individual justice and the latter requires moral sensitivity to the perplexities of social injustice.

Later in his philosophical oeuvre, Murphy examines the Christian virtue of agape and considers its implications for criminal justice, claiming that giving offenders what they deserve is not incompatible with the ethics of love. In his view, it is possible to both punish offenders and express loving care towards them, especially if we can create penal practices that embody both justice and

26 Halil Cesur, *Ödetmeci Ceza Adaletinin İki Yüzü* (Pinhan Yayıncılık 2024).
27 Murphy, *Retribution, Justice, and Therapy: Essays in the Philosophy of Law* p.90.

love. Imprisonment, he thinks, could serve as one such practice, allowing offenders' humanity to be acknowledged in a caring way. However, he does not address the complex and perhaps inherent challenges of reconciling the intentional deprivation of offenders' liberty with an ethic of genuine, loving concern for their well-being. Nor does he offer a critical reflection on the limitations and potential blind spots of retributive thinking in the way he did in his earlier work. This leaves an ongoing unresolved tension between the demands of legal justice and those of loving ethics within his retributive thinking, which I call a 'theoretical deadlock'.

In Chapter 1, I will explore Murphy's ambivalent reflections on retributivism in greater depth, incorporating brief analyses of other neo-retributivists where relevant – especially those who, like Murphy, find themselves caught in a similar theoretical deadlock. The aim is to convince the reader that two conflicting strands within neo-classical retributive thinking resist easy reconciliation. On the one hand, neo-classical retributivism upholds punishment as a strict demand of justice rooted in the concept of desert: legal justice. On the other hand, there is a competing impulse within the framework – a humanistic strain that questions its core assumptions: loving ethics. I will give more flesh to these two competing strands in Chapters 2 and 3 through a detailed examination of Hegel's early and later works, clarifying how legal and ethical retributivism each stand independently on their own terms. This will then set the ground for a thorough understanding of neo-classical retributivism in the following chapters, where I will engage in an in-depth critique of the punishment theories proposed by Hampton, Duff and Brudner.

To provide an early roadmap, I will begin by diagnosing the 'disease' within neo-retributivism, so to speak, using Murphy as a starting point. I will then offer the reader a comprehensive explanation of this 'disease' through Hegel's works. Following that, to substantiate my arguments, I will examine other neo-retributive theories, focusing on the three parties with a stake in crime (the victim, offender, state). Let me now explain how I will engage with these theories.

3. Neo-retributive theories of punishment

Since the declaration of the demise of the rehabilitative ideal by Robert Martinson, with the slogan 'nothing works' in 1974,[28] a wave of retributive theories had already started to come back to penal thinking in the Anglo-American world.[29] It was in his 1979 paper that John Cottingham attempted

28 Robert Martinson, 'What works?-Questions and answers about prison reform' (1974) 35 *The Public Interest* 22.

29 Morris, 'Persons and Punishment'; Murphy, *Retribution, Justice, and Therapy: Essays in the Philosophy of Law*; Hirsch, *Censure and Sanctions*; Duff, *Punishment, Communication, and Community*.

'to combat ambiguity and muddle' about the justification of punishment by identifying nine varieties of retributivism.[30] Forty years later, the number of retributive theories has multiplied, which perhaps makes the field blurrier than ever.[31] My aim is not to resolve the conceptual and theoretical ambiguities embedded in the multivocal discourse of retributivism. Neither is it to add a new theory to an already full-blown literature. It is rather to provide a wider, critical lens through which to shed more light on these theories.

As stated earlier, I take retributivism as a theory that is concerned not only with the deserved punishment of offenders in socio-political settings (legal retributivism) but also with the suffering they experience in their moral world as a result of criminal violation (ethical retributivism). I have also stated that contemporary theorists not only hold on to the standard legalistic retributivism but also add a new dimension that goes beyond the idea of desert and an abstract restoration of rights. They do so by giving the legal image of punishment an ethical and intersubjective grounding, where the imposition of suffering is understood in relational terms.

Behind this new model of retributivism, though not expressly set out, lies the idea that more attention should be paid to relevant parties who have a stake in crime and punishment. What is particularly crystallising is a triadic model of relationships that is moulded by the victim, offender and state. Differentiating it from the model of restorative justice where relationships are shaped by the victim, offender and community, I view the relational dimension of neo-classical retributivism as state-centric.[32] Unlike restorative justice, where the parties constructively engage with each other in dialogue, within a supportive environment, to reach a mutually agreed outcome, neo-classical retributivism is relational only in the sense that state punishment relates to the three stakeholders. That is, punishment is restorative only in relation to those who benefit from it.

From the perspective of the victim, punishment means a legal form of counteraction that reaffirms equality between the victim and the offender in the face of the offender's denial of the victim's dignity. It repairs the moral injury caused by crime by acknowledging that the victim is violated: ***punishment as vindication***. In this conception of punishment, which is mainly developed by Jean Hampton, the ethical voice of the victim is animated by the idea of recognition, acknowledging the wrong done to the victim as *wrong* and

30 John Cottingham, 'Varieties of retribution' (1979) 29 *The Philosophical Quarterly* 238.

31 Nigel Walker, 'Even more varieties of retribution' (1999) 74 *Philosophy* 595; Berman, 'Two kinds of retributivism'.

32 Why the community is replaced by the state in my account may not be too obvious. But I believe that the modern state is often presented as a neutral regulatory power through which a just social balance is maintained. And retributivism in its standard form is concerned with an idea of justice that is delivered by a political authority.

restoring their moral worth.[33] It is therefore argued that punishment equalises the score when it repairs the normative harm inflicted on the equal relations between the victim and others: legal restoration.[34]

But the major problem with this is that the interests and overall well-being of the victim are reduced to the demand for giving offenders their just deserts.[35] What the victim needs, however, is a genuine addressing of the harm they suffer in a supportive environment where they are given the opportunity of grieving and mourning and thereby recovering from what has happened. This requires, of course, more than punishment of the offender, pointing in the direction of another level of restoration that heals the wounds of the victim in a way that re-establishes their moral and psychological integrity: ethical restoration.

From the perspective of the offender, legal punishment serves as a means of extracting the debt they owe to society, a debt that is derived from their public wrong. Crimes create a rupture in the offender's relationship with society, undermining the trust that binds individuals within the social framework. In this sense, restoring the trust and solidarity the offender has violated, at least in a formal sense, punishment repairs the harm done to their normative status within society. When punished, the offender bears the consequences of their harmful actions (payback) and re-establishes their place within the social and legal order. Doing so, they are released from their debt and regain their normative standing within society: legal restoration.

Ideally, as Duff emphasises, we could expect retributive penal sanctions to operate in a way that does good to the offender in a substantial sense. In this sense, punishment can also be seen as bringing them to understand the moral consequences of their crime and express repentance: punishment as reform. In Duff's terms, understood this way, punishment can also be seen as a secular penance that is imposed on the offender so that they could reconcile with themselves as well as others and restore their moral sense of self not only in the eyes of others but also themselves: ethical restoration.[36] Nevertheless, retributivism finds the release of debts sufficient for justice to be done, often

33 Hampton, 'Correcting harms versus righting wrongs: The goal of retribution'; George P Fletcher, 'The place of victims in the theory of retribution' (1999) 3 *Buffalo Criminal Law Review* 51; Richard L Lippke, 'Victim-centered retributivism' (2003) 84 *Pacific Philosophical Quarterly* 127.

34 For more detailed analysis about his see Halil Cesur, 'Retributive punishment: between vindication and healing' (2025) 31(2) *International Review of Victimology* pp.185–202.

35 Nicola Lacey and Hanna Pickard, 'A dual-process approach to criminal law: Victims and the clinical model of responsibility without blame' (2019) 27 *Journal of Political Philosophy* 229 p.10.

36 Duff, *Punishment, Communication, and Community*; Bennett, *The Apology Ritual: A Philosophical Theory of Punishment*; Herbert Morris, 'A paternalistic theory of punishment' (1981) 18 *American Philosophical Quarterly* 263; Jean Hampton, 'The moral education theory of punishment' (1984) 13(3) *Philosophy & Public Affairs* 208.

stopping short of requiring the deeper moral and relational transformation that ethical restoration entails.

Finally, from the perspective of the state, punishment is an act of correction, the correction of the wrong and injustice at a political level. It restores the *infringed* order of rights by upholding the law that has been violated: *punishment as restoration of the rightful order*. In other words, punishment is meant to reaffirm the state's presence within the public sphere when its authority is challenged by the offender. More technically, as Brudner points out, legal punishment vindicates the system of mutual recognition of free agents by restoring formal relations from which the state derives its legitimate power. In this sense, it can be taken as reasserting the state's *vertical* authority in the face of its denial: legal restoration.[37]

There is, however, a deeper sense of restoration that has often been neglected by the state's legal intervention. Punishment may restore the law and state's public authority when challenged by crime. But it does little to address the previous underlying harms that cause crime within society in the first place. Equally significant is the idea that intersubjective relations of mutual recognition should be restored alongside formal relations, through which the state exercises its political power. Retributive punishment, as Brudner argues, may be conceived of as a penal sanction that restores the normative power of political authority. However, it is doubtful whether it can achieve the ethical restoration of horizontal societal relations.

It is worth noting that retributive punishment ideally restores the whole triadic model. Put differently, all theories concern themselves with the restoration of the three parties in some way. But it is their point of focus that differs from one other. For instance, Duff's communicative theory views punishment as a dialogic process, centred on the offender's recognition of wrongdoing. But it also addresses the victim's need for acknowledgement and the state's role in upholding justice. The same can be said of Hampton and Brudner. Thus, each of these theories constructs a relational model of punishment, but they diverge in terms of whose restoration is prioritized and how it is achieved.

What is common in all the neo-retributive accounts, however, is the fact that restoration is modest and one dimensional while the three parties talk past each other when dealing with the violation and lack the resources to come together to achieve a fuller reconciliation. Punishment might embody a moment of recognition of the violation which vindicates the victim, and yet it usually does so by becoming 'vindictive' towards the offender. Likewise, the offender is often pushed away for the sake of restoring law and justice. When being punished, they are, as it were, locked away with no reason to think about what they have done. In a traditional retributive framework, the state also

37 Morris, 'Persons and punishment'; Brudner, *Punishment and Freedom*;

withdraws from the process after having punished, leaving both the offender and the victim alone when working through what has happened.

Restoration, however, is capable of expansion in an ethical retributivist framework while setting the scene for the parties to come together to heal the shared wounds. From the perspective of the victim, restoration can mean a thorough engagement with criminal violation and perhaps also finding a higher ground than law on which they are prepared to forgive the offender. What underlies the process of mourning and getting ready for forgiveness is an ethical structure that relies on a more constructive dialogue than punishment provides. On the other hand, restoration for the offender can mean discovering an ethical zone where they are given a chance to renew their relationships with themselves, as well as their victim and community, with serious moral reflection in light of the injury done by violation. At work in this sort of restorative process is a moral and emotional coming to terms with what the offender *was*, how they *would like to be* and how *they should relate to others, change and grow*. And finally, from the perspective of the state, restoration can mean reviewing and refreshing the conditions of mutual recognition, with a particular focus on the prior existence of imbalance and disharmony that generates crime. The restorative ethos that underpins the state may then include rethinking about relationships in a way that pays due regard to the initial withdrawals of recognition and reconstruction in the light of what has happened.

The meaning of restoration through punishment in an ethical retributivist setting can therefore encompass a move beyond the legal '*restoring back to*' and embody broader ethical ideas of '*renewing, re-constructing and flourishing*' for all parties involved in violation.[38] This is to say that there are two senses of restoration that can be produced by the retributive experience. Yet, being structurally limited, neo-classical retributivism is in a theoretical deadlock that must be broken or overcome.

4. Restoration at two levels: seeking a shared ground between legal justice and ethical love

I will reinforce the idea that there exists an unresolved split between the legal and ethical approaches in neo-classical retributivism in Part III (Chapters 4, 5 and 6). I will then move on to address the question of whether there is a way forward beyond the impasse in Chapter 7, in which I will visit Lacey and Pickard's therapeutic theory of punishment and Norrie's theory of mature retributivism.[39] I will argue that critical criminal justice accounts take

38 Amanda Wilson and Henrique Carvalho, *Rethinking the Restorative Dimension of Criminal Justice* (Wiley Online Library 2022) p.8.

39 Nicola Lacey and Hanna Pickard, 'From the consulting room to the court room? Taking the clinical model of responsibility without blame into the legal realm' (2013) 33 *Oxford Journal of Legal Studies* 1; Lacey and Pickard, 'To blame or to forgive? Reconciling punishment and forgiveness in criminal justice'; Lacey and Pickard, 'A dual-process approach to criminal law:

a significant progressive step by preserving respect for rational agency while rejecting the notion of moral desert. In other words, there are non-punitive ways to hold the offender accountable for what they did without adhering to the principles of standard legal retributivism. In this sense, the theoretical impasse in neo-retributivism appears largely resolvable, suggesting that the ideal of loving justice is not an unattainable utopia but a viable project, even under current conditions. However, this does not compel us to conclude that legal and ethical retributivism are fully reconcilable.

Lacey and Pickard propose a therapeutic conception of punishment to avoid the pitfalls of legal retributivism. They suggest that just as clinics are designed to motivate patients to change their life course and take responsibility for healing, criminal justice processes can be structured to encourage offenders to take responsibility without resorting to blame. Key to the therapeutic criminal justice system is a forgiving disposition towards offenders while confronting them with the negative yet reparative consequences of their actions. This approach requires *radical reform* that fundamentally transforms main justice practices, including imprisonment. But because criminal justice systems are inherently offender-focused, a separate system should be established to meet the distinct needs of victims.

The central worry I will raise in relation to the therapeutic conception of punishment will be largely the same as with neo-classical retributivism: despite radical reforms, carceral practices may inevitably retain a coercive residue, reflecting the persistent undercurrents of control and domination inherent in the system. However, unlike neo-retributivism, the therapeutic model recognises these coercive practices as a failure or, at best, a second-best outcome. As such, the therapeutic approach can be understood as a form of what I call 'loving justice', even though it does not fully reconcile the legal and ethical dimensions of punishment. In this way, the therapeutic approach seeks to reduce coercion but acknowledges that the demands of ethical retributivism remain elusive within current institutional frameworks.

On the other hand, Norrie's mature retributivism aims to demolish and rebuild the criminal justice system with a new set of penal grammar. He argues that we should stop using the language of 'crime and punishment' and instead speak of 'violation and making amends'. His proposed model is rooted in a moral psychological ethics where the offender suffers and makes amends in response to their violative behaviour, which causes harm to the victim. Though ethically satisfactory this critical account might be, Norrie does not fully develop

victims and the clinical model of responsibility without blame'; Nicola Lacey and Hanna Pickard, 'Why standing to blame may be lost but authority to hold accountable retained: Criminal law as a regulative public institution' (2021) 104 *The Monist* 265; Alan Norrie, 'Taking guilt seriously: Towards mature retributivism' in Iyiola Solanke (ed), *On Crime, Society, and Responsibility in the Work of Nicola Lacey* (Oxford University Press 2021); Alan Norrie, *Rethinking Criminal Justice Punishment, Abolition and Moral Psychology* (Cambridge University Press 2025).

what I call his 'radical reconstructive' project under these terms. In a sense, his victim-centred, mature retributivism remains practically underdeveloped. Nevertheless, he elaborates on his vision through the example of the Barlienne Special Unit in Glasgow Prison, arguing that we should both improve how prisons are administered and deconstruct them from within. These types of reconstructive projects can be viewed as non-reformist reforms – reforms that challenge the current approach to criminal violation and offer potential loving ways of achieving justice.

Both critical criminal justice theories seek ways to radically transform the standard understanding of criminal justice. That said, Norrie's moral psychological account (unlike Lacey's therapeutic theory) does not develop *from within* 'the legal' in order to be pitted *against* it but develops from *within the ethical* in order to be *against* 'the legal'. In this sense, its ultimate aim is not reform but abolition. Still, a tension persists between penal reform and abolition, despite the potential success in achieving the ideal of loving justice in current practices. In this book, I will not take a definitive stance on the debate between penal reform and abolition. Instead, I adopt an intentionally ambivalent position, one that could be seen as a "moral oscillation" between radical penal reform and abolition.

Let me now provide a broad outline of the book: Part I (Chapter 1) offers a diagnosis of neo-classical retributivism through Murphy's retributive accounts, arguing that the theory has reached a deadlock. Part II (Chapters 2 and 3) juxtaposes two contrasting ways of thinking about punishment, in which Hegel's later state-based account is placed against his early intersubjective thoughts. The aim is to explore the origins of two radically different approaches to retributivism and show the sharply divided theoretical elements that exist in neo-classical retributivism: legal justice versus loving ethics. Part III (Chapters 4, 5 and 6) is the loadbearing block of this work and investigates whether the legal and ethical approaches are sufficiently reconciled in recent retributive theories. Here, by following a tripartite model (the victim, offender, state), this book will seek to pay due justice to the merits of neo-classical retributivism and its limitations. Finally, Part IV (Chapter 7) explores possible ways to move beyond the limitations of neo-classical retributivism. The aim is to resolve the problems that are diagnosed in retributive thoughts and bring to light the constructive critical approaches to criminal justice.

Bibliography

Armstrong J, 'Rethinking the restorative–retributive dichotomy: is reconciliation possible?' (3 July 2014) 17(3) *Contemporary Justice Review* 362–374

Bennett C, *The Apology Ritual: A Philosophical Theory of Punishment* (Cambridge University Press 2008)

Berman MN, 'Two kinds of retributivism' (2010) U of Texas Law, Public Law Research Paper No. 171. http://dx.doi.org/10.2139/ssrn.1592546

Binder G, 'Punishment theory: moral or political?' (2002) 5 *Buffalo Criminal Law Review* 321

Brooks T, 'Punitive restoration and restorative justice' (2017) 36 *Criminal Justice Ethics* 122

Brudner A, *Punishment and Freedom* (Oxford University Press 2009)

Burchard C, Chiao V, Lorca R and Wilenmann J (eds), *The Political Turn in Criminal Law Scholarship* (Hart 2024)

Caruso GD, *Rejecting Retributivism: Free Will, Punishment, and Criminal Justice* (Cambridge University Press, 2021)

Cesur H, *Ödetmeci Ceza Adaletinin İki Yüzü* (Pinhan Yayıncılık 2024)

Chiao V, *Criminal Law in the Age of the Administrative State* (Oxford University Press 2018)

Chiao V, 'What is the criminal law for?' (2016) 35(2) *Law and Philosophy* 137–163

Cottingham J, 'Varieties of retribution' (1979) 29 *The Philosophical Quarterly* 238

Duff A, 'Criminal law and the constitution of civil order' (2020) 70 *University of Toronto Law Journal* 4

Duff A, *Punishment, Communication, and Community* (Oxford University Press 2001)

Duff A, 'Responsibility, restoration and retribution' in Tonry M (ed), *Retributivism Has a Past: Has it a Future?* (Oxford University Press 2011)

Duff A, 'Restoration and retribution' in Julian Roberts V, Von Hirsch A, Bottoms AE, Roach K and Schiff M (eds), *Restorative Justice and Criminal Justice: Competing or Reconcilable Paradigms* (Bloomsbury Publishing 2003)

Duff A, 'Retrieving retributivism' in White MD (ed), *Retributivism: Essays on Theory and Policy* (Oxford University Press 2011)

Fletcher GP, 'The place of victims in the theory of retribution' (1999) 3 *Buffalo Criminal Law Review* 51

Fletcher GP, 'Political theory and criminal law' (2006) 25(1) *Criminal Justice Ethics* 18

Gardner MR, 'The renaissance of retribution-an examination of doing justice' (1976) *Wisconsin Law Review* 781 781–815

Garvey SP, 'Restorative justice, punishment, and atonement' (2003) 1 *Utah Law Review* 303

Hampton J, 'Correcting harms versus righting wrongs: the goal of retribution' (1992) 39 *UCLA Law Review*1659–1702

Hampton J, 'A new theory of retribution' in Morris CW, Frey RG and Postema G (eds), *Liability and Responsibility: Essays in Law and Morals* (Cambridge University Press 1991)

Hampton J, 'The moral education theory of punishment' (1984) 13(3) *Philosophy & Public Affairs* 208

Hayes D, *Confronting Penal Excess: Retribution and the Politics of Penal Minimalism* (Bloomsbury Publishing 2019)

Husak D, 'Holistic retributivism' (2000) 88 *California Law Review* 991.

Johnstone G, *Restorative Justice Ideas, Values, Debates* (Routledge 2013)

Lacey N and Pickard H, 'To blame or to forgive? Reconciling punishment and forgiveness in criminal justice' (2015) 35 *Oxford Journal of Legal Studies* 4

Lacey N and Pickard H, 'A dual-process approach to criminal law: victims and the clinical model of responsibility without blame' (2019) 27 *Journal of Political Philosophy* 229

Lacey N and Pickard H, 'From the consulting room to the court room? Taking the clinical model of responsibility without blame into the legal realm' (2013) 33 *Oxford Journal of Legal Studies* 1

Lacey N and Pickard H, 'Why standing to blame may be lost but authority to hold accountable retained: criminal law as a regulative public institution' (2021) 104 *The Monist* 265

Lippke RL, 'Victim-centered retributivism' (2003) 84 *Pacific Philosophical Quarterly* 127

Martinson R, 'What works?-Questions and answers about prison reform' (1974) 35 *The Public Interest* 22

Matravers M, 'Is twenty-first century punishment post-desert?' in Tonry M (ed), *Retributivism Has a Past Has it a Future* (Oxford University Press 2011)

Moore MS, 'The moral worth of retribution' in Schoeman F (ed), *Responsibility, Character, and the Emotions: New Essays in Moral Psychology* (Cambridge University Press 1987)

Moore MS, *Placing Blame: A Theory of the Criminal Law* (Oxford University Press 2010)

Morris H, 'A paternalistic theory of punishment' (1981) 18 *American Philosophical Quarterly* 263

Morris H, 'Persons and punishment' (1968) 52(4) *The Monist* 475

Murphy JG, *Retribution, Justice, and Therapy: Essays in the Philosophy of Law* (Springer Science & Business Media 1979)

Norrie A, *Rethinking Criminal Justice Punishment, Abolition and Moral Psychology* (Cambridge University Press Forthcoming)

Norrie A, 'Taking guilt seriously: towards mature retributivism' in Solanke I (ed), *On Crime, Society, and Responsibility in the Work of Nicola Lacey* (Oxford University Press 2021)

Pereboom D, *Free Will Skepticism and Criminal Punishment The Future of Punishment* (Oxford University Press 2013)

Pereboom D, *Wrongdoing and the Moral Emotions* (Oxford University Press 2021).

Ramsay P, 'The responsible subject as citizen: criminal law, democracy and the welfare state' (2006, January) 69(1) *The Modern Law Review* 29–58

Thorburn M, 'Punishment and public authority' in Ulväng M, Asp P and Bois-Pedain A (eds), *Criminal Law and the Authority of the State* (Hart Publishing 2017)

Von Hirsch A, *Censure and Sanctions* (Oxford University Press 2003)

Von Hirsch A, Roberts JV, Bottoms AE, Roach K and Schiff M (eds), *Restorative Justice and Criminal Justice: Competing or Reconcilable Paradigms* (Bloomsbury Publishing 2003)

Walker N, 'Even more varieties of retribution' (1999) 74 *Philosophy* 595

Wilson A and Carvalho H, *Rethinking the Restorative Dimension of Criminal Justice* (Wiley Online Library 2022)

Wright M, 'Is it time to question the concept of punishment?' in Walgrave L (ed), *Repositioning Restorative Justice* (Willan 2012)

Part I

Diagnosing the deadlock

1 Two faces of retributivism

Introduction

This work could have been an extensive analysis of the complete oeuvre of Jeffrie Murphy, an interesting retributivist scholar who has written widely on almost every aspect of penal theory. In fact, it is in some way all about Murphy, in the sense that it seeks to cover a broad range of topics that he addresses from the moral psychological aspects of crime and punishment to critical theory, and that it seems to be specifically structured to shed light on his remarkable ambivalence with regard to retributivism. Yet, in this chapter, I will focus on his varying conceptions of punishment, specifically to highlight the theoretical impasse of neo-retributive thinking.

At the heart of this impasse lie two contrasting ideas in relation to legal punishment. The first is based on the standard well-known principle that offenders deserve to suffer in response to their crime. The claim, or perhaps assumption, that underpins this principle is as follows: we respect their rational agency when we punish them, as they rightly confront the consequences of their rational choice. Within neo-retributivist thinking, there is, however, also a second idea that offenders must experience something that makes them better, not worse. In other words, it is also believed that the imposition of pointless suffering on offenders is unjust or at the very least not morally and politically desirable. This creates a dilemma, as both ideas present compelling reasons for their respective positions, yet they are difficult to reconcile in a coherent understanding of legal punishment.

Another problem with this refined retributive thinking is its exclusive focus on individual justice, which is called into question by the moral uneasiness it generates in the context of prevalent social injustices. As Murphy indicates in his early works, retributivism may function in societies where burdens and benefits are fairly distributed. In such societies, it may be appropriate to punish offenders who have harmed reciprocal social interactions. However, when justice is defined in terms of reciprocity, as is often claimed, it becomes problematic to justify punishment where individuals have not been given fair access to societal benefits. The problem of doing justice in an unjust world is

DOI: 10.4324/9781003563150-3

then a further challenge that complicates the theoretical foundation of neo-retributivism, especially when crimes are isolated from social conditions.

I begin this chapter by diagnosing the impasse in neo-classical retributivism, where the idea of respect for individual autonomy clashes with the intentional infliction of suffering. I then analyse Murphy's two contrasting conceptions of punishment in his early period, where he is first drawn to fair play theory and later becomes a critic of it. Finally, I move on to his two different theories of punishment, one shaped by moral hatred and the other by Agapic love. This chapter primarily focusses on Murphy's evolving ambivalent views on retributive justice, but where relevant, I also give a brief analysis of other neo-retributivists who find themselves in the same deadlock as Murphy.

1. Diagnosing the impasse within neo-classical retributivism

Morris is a remarkable philosopher, as he reset the retributivism game about 50 years ago. To continue with that analogy, Murphy is a philosopher who has played that game for 50 years, albeit in a way that his critics might see as clumsy. He never fully stepped away from the game, but he always wanted it to be revised and reformed to make it more attractive, producing works that do not stand peacefully. Norrie describes Murphy's moving positions as 'a parabola', changing from 'a more mature account of retributive punishment in the 1970s to a more primitive one in the 1980s, and then back to a more mature approach in the new millennium'.[1]

I am doubtful about the terminology and periodisation that he offers, as there has always been some confusion in Murphy's views on retributive justice. Yet it is clear that Murphy's oeuvre represents a wide variety of retributive thoughts worth considering, particularly in terms of how punishment is linked with the idea of restoration. I also find his works particularly useful for understanding neo-classical retributivism, as he serves as a significant representative figure, engaging with almost every challenge the theory has faced while also holding an ambivalent position in relation to them. At one point in his intellectual journey, he became an adamant supporter of retributive punishment, for example, arguing that it respects the rational agency of individuals as it gives an appropriate response to their wrongful behaviour. Subsequently, he became suspicious of it, albeit not fully abandoning it, questioning whether the individual responsibility emphasised by retributivism sets ground for justice in social circumstances which may limit the choices of individuals. At another time, he thought of retributive punishment as a legitimate response to morally atrocious wrongs, as it manifests our rightful hatred towards the offender. Yet he radically transformed and developed his understanding of retributivism in his later works, seeking to reconcile desert with the Christian ethics of

1 Alan Norrie, *Rethinking Criminal Justice Punishment, Abolition and Moral Psychology* (CUP 2025) chapter 8.

agape. Throughout this book, I will argue that these sorts of ambiguities and confusions in the approach to punishment are prevalent in all the neo-retributivist accounts. Although ultimately unsuccessful, they all attempt, like Murphy, to meet the demands of what I call 'legal justice' and loving ethics at the same time. For this reason, to grasp Murphy's thoughts is somehow to distill the antinomical essence of 50 years of retributivist thought.

Perhaps what makes Murphy unique among others is his awareness of the dual or ambivalent nature of retributivism. Indeed, he candidly acknowledges the tensions and contradictions inherent in retributivism in his self-reflective book *Punishment and the Moral Emotions* and his latest article. There are two faces of retributivism, he says: 'one face that draws us, in its stress on moral desert, toward the recognition of human dignity and responsibility and another face that tempts us to self-deceptive cruelty'.[2] I do not think moral desert is necessarily a block to cruelty; as will be discussed shortly, perhaps it is the opposite in many cases. Yet I do believe there are two faces or elements in retributive theory which conflict with each other. Indeed, at the end of the day, Murphy identifies his position as that of a 'reluctant retributivist': a retributivist who has realised the dangers inherent in the central tenets of retributivism yet continues to hold on to it, though much more cautiously than previously.[3] For me, his reluctance, like that of others, is to do with finding himself in a theoretical deadlock, or at least sensing it, yet being unable to break free due to the limitations embedded in the theory.

On the one hand, there is the unwavering belief that retributivism is the only framework for holding people responsible for what they have done: offenders must confront the painful consequences of their freely chosen bad choice, as they deserve. On the other hand, there exists the fear that the infliction of suffering is insidiously derived from the basic – sometimes barbaric – passions we harbour towards those who have done wrongs: offenders must experience something from which there is no way out but suffering, but in a way that makes them better, not worse. This is the deadlock Murphy and other neo-classical retributivists face. They must either abandon the idea that offenders deserve punishment and move towards more supportive and rehabilitative legal interventions or further explain how the deliberate infliction of pain chimes in with the idea of respecting, and even caring for, them.

Strikingly, in his 'last words on retribution', Murphy sought to move beyond the deadlock, opening the way towards a 'reconciliatory' zone between the strict demand for justice and punishment and the moral sensitivity that searches for constructive sanctions. In his view, deserved punishment should be defined not only by the deliberate infliction of pain but also by the endurance of suffering that brings about self-growth and moral reckoning for

2 Murphy, 'Last words on retribution' p.29; Murphy, *Punishment and the Moral Emotions: Essays in Law, Morality, and Religion* p.85.

3 Murphy, *Punishment and the Moral Emotions: Essays in Law, Morality, and Religion* p.86.

one's actions.[4] He suggests that, if understood in a wider sense than usually held, desert need not be solely associated with someone punishing the other as the latter's actions require bad treatment. Instead, it can also be seen as a kind of reward for the offender, out of which 'a sense of wisdom' can emerge. In other words, desert does not necessarily lead us to think of a one-sided practice that hurts and objectifies the one deserving punishment but rather of a two-way process that invites active responsibility.

For Murphy, if burdened with patience, humility and good temper, punishment as deserved suffering can also be viewed as 'the dispensing of what is due' as well as an educational tool for the offender that makes him 'suffer unto truth'.[5] That is, alongside its negative connotation of 'being treated as he deserves to be treated' in a criminal justice context, desert for him can also have a positive (restorative) meaning. At the very least, it should be understood in a neutral way: 'getting his due as a matter of justice'.[6] Rather than advancing the progressive understanding of desert, however, he adheres to the standard conception in his latest work, arguing that desert remains the virtuous side of retributivism. He contends that it can 'weaken the temptations posed by the bad face' and help ensure a just and proportionate punishment within our excessively punitive environment.[7]

As will be discussed in more detail in the following chapters, not only Murphy but all neo-classical retributivists tend to view the principle of desert as inherently tied to the concept of justice. Hampton, for example, associates desert with reaffirmation of equality between the victim and the offender. For her, it is just to punish the offender, as it rectifies the message conveyed by the crime, which seeks to diminish the victim's value.[8] Duff, on the other hand, links desert to the obligation of the offender to pay back for what they have done. In his view, the offender must, or deserves to, be subject to the moral disapproval or condemnation of the community in response to their wrongful behaviour.[9] Finally, Brudner connects desert to the restoration of relations of mutual recognition disrupted by crime. He argues that the state is justified in responding to crimes with sanctions that reaffirm its public authority, as the offender's actions challenge the whole system of rights that sustains just social order.[10]

At the core of all these legalistic approaches lies the idea that desert is the only element that can stand in the way of punitiveness, being respectful of

4 Murphy, 'Last words on retribution' p.30.
5 Murphy, 'Last words on retribution' p.40.
6 Murphy, 'Last words on retribution' p.30.
7 Murphy, 'Last words on retribution' p.36. For a similar view: Jonathan A Jacobs, *The Liberal State and Criminal Sanction: Seeking Justice and Civility* (Oxford University Press 2020).
8 Jean Hampton, 'Correcting harms versus righting wrongs: The goal of retribution' (1992) 39 *UCLA Law Review* 1659–1702.
9 Antony Duff, *Punishment, Communication, and Community* (Oxford University Press 2001).
10 Alan Brudner, *Punishment and Freedom* (Oxford University Press 2009).

the dignity and rights of the offender and giving them no more nor less than what they deserve. In other words, desert is seen as providing a legitimate basis for punishment by saving it from excessive utilitarian approaches or punitive extremes. Yet, it is also ill-suited to control the level or severity of punishment. Perhaps the most visible reason for this is that desert does not establish clear boundaries for how much the state should interfere in people's lives or how strict it should be. Is mandatory life imprisonment, for example, a deserved punishment for murder? Or how much should an offender suffer, and what specific punishment should he receive for violating someone's property rights?

For sure, the state can classify crimes ordinally, which means that 'offenses of similar seriousness receive punishments of similar severity and that the punishments increase in severity as offense seriousness increases'. In other words, the state may endure a form of ordinal proportionality. However, it is much less clear how it can endure cardinal proportionality, the sort of proportionality which 'concerns the severity of the entire scale of ordinally proportionate punishments'. In this sense, how the state determines the ultimate harshest or lightest possible punishment appears to be a contingent question of social convention, one that cannot be resolved by the principle of desert alone.[11] From this, it should follow that desert is not necessarily the good face of retributivism that blocks punitiveness but, at best a neutral face that is dependent on social and political conditions.

In fact, paradoxically, desert can also be the element that can feed into punitiveness and take a bad face. As will be discussed later, in Murphy's conception of punishment as retributive hatred, desert can also be associated with, or worse, conceptually related to, punitiveness. It might be shaped and channelled by our basic emotions, such as anger and hate, moving us towards holding a vindictive or vengeful stance against the offender. In other words, what initially seems to be the sole means of respecting the dignity and rational agency of offenders can dramatically transform into a mechanism for diminishing or instrumentalising them.

One could argue that respect for individual agency makes up the good face of retributivism, especially when coupled with the idea of holding individuals responsible without necessarily adhering to the concept of desert. This is to mean that accountability and retributivism can coexist without the need for the latter to be tied exclusively to what one deserves. However, Murphy and other retributivists have not been able to fully disassociate desert from the respect for individual agency. Instead, they have insisted on treating the two as if they are intrinsically connected, reinforcing the idea that individual responsibility is inherently linked to the notion of just deserts. For sure, not all philosophers have grounded the concept of desert in their theory in such a fundamental way, but they have, in one way or another, adopted a legalistic vision that equates justice with the deserved suffering of the offender.

11 Ramsay, 'A democratic theory of imprisonment' p.87.

Interestingly, moving away from the idea of retributive hatred in his later work, Murphy came to believe that the concept of desert can be married to ideas of reform and restoration if reconciled with the Christian ethics of agape. For him, our love for offenders along with our commitment to justice can lead us to think that they deserve both suffering and reform at the same time. In this chapter and various parts of this book, I will argue the opposite, asserting that desert functions as a barrier to the progression of retributivism, creating an impasse that must be overcome. There must be an alternative way to respect the rational agency of offenders without insisting that they must suffer in response to their wrongful behaviour. To elaborate further on how neo-classical retributivism is caught in an impasse, I will now take a closer look at Murphy's evolving conceptions of retributive punishment.

2. The early period: from fair play theory to critical theory

Being discontented with the injustices associated with penal welfarism in the 1960s, Murphy's early works were initially influenced by Herbert Morris's theory of punishment, in which the social control model of treatment is sharply contrasted with a 'rational choice' model, that centrally locates the ideas of responsibility and moral desert within retributive thinking, first proposed and developed in *Persons and Punishment* (1968).[12] Like other retributivists who complain that there is insufficient regard for the dignity of human beings in the excessive disciplinary control of the therapeutic state,[13] Murphy was attracted to fair play theory, a theory that takes the idea of free individual agency seriously. Fair play theory, Murphy argues, 'respects the dignity of persons through holding them responsible and sometimes resenting or even punishing them for what they do instead of insulting them by regarding them as sick or helpless victims of their fixed natures or social circumstances'.[14] His early conception of punishment was, thus, constituted mainly by the principle of desert, which regards offenders as capable of agency and responsibility.

According to this version of retributivism, desert is understood by reference to the notion of the debt owed by offenders to other fellow citizens when they commit crime and disturb the balance of society or the rule of law formed by a mutually beneficial scheme of social cooperation.[15] Unlike others who are loyal and obedient, and who bear the burden of self-restraint necessary to keep the legal system functioning, offenders enjoy a 'free ride' on others' cooperation and owe a debt for their transgression to the system from which they gain the benefits of peace, security and freedom. They derive an unfair

12 Morris, 'Persons and punishment'.

13 Hirsch, *Censure and Sanctions*; Andrew Ashworth and Andrew Von Hirsch, *Proportionate Sentencing: Exploring the Principles* (Oxford University Press 2005).

14 Murphy, 'Last words on retribution' p.28.

15 Murphy, *Retribution, Justice, and Therapy: Essays in the Philosophy of Law* p.83.

advantage from 'living under our rule of law without being willing to make the necessary sacrifices (obedience, self-restraint) required'.[16] Thus, by virtue of the principle of reciprocity and mutuality of restrictions, justice demands that offenders should 'pay a debt' by shouldering some burden or getting their just deserts. Put otherwise, fair play theory suggests that punishment should aim at extracting the debt that offenders owe to others, re-establishing the broken balance caused by criminal behaviour and maintaining the equilibrium of benefits and burdens.[17] In my own terms, punishment restores formal, legal relations of recognition that have been challenged by crime: legal restoration.

This theory has been subject to a great deal of criticism since its early development, in terms of both the way it conceives of crime and the way it justifies the infliction of punishment.[18] Restricted by the scope of this work, all of this criticism cannot be included here. Rather, the focus will be on what I call Murphy's 'incomplete loving in his critical post-reflection on the idea of justice and reciprocity in the fair play model of punishment.

In his radical essay on Marxism and retribution first published in 1973, Murphy raised grave doubts about the idea that there is a fair balance of benefits and burdens in society.[19] For him, most offenders 'neither benefit nor participate but rather operate at a built-in economic or racial disadvantage which is in fact, if not in theory, permanent'.[20] Having failed to access the basic resources and services of society, they are drawn from the poorer classes and suffer from what Marx calls alienation'. If justice consists in reciprocity, as is usually claimed, Murphy writes, 'it is hard to see what these persons are supposed to reciprocate for'.[21] That is, the initial distribution of benefits and burdens is unjust or imbalanced such that the state can lose its right to be obeyed and 'largely lack the moral right to punish'.[22] Nonetheless, the state 'pretends' that the conditions of legal coercion are met and justice is done, but what it actually does is to 'provide a "transcendental sanction" for the status quo'.[23]

'Instead of looking upon offenders as the mere object[s], and the slave[s] of justice', Murphy quotes Marx, noting that retributive justice elevates them

16 Jeffrie G Murphy, 'Retributivism and the state's interest in punishment' in J. Roland Pennock and John W Chapman (eds), *Criminal Justice* (New York University Press 1985) p.161.

17 Murphy, *Retribution, justice, and therapy: essays in the philosophy of law* p.83.

18 Matt Matravers, *Justice and Punishment: The Rationale of Coercion* (Oxford University Press on Demand 2000); Antony Duff. 'Penal communications: Recent work in the philosophy of punishment' (1996) 20 *Crime and Justice* 1; Michael Tonry, *Why Punish? How Much?: A Reader on Punishment* (Oxford University Press 2011).

19 Murphy, 'Marxism and retribution'; Murphy, *Retribution, Justice, and Therapy: Essays in the Philosophy of Law.*

20 Murphy, *Retribution, Justice, and Therapy: Essays in the Philosophy of Law* p.80.

21 Murphy, *Retribution, Justice, and Therapy: Essays in the Philosophy of Law* p.107.

22 Murphy, *Retribution, Justice, and Therapy: Essays in the Philosophy of Law* p.95.

23 Murphy, *Retribution, Justice, and Therapy: Essays in the Philosophy of Law* p.95.

to the position of free self-determined beings.[24] In other words, 'it manifests at least a formal or abstract respect for rights, dignity, and autonomy' by seeking ways to link state coercion to the rational will of offenders.[25] Nevertheless, where the actual world is structurally unjust and poses a great obstacle to the actualisation of freedom, retributivism is 'largely inapplicable'. Even if it seems the only 'morally defensible' and 'formally correct' theory of punishment, it is 'materially inadequate' and 'politically unjust'.[26] As Norrie puts it in his analysis of Murphy's Marxist period, the individualist, formalist construction of retributive justice 'hides links between individual agency and underlying structural violence' while also obscuring 'the underlying social explanation of that violence'. Therefore, it 'stabilises (social) injustice in the name of (legal individual) justice'.[27]

It is remarkable that Murphy 'deconstructs' the political conception of punishment formed by the liberal precepts of justice, fairness, and reciprocity. He challenges the idea of balance and any sense of restoration that is supposed to preserve the just public order. In this sense, he is even suspicious about what I call 'legal restoration', the sort of restoration that reaffirms formal relations of society. Reflecting upon contradictions or antagonisms that are inherent in retributive justice, Murphy appears to encourage us to think beyond the law towards the intersubjective relations within society which should be restored in the first instance. Yet he ultimately stops at this point, remaining 'conflicted', 'tentative' and 'hesitant' about retributive justice.[28] He is drawn to it because of the belief that it is based on the Kantian idea of human dignity along with that of responsibility: when offenders are punished and receive what they deserve, they are seen as being treated with due respect and acknowledged as rational agents. Yet Murphy is also critical of it, suggesting that it moves us to a kind of 'blindness to the way things really are' and 'give[s] rise to smugness and self-righteousness': after all, the challenge of social injustice stands as a formidable barrier to individual legal justice, urging us to adopt a morally sensitive stance on punishment. Concluding in an indecisive manner, Murphy writes, retributivism is 'a theory built on tension – tension between justice and utility, tension between ideal states and actual states, tension between righteousness and humility'.[29]

As will be seen in Chapter 6 in more detail, though not as sharply critical as Murphy, Brudner also addresses the long-standing issue of doing justice in an unjust world. He largely accepts that social injustice causes crime,

24 Karl Marx, 'Capital punishment. Mr Cobden's pamphlet: Regulations of the Bank of England' (1853) 28 *New York Tribune Marxists Internet Archive* https://www.marxists.org/archive/marx/works/1853/02/18.htm accessed on 28.04.2025.

25 Murphy, *Retribution, Justice, and Therapy: Essays in the Philosophy of Law* p.102.

26 Murphy, *Retribution, Justice, and Therapy: Essays in the Philosophy of Law* p.108.

27 Norrie, *Criminal Justice and Moral Psychology.*

28 Murphy, 'Last words on retribution' p.40.

29 Murphy, *Retribution, Justice, and Therapy: Essays in the Philosophy of Law* p.90.

and real-world conditions can create circumstances where individuals feel marginalised or alienated from the community. However, unlike Murphy, who sees these injustices as a basis for reconsidering or even dismantling the whole criminal justice system, Brudner holds that retributivism remains justified.[30] For him, the legitimacy of punishment depends on whether we respect the offender's rational choice, at least in a formal sense, and whether the offender *could* acknowledge their punishment as just and deserved. Whether they *actually* internalise their punishment is a secondary problem, one that should be addressed by criminologists, social workers and correctional officers. In fact, this is why, Brudner thinks, we need restorative justice mechanisms. We need to supplement retributive punishments with more constructive and communitarian sanctions that seek to repair broken relationships. Nevertheless, he does not tell us whether restorative justice can adequately address the old problem of doing justice in an unjust world.[31]

Although they diverge in their conclusions, both Murphy and Brudner recognise the flaws or shortcomings of retributive justice. While this chapter cannot delve into the full complexities of Brudner's theory, we can, for now, frame their (either hidden or overt) ambivalence towards retributivism as being driven by an "incomplete loving impulse", an impulse triggered by a 'negative dialectic' that helps explore the irreducible contradictions and unresolved tensions between opposing principles.[32] Neo-classical retributivism involves a kind of 'moral restlessness' or 'dissatisfaction' because of the binary rift between what I call the 'demands of legal justice' and those of 'loving ethics'. It seeks to enrich the legal and pushes us towards a 'better' retributivism. But it does not give us a roadmap on how to deal with the unaddressed questions of retributivism. In this regard, perhaps one of the most fundamental questions here is whether or how retributivism operates in an unjust world. Equally significant is also the question of whether or how retributive punishment respects the dignity of offenders when it intentionally inflicts suffering on them.

Murphy did not directly address these questions in *Marxism and Retribution* or in his other works from the 1970s. Neither did he fully renounce his allegiance to it despite the serious doubts he raised. By contrast, having associated moral desert with rightful hatred towards offenders, he ended up advocating a punitive version of retributivism in *Forgiveness and Mercy,* co-authored with Jean Hampton in 1988. Later in his career, however, he re-questioned his views and became once again an ambivalent supporter of retributivism, especially in *Punishment and the Moral Emotions* (2008). In this later work, he sought to marry love to moral desert. In other words, he appears to have been drawn into the "vortex" of retributivism twice. In the first

30 Alan Brudner, *Punishment and Freedom* (Oxford University Press 2009) s.324.

31 Brudner, *Punishment and Freedom* s.307.

32 Theodor Adorno, *Negative Dialectics* (Continuum 1983).

instance, he tried to escape its pull by criticising the individualistic conception of responsibility and by pointing out the issue of social injustice, though this effort ultimately failed. In the second, he sought to change the lens through which retributivism is viewed, this time focussing on love. Was this attempt more successful? The following section will answer this question by tracing the 'maturation' of Murphy's views as he moved from hatred to love.

3. Retributive maturation: from hatred to love

The opening lines of Murphy's *Forgiveness and Mercy* are as follows: 'a full philosophical grasp of law and [punishment] requires an examination of the underlying causal forces that in part generate both the doctrines and the intellectual rationales for them'.[33] For him, the causal forces of punishment in contemporary societies are largely shaped by certain moral emotions that we experience when coming to terms with criminal violations. Murphy argues that, alongside the feelings of anger and resentment that the criminal law institutionalises in order to support victims and promote their self-respect, retributive hatred should also deserve 'a certain amount of respect'. It involves a legitimate form of 'moral outrage against an injustice suffered' while being coupled with 'a desire to make sure the perpetrator of the outrage gets his just deserts'.[34] Thus, it is in principle a 'natural', 'fitting' and 'proper' response to certain (usually atrocious) kinds of wrongs.

Admittedly, he says, 'it is generally both irrational and immoral to be led, to use Spinoza's phrase, by this dangerous and often blind passion', and thereby it should be overcome in most cases.[35] Nonetheless, it is not necessarily 'irrational or immoral'. In fact, at times, it may become 'therapeutic for the victim' if it is 'appropriately directed toward the wrongdoer'. Therefore, it should not be 'dismissed with a few pious cliches' but seen as 'both respected and dangerous'.[36]

What drove Murphy to defend retributive hatred was the fact that he had grave doubts about Augustine's 'hate the sin but not the sinner' counsel, especially in cases of cruel and inhuman sorts of violation. For him, it is sometimes impossible to separate the sin from the sinner because a sinner can be so intimately linked with the sin or 'the evil upon which he acts that he seems to be, in and of himself, a kind of sin, irredeemably 'rotten'.[37] In these cases, we should respect the victim's feelings and the moral satisfaction that

33 Murphy and Hampton, *Forgiveness and Mercy* p.1.

34 Murphy and Hampton, *Forgiveness and Mercy* p.107.

35 Jeffrie Murphy, 'Hatred: A qualified defense' in Jeffrie Murphy and Jean Hampton (eds), *Forgiveness and Mercy* (CUP 1988) p.108.

36 Murphy, 'Hatred: A qualified defense' p.90.

37 This is how Hampton rephrases Murphy's conception of hatred. Hampton, 'The retributive idea' in Murphy J and Hampton J (eds), *Forgiveness and Mercy* (Cambridge University Press 1988) p.146.

stems from seeing justice done, when the perpetrator gets his just deserts. In turn, hatred for Murphy is, in principle, a justified emotion that one feels towards the perpetrator, in terms of both expressing self-respect and providing therapeutic relief for victims.

As will be discussed in greater detail in Chapter 4, we may agree that retributive punishment addresses the victim's sense of injustice by correcting the false message conveyed by crime, which seeks to diminish the victim's value. Following Hampton's account, we might also partially accept that punishment restores a sense of equality between the victim and the offender by defeating the latter when it dispels their hubris.[38] However, this should not lead us to assume that hatred is a justified response towards the offender as a means of vindicating the victim. Hatred, particularly when it fosters a vindictive and excessively punitive attitude, is more likely to be self-deceptive and even self-destructive for the victim. This is especially the case when victims are swayed by a primitive, hostile anger that does neither themselves nor their offenders any good and when they see no way other than revenge when rebuilding their self-respect. Equally significant is the fact that hatred is intrinsically indifferent to the ethical harm that victims suffer, the sort of harm that disrupts the way victims look at themselves and the world. It stands in the way of the process of grief while also standing as a barrier to moral and emotional recovery. Here is where we should realise that retributivism has a tendency to imprison us in a mental state consumed by the passions of anger and hostility, in which we hold a distorted image of the world and offenders, move towards moral insensitivity and even cruelty, and do not attend to the moral damage inside ourselves.

As incisively articulated by Craig Reeves, who interprets contemporary penal thinking in light of Klein's psychoanalysis, retributive moral psychology is inclined to treat offenders as 'all bad objects' that must be 'destroyed'[39] – for it often presupposes 'a partial view' of them, by only looking at what they have done and abstracting it from 'their actual social and psychological formation'. When offenders are abstracted from an experience of their concrete wholeness as real persons, 'aggressive, punitive, retaliatory, destructive, or even annihilating, impulses make emotional sense'.[40] But, viewing offenders as part objects that possess no goodness, these punitive impulses are based on a kind of 'distortion or delusion rather than realistic apprehension' of what offenders look like in a moral psychological sense.[41]

Alongside distortion in the perception of offenders, the moral psychology of retributive punishing comes also with a distortion of self-image. The

38 Hampton, 'Correcting harms versus righting wrongs'.

39 Craig Reeves, 'What punishment expresses' (2019) 28 *Social & Legal Studies* 31, 40.

40 Reeves, Norrie and Carvalho, 'Between persecution and reconciliation: criminal justice, legal form and human emancipation' p.390.

41 Reeves, Norrie and Carvalho, 'Between persecution and reconciliation: criminal justice, legal form and human emancipation' p.391.

retributive motivation to punish, as Carvalho and Chamberlen comment, is usually geared towards the release of certain negative emotions, such as anxiety, insecurity, anger and frustration.[42] It also produces a kind of negative solidarity that bonds individuals together when confronting the 'threat' of crime and gives them a sense of belonging and community. But the punitive urge in individuals often 'generates and reinforces solidarity through hostility', not through more constructive feelings, such as care, compassion and love. When doing so, it also blocks a thorough engagement with the root question of why they feel 'insecure', 'threatened' and 'vulnerable' in the first place.[43]

Having engaged in a kind of self-analysis in his recent work, perhaps in a manner that Carvalho and Chamberlen would approve, Murphy regretfully accepts that his previous retributive thoughts are drawn in part by what Nietzsche calls the destructive passion of *ressentiment*, 'an evil brew of malice, spite, envy, and cruelty'.[44] In Murphy's view, Nietzsche is right to caution us when he maintains that 'whoever fights with monsters should take care that in the process he does not become a monster'.[45] Finding his soul 'troubled' by this famous insightful remark, he notes that 'with their scorekeeping and their tit for tat', retributivists, including himself, 'have the sensibilities of accountants'.[46] They carry 'a soul that squints'. What is more, very unusually for a philosopher who is supposed to keep a certain distance from all the psychological or autobiographical factors, he comes to confess:

> I remain a prisoner – in ways of which I am often unaware – of my own resentful and vindictive Irish nature, some tendencies toward self-righteousness, a certain rigidity of character, and my lifelong back-and-forth struggle between the gospel of love stressed in my Christian upbringing and my not always- loving personality. … If I had been a kinder person, a less angry person, a person of more generous spirit and greatness of soul, would robust retributivism have charmed me to the degree that it at one time did? I suspect not.[47]

42 Carvalho and Chamberlen, 'Why punishment pleases: Punitive feelings in a world of hostile solidarity' p.1.

43 Carvalho and Chamberlen, 'Why punishment pleases: Punitive feelings in a world of hostile solidarity' p.12.

44 Murphy, *Punishment and the Moral Emotions: Essays in Law, Morality, and Religion* p.xii.

45 Friedrich Nietzsche, *Beyond Good and Evil* (Vintage Books 1989) p.89.

46 Murphy, *Punishment and the Moral Emotions: Essays in Law, Morality, and Religion* p.22

47 Murphy, *Punishment and the Moral Emotions: Essays in Law, Morality, and Religion* p.88; 'Those who knew Murphy best would often note, with a slight ribbing, that his views on retribution and repentance might be influenced, just slightly, by the obvious fact that he loved dogs more than people!' (Julie Tenney, 'ASU honors the passing of Professor Jeffrie G. Murphy, notable philosopher and author on forgiveness' (17 September 2020) <https://news.asu.edu/20200917-asu-honors-passing-professor-jeffrie-g-murphy-notable-philosopher-and-author-forgiveness>.

This is an interesting self-observation that may seem unsuitable and unhelpful to quote when defending a particular view or argument: *ad hominem*. That said, it helps us to see the mental or psychological bridge that Murphy builds when he transitions from a primitive, score-keeping version of retributivism to a mature one driven by a more 'generous spirit'. That bridge points towards another – kinder – conception of retributivism that has been blocked or suppressed by rigid legality, anger and self-righteousness.

Reflecting on the question of what the institution of punishment would look like if it is not solely driven by Rawlsian precept of justice but by the Christian virtue of *agape*, he argues that it would, first of all, be an institution purged of moral hatred or other vindictive passions, which he had earlier endorsed.[48] It would also be an institution that is not 'pursued with righteous enthusiasm but always with caution, regret, and humility'.[49] Despite his belief in the transformative power of Christian love, Murphy does not think that agape necessarily paves the way for penal abolitionism or radical reform. For him, agape can direct us towards more humane forms of penal practices, in which we could express our anger by integrating it with love and even forgiveness. In this more mature response, we can convey to offenders the message that 'they are still loved and not hated, that their essential humanity is still being acknowledged, and that we have not presumed to banish them from the domain of loving concern'.[50] This requires, of course, as Reeves puts it, a more nuanced and complex emotional processing, animated by 'love and hope as well as hurt and disappointment'.[51] If we could do so and recognise offenders as whole persons, we could have more spacious room for what I call 'ethical restoration'.

Reflecting on the interface between punishment and loving ethics, Murphy gives the example of the Prison Dog Project, a programme in which offenders are asked to care for dogs and expected to 'develop some of the virtues that come from the receiving and giving of love they have been missing in their prior lives'.[52] As happened in these kinds of restorative practices, retributive punishment, Murphy thinks, might be compatible with love and even forgiveness, if our motivation to punish is grounded only in considerations of justice and moral desert, not vindictive anger, and if punishment is constructed as 'instrumental in the moral and spiritual transformations of offenders'.[53] It seems doubtful whether we could inflict a 'deserved' suffering on offenders and then expect them to morally grow – for the former is concerned with whether the offender suffers an appropriate amount of pain, while the latter

48 Murphy, *Punishment and the Moral Emotions: Essays in Law, Morality, and Religion* p.43.
49 Jeffrie G. Murphy, *Getting even: Forgiveness and its limits* (Oxford University Press 2003) p.111.
50 Murphy, *Punishment and the Moral Emotions: Essays in Law, Morality, and Religion* p.60.
51 Reeves, 'What punishment expresses' p.51.
52 Murphy, *Punishment and the Moral Emotions: Essays in Law, Morality, and Religion* p.51.
53 Murphy, *Punishment and the Moral Emotions: Essays in Law, Morality, and Religion* p.59.

aims to encourage 'reflection, repentance, and spiritual rebirth'. Likewise, the former associates the idea of payback with justice, while the latter is concerned with achieving reform and reconciliation. There is, thus, a notable tension between the ideas of desert and reform, a tension that will be examined at some points of this work.

At this point, perhaps what is most remarkable and worth noting is a similar kind of deadlock Duff's communicative retributivism finds itself in. It offers a unique framework in which the offender is punished both because they deserve and because they are encouraged to repent and reconcile with themselves and others. On the one hand, Duff maintains that the offender deserves the condemnation of society in response to their wrongs: it is just to inflict an appropriate level of suffering upon them, a suffering that is proportionate to their moral desert. This reflects the classical retributive idea that punishment is justified by the past wrong committed. On the other hand, however, he contends that the offender's suffering should take place within a framework of moral dialogue: we should impose a morally suitable form of burden on them with the aim of reform, repentance and reconciliation.[54] This is where Duff diverges from traditional retributivism, proposing that punishment should not simply be a means of expressing society's moral condemnation but also an invitation to the offender to reflect on their wrongdoing, accept responsibility and make efforts to repair the harm caused. Where these aims conflict or become tense with the strict demands of justice, Duff remains committed to the core of retributivism, asserting that the offender should pay their debt through suffering.[55]

In no way do I mean to simplify Duff's theory of punishment. On the contrary, I will engage more deeply with his complex ideas on retributivism in Chapter 5. For the purposes of this chapter, however, it is important to highlight that neo-classical retributivists often find themselves caught in an unresolved tension between what I call 'legal justice' and 'loving ethics'. In this regard, Murphy is not the first and only author who drew attention to the potential for a *loving* dimension within retributive thought. But he is the author who has produced works which remain of considerable representative value within neo-classical retributivism. He is in a deadlock, as are the others.

Conclusion

In this chapter, I have wandered through a broad spectrum of retributive thinking using Murphy's works, from its strictly legal and formalist interpretations to its more expressive and symbolic dimensions, highlighting the diverse ways in which it is conceptualised and justified. I have made a diagnosis of the

54 Antony Duff, 'Punishment as communication' in Ryberg J (ed), *Oxford Handbook of Punishment Theory and Philosophy* (Oxford University Press 2022) p.16.

55 Duff, 'Punishment as communication'.

recent neo-retributivists through Murphy. In this regard, I have first explored the inherent contradiction between loyalty to the precept of desert and the moral uneasiness about the deliberate infliction of suffering on offenders. Attempting to navigate this contradiction, the neo-classical retributivists strive to keep a double rein: one firmly holding onto the principles of fairness and accountability (legal restoration), while the other seeks to avoid or temper the rigidity of punishment with moral sensitivity (ethical restoration).

To delve deeper into the tension between legal justice and ethical love, I have critically examined Murphy's evolving engagement with the fair play theory of punishment. Initially, he embraced its penal model, which prioritises restoring fairness between lawbreakers and society. However, he later expressed scepticism, questioning whether genuine reciprocal relations can exist between disadvantaged offenders and others. I interpret his later critique as stemming from a loving impulse, but this does little to address the structural issues within retributivism. The core impasse arises from a failure to grapple with the challenge of pursuing individual justice in the context of broader social injustice.

In the final section of this chapter, I have examined the limitations of strict reliance on moral desert, especially when it is intertwined with negative emotions, while asking whether moral desert can coexist with the ethics of love. As detailed earlier, Murphy initially took retributivism as a channel for expressing justified moral hatred towards offenders. However, he later moved away from this approach, as his understanding of retributivism 'matured', incorporating the Christian ideal of agape. His aim was to craft a more humanistic approach to just deserts. Yet his works leave unresolved the tension between the demands of legal justice and those of ethical love.

To repeat, I have sought to demonstrate, where relevant, how other neo-retributivists encounter a similar kind of deadlock. However, I will address those theorists more thoroughly in Part III, where I analyse retributivism through the lenses of the victim, offender and state. Before turning to that discussion, it is essential to first clarify the distinct features of legal and ethical retributivism as they stand on their own. To this end, the next part focusses on Hegel's two contrasting approaches to punishment.

Bibliography

Adorno T, *Negative Dialectics* (Continuum 1983)

Brudner A, *Punishment and Freedom* (OUP 2009)

Duff A, 'Penal communications: recent work in the philosophy of punishment' (1996) 20 *Crime and Justice* 1

Duff A, 'Punishment as communication' in Ryberg J (ed), *Oxford Handbook of Punishment Theory and Philosophy* (2022) 16

Duff A, *Punishment, Communication, and Community* (OUP 2001)

Hampton J, 'Correcting harms versus righting wrongs: The goal of retribution' (1992) 39 *UCLA Law Review* 1659–1702

Jacobs JA, *The Liberal State and Criminal Sanction: Seeking Justice and Civility* (OUP 2020)
Marx K, 'Capital punishment. Mr Cobden's pamphlet: regulations of the bank of England' (1853) 28 *New York Tribune*
Matravers M, *Justice and Punishment: The Rationale of Coercion* (OUP 2000)
Morris H, 'Persons and punishment' (1968) 52(4) *The Monist* 475
Murphy J, *Getting Even: Forgiveness and Its Limits* (OUP 2003)
Murphy J, 'Hatred: a qualified defense' in Murphy J and Hampton J (eds), *Forgiveness and Mercy* (Cambridge University Press 1988)
Murphy J, 'Last words on retribution' in Jacobs J (ed), *The Routledge Handbook of Criminal Justice Ethics* (Routledge 2016)
Murphy J, 'Marxism and retribution' (1973) 2 *Philosophy and Public Affairs* 21
Murphy J, *Punishment and the Moral Emotions: Essays in Law, Morality, and Religion* (OUP 2012)
Murphy J, *Retribution, Justice, and Therapy: Essays in the Philosophy of Law* (Springer Science & Business Media 1979)
Murphy J, *Retribution Reconsidered: More Essays in the Philosophy of Law* (Springer Science & Business Media 1992)
Murphy J, 'Retributivism and the state's interest in punishment' in Pennock JR and Chapman JW (eds), *Criminal Justice* (New York University Press 1985)
Murphy J, 'Shame creeps through guilt and feels like retribution' (1999) 18 *Law and Philosophy* 327
Murphy J and Hampton J, *Forgiveness and Mercy* (Cambridge University Press 1988)
Nietzsche F, *Beyond Good and Evil* (Vintage 1989) 89
Norrie A, *Rethinking Criminal Justice Punishment, Abolition and Moral Psychology* (Cambridge University Press Forthcoming)
Ramsay P, 'A democratic theory of imprisonment' in Dzur AW, Loader I and Sparks R (eds), *Democratic Theory and Mass Incarceration* (OUP 2016)
Reeves C, Norrie A and Carvalho H, 'Between persecution and reconciliation: criminal justice, legal form and human emancipation' in Christodoulidis E (ed), *Research Handbook on Critical Legal Theory* (Edward Elgar Publishing 2019)
Reeves C, 'What punishment expresses' (2019) 28 *Social & Legal Studies* 31
Tenney J, 'ASU honors the passing of Professor Jeffrie G. Murphy, notable philosopher and author on forgiveness' (September 17, 2020) <https://news.asu.edu/20200917-asu-honors-passing-professor-jeffrie-g-murphy-notable-philosopher-and-author-forgiveness>
Tonry M, *Why Punish? How Much?: A Reader on Punishment* (OUP 2011)

Part II

Back to origins

2 Legal retributivism

Introduction

If going back to the classics is not to be a step backwards, it should be a refreshing exercise that illuminates the world in which we live today. This is all the more so with regard to institutions which are subject to constant change, such aslaw and punishment, depending on the historical and social contexts. Thoroughly investigating the moral and political foundations of modern life, perhaps no philosophy other than Hegel's in the classical period provides a satisfactory set of materials when seeking to understand the central pillars of contemporary legal thought. In his *Philosophy of Right*, where human freedom is taken as both the departure and arrival point to explore the main tenets of ethical and political life, Hegel presents various themes that have been shared and developed by many legal scholars, including penal theorists.

His thoughts about punishment are largely built into his overall vision of the world. This thus leads me to his general philosophical system before scrutinising his theory of punishment. What is most well-known in Hegel's philosophy is the dialectical method, through which he seeks to grasp the world as it is. Simply put, this method demands that our thoughts over a particular subject become complicated in a process where contradictory elements between opposing sides are reconciled at a higher level, with a linear evolution from less sophisticated understandings to more coherent and consistent ones. I will argue that, under a dialectical gaze, punishment in Hegel should be understood as the end product of a process in which retaliation is followed by self-punishment and then turned into legal sanction at an institutional level. Following Hegel's own methodological track, I will formulate legal punishment as the reconciliation of *the moral* (desert and self-punishment) and *the political* (the restoration or re-affirmation of state authority).

Formed by the notions of desert and self-punishment at the lower level of thinking, the moral provides a normative basis for the conditions of

DOI: 10.4324/9781003563150-5

responsibility.[1] The offender is held accountable and deserves punishment because his violation of others' rights makes him due for punishment: 'as the criminal has done, so should it be done to him'.[2] But the offender should make sense of how crime is followed by punishment and come to see his crime as a wrong that damages the freedom of others as well as his own. Otherwise, punishment would not go beyond mere retaliation. Punishment, as it were, should be self-imposed: self-punishment.

These moral conditions, however, are still insufficient without a socio-political institutional setting in which punishment is imposed by a legal authority. Violation at the political level becomes public and an act of attack that concerns all the members of the society. At a higher stage of thinking, the focus is shifted from the question of how crime morally entails punishment to an enquiry about whether it raises a direct challenge to the state's authority. Here is where the *legal* in Hegel's theory comes onto the scene: only the wrongs that are legally prohibited injure the normative status of the state, *challenge* freedom all the way through and thereby require a retributive response. As famously stated, while crime is a negation of law (Recht), punishment is the negation of that negation.[3] So being, it restores the law that has been infringed.

By combining the ideas of desert and self-punishment with the reaffirmation of the state's authority, the moral in Hegel is reconciled with the political and constructs the legal. In this chapter, I will take this as constructing what I have termed 'legal retributivism'. Legal retributivism provides a complex conception of punishment, in which various elements (the moral, ethical, and political) are brought together to produce a comprehensive normative theory. I claim that, despite its intricacy, legal retributivism produces an *unevenly integrated* conception of punishment in which the principles of desert and self-punishment do not stand in harmony with the restoration of law. Equally significant is the fact that legal retributivism is also *ethically truncated*, in that the ethical possibilities inherent in the moral are often overshadowed by the political.

To form a basis for my reading of Hegel's theory of punishment, I will begin this chapter with a summary of his dialectical method. This is followed in the second section by a brief outline of how his dialectics generates a theory of formal ethical life that creates a tension between subjective freedom and law. The third section is concerned with an analysis of the internal elements of legal punishment. Finally, this chapter concludes with the idea that legal

1 Note that I draw on the term 'moral' in a broad sense, not in the sense that Hegel uses in the Philosophy of Right as a concept that explains the transitional sphere between Abstract Right and Ethical Life.

2 Hegel, *Outlines of the Philosophy of Right* para.101.

3 The German term Recht has a wider meaning than any English word. When Hegel uses this term in the context of crime and punishment, he means the whole structure of moral life, including both legal norms and institutions and individual morality. Michael James Inwood, *A Hegel Dictionary* (Blackwell 1992) p.259.

retributivism is a political theory of punishment that compromises the ethical world from which it takes its legitimacy and privileges a legalistic conception of punishment over a deeper account of self-punishment.

1. The philosophical ground: Hegel's logic

Located squarely in the modern idealist tradition, Hegel is a philosopher of change, contradiction and disunity. But he is also a philosopher of synthesis, reconciliation and unity. Hegel is well known for what is usually called 'speculative logic', where the complex nature of reality is discovered by a peculiar way of thinking.[4] Speculative logic gives us a systematic method to shed light on reality in its complexity and contradictions. Yet it is also derived from the very nature of reality by disclosing how reality operates.[5] Loosely speaking, how we think in Hegel is inextricably linked up with how things exist as they are. 'To say that certain conceptual structures must apply to the world', as Taylor comments on Hegel's philosophy, 'is surely to say something about the nature of things'.[6] In this sense, speculative logic is somehow meant to produce a theory of ontology alongside that of epistemology by providing heuristic instruments for an understanding of not only the reasoning process but also the nature of the external world.[7]

The underlying principle in this logic is that there is a driving force in both thought and being to unify and reconcile what is contradictory: dialectic.[8] Dialectic is the 'dynamo' of the process of reasoning, where reality is unravelled through increasing levels of sophistication and comprehensiveness, by way of what Hegel calls 'sublation' or 'supersession' (*Aufhebung*).[9] In other words, dialectical reasoning grasps reality on many levels, each level calling for different sorts of explanation. In the process of thinking, simple and abstract forms of thought are negated, preserved and superseded by more complex explanations so that a total and complete grasp is brought out in a progressive movement.

4 Alan Norrie, *Dialectic and Difference: Dialectical Critical Realism and the Grounds of Justice* (Routledge 2010) p.54. Stephen Houlgate, *The Opening of Hegel's Logic: From Being to Infinity* (Purdue University Press, 2005).

5 Stephen Houlgate, 'G.W.F Hegel: An introduction to his life and thought' in Stephen Houlgate and Baur Michael (eds), *A Companion to Hegel* (Blackwell 2011) p.7.

6 Charles Taylor, *Hegel* (2005) p.227.

7 Pippin describes speculative logic as 'a new kind of metaphysics'. Robert B Pippin, 'Hegel on logic as metaphysics' in Moyar (ed.), *The Oxford Handbook of Hegel* (Oxford University Press, 2017) pp.199–218, p.199. see also Paul Redding, 'Georg Wilhelm Friedrich Hegel' in Zalta EN and Nodelman U (eds), *The Stanford Encyclopedia of Philosophy* (Fall 2024), https://plato.stanford.edu/cgi-bin/encyclopedia/archinfo.cgi?entry=hegel accessed on 28.04.2025. .

8 Hegel draws on the concept of dialectic in two senses. While the first is a narrower term that signifies the middle stage of thought process, the second is a general term that describes the entire process.

9 Norrie, *Dialectic and Difference: Dialectical Critical Realism and the Grounds of Justice* p.55.

This takes place in a tripartite model of thinking: 'understanding', 'dialectic' and 'speculation'. While 'abstract understanding' sees the world as composed of distinct particular things, 'dialectic' or 'negative reason' reveals the dynamic and contradictory nature of things. When things stand in opposition at the level of 'negative reason', 'speculative reason' repairs the opposition by showing that a sort of unity and wholeness is present within the contradictions. For Hegel, this sort of systematic thinking presents a wider lens through which to grasp how varied and conflicting things come together in a rational whole.[10] As stated earlier, this method or reasoning is derived precisely, Hegel would say, from the way reality manifests itself in the external world.

Drawing on an analogy to clarify his method, Hegel appeals to the example of the development of a tree. 'The buds', writes Hegel, 'have the tree implicit within them and contain the tree's whole strength, although they are not yet the tree itself'.[11] To be able to call a bud 'a fully developed tree', which is a whole involving the earlier forms of a tree (namely seed, trunk, branches and fruit), it must actualise itself and become a concrete unity in the external world. It is the demand of reason that a tree exists as a tree when it takes its most developed form.[12] But it is also the nature of the tree from which the demands and principles of reason originate.

Hegel goes further than this. He claims that reason does not only tell us *how* the world works; it also explains *why* the world works that way. This means that there is a teleology or purpose within his conception of reason that moves beyond describing the world as it is. In other words, Hegelian reason is normative, and its normative character is particularly key to the understanding of his law and ethical life. This is perhaps best encapsulated in the dictum that 'what is rational is actual and what is actual is rational'.[13] To provide more insights into how reason is embedded in and directs normative world, let us move on to his conception of freedom and ethical life.

2. Dialectical ethics: progression of freedom

Just as the physical world can be explored by a certain conception of reasoning in Hegel, so too in the moral and social world, there is an internal rationality governing how human beings live or should live. Reason both makes and is made by the building blocks of morality, laws and socio-political arrangements upon which human freedom is founded.[14] In this sense, incorporating a

10 Georg Wilhelm Friedrich Hegel, *The Encyclopaedia Logic: Part I of the Encyclopaedia of Philosophical Sciences with the Zusätze* (Hackett Publishing 1991) p.125.

11 Hegel, *Outlines of the Philosophy of Right* para.1.

12 Hegel, *Outlines of the Philosophy of Right* para.1.

13 Hegel, *Outlines of the Philosophy of Right* p.14.

14 Stephen Houlgate, *Freedom, Truth, and History: An Introduction to Hegel's Philosophy* (Blackwell 2005) p.181.

developing notion of freedom at its heart, Hegel's ethical and political theory stand in close connection with his speculative logic and metaphysics.[15]

Hegel contends that within the actual structure of social interactions, human freedom gets complicated in a threefold mode, in correspondence with the three layers of reasoning: Abstract Right, Morality and Ethical Life. Each of these spheres embodies a model in which institutions and practices underpin and sustain the ways in which freedom is actualised. At the basic level of freedom, human beings are taken as right holders or juridical individuals, defined by relations of property and contract.[16] Establishing the equality of all, Abstract Right views human beings as persons having a claim on an external sphere for the exercise of their free choice.[17] They want their choice to be respected and recognised by others at this level, where they are bound by minimum social ties. But freedom here is likely to be shattered by violations of the boundaries when subjective choices clash in tort, especially crime. The ignorance of others' rights results in a kind of punishment to develop a normative possibility of mutually agreed rights.[18]

From the perspective of the offender, punishment in Abstract Right is nothing more than retaliation imposed by others. Because of the lack of resources to understand the moral nature of punishment at this level, there is a need to engage with the meaning of violation so that the response to

15 It is noteworthy that there is a debate in the literature about how much Hegel's logic (metaphysics) is related to his conception of ethics. Because I believe that there is enough textual evidence that his conception of ethics is shaped by his dialectical logic, at least on the themes of crime and punishment, I will read Hegel's conception of ethical in the light of his dialectical method; for a similar view see: Peter J Steinberger, 'Hegel on crime and punishment' (1983) 77 *American Political Science Review* 858; Thom Brooks, *Hegel's Ambiguous Contribution to Legal Theory* (HeinOnline 2005) Some think that the link between Hegelian ethics and logic is not as strong as Hegel claims. On this see: Zbigniew Andrzej Pelczynski, *An Introductory Essay' in G. W. F. Hegel, Hegel's Political Writingstrans. T. M. Knox* (Oxford: Clarendon Press 1964) Allen W Wood, *Hegel's Ethical Thought* (Cambridge University Press 1990). For the problems of this view, see: Stephen Houlgate, 'Hegel's Ethical Thought' (1992) 13 *Hegel Bulletin* 1

16 It is significant to note that Hegel understands the term property in a very broad sense. 'A person's right to life and free status, which Hegel regards as inalienable and imprescriptible, depend on the fact that a person's body and life are paradigmatically that person's property, constituting an external sphere that is inseparable from personality itself'. Allen W Wood, 'Hegel's ethics' in C Beiser (ed), *The Cambridge Companion to Hegel* (Cambridge University Press 1999) p.220.

17 Terry Pinkard, *Hegel: A Biography* (Cambridge University Press 2001) p.477.

18 If we interpret the Philosophy of Right as a theory of mutual recognition, Abstract Right would be the most basic form of recognition as 'it is formal, limited, and impersonal.' See for a detailed discussion of the debate: Robert R Williams, *Hegel's Ethics of Recognition* (University of California Press 1998) p.138 for a similar reading see Axel Honneth, *The Pathologies of Individual Freedom: Hegel's Social Theory* (Princeton University Press 2021) p.33; for the opposing view: Karin de Boer, 'Beyond recognition? Critical reflections on Honneth's reading of Hegel's philosophy of right' (2013) 21 *International Journal of Philosophical Studies* 534.

crime becomes justice rather than revenge.[19] Morality then replaces Abstract Right, providing a wider horizon through which individuals gain a sense of moral rightness and wrongness about what they have done and what is done to them. Concerning the inner life of individuals, this is a sphere of freedom in which they come to adopt a set of moral values and principles, while also taking responsibility for the actions which they see as their duties. Morality brings about a universalistic conception of a human being that is independent of any social status or role, developing a conscience that gives individuals a moral subjectivity. And yet, it leaves individuals on their own, accepting that they are self-sufficient about deciding how to act morally. As Beiser comments, 'the standpoint of morality is one-sided and abstract because it separates the individual from his place in the social whole, which gives the individual his very identity'.[20]

For Hegel, without social and public arrangements that would back up individuals as autonomous beings, freedom would be insufficiently realised. There is therefore a requirement for a social complement to fill up the 'emptiness' individuals face at the Morality stage, which would yield certain normative guidelines: Ethical Life (*Sittlichkeit*).[21] The modern family, market society and constitutional state make up the multilayered identity of modern individuals (family member, self-interested trader, citizen).[22] In the social life of modernity, everyone recognises that they are separate and independent from others. And yet, they are also aware that they 'bond into a reflective ethos of a developed ethical life'.[23] In Hegel's view, human freedom at this stage arrives at a point where individuals 'live at peace with the world' while also identifying with their social environment such that public institutions seem like their 'second nature'.[24] At the stage of Ethical Life, laws regulated by the political authority are not commands, but rather, they stipulate what individuals already want to have in accordance with their freedom.[25] They recognise

19 For a similar reading: Katerina Deligiorgi, 'Hegel's moral philosophy' in Dean Moyar (ed), *The Oxford Handbook of Hegel* (Oxford University Press 2017) p.501.

20 Frederick C. Beiser, *Hegel* (London: Routledge 2005) p.234.

21 What is called 'emptiness charge' in the Philosophy of Right is posited against Kant's moral philosophy. Very crudely put, Hegel thinks that from a moral point of view 'we may intend good but our only guide is our individual conception of the good', so what we need to do is to reflect about ourselves acting in relation to others in Ethical Life. Hegel, *Outlines of the Philosophy of Right* para.140; for a brief critique of this emptiness criticism see: Thom Brooks, 'Hegel's Social and Political Philosophy' in Zalta EN and Nodelman U (eds), *The Stanford Encyclopedia of Philosophy* (Summer 2025), https://plato.stanford.edu/entries/hegel-social-political/ accessed on 28.04.2025'.

22 Honneth, *The Pathologies of Individual Freedom: Hegel's Social Theory* p.43.

23 William Conklin, *Hegel's Laws The Legitimacy of a Modern Legal Order* (Stanford University Press 2008) p.45.

24 Hegel, *Outlines of the Philosophy of Right* para.151.

25 Tunick, *Hegel's Political Philosophy: Interpreting the Practice of Legal Punishment* p.95.

law as identical to their moral values and obey its authority as an extension of their own.

It is worth noting that moving from Abstract Right to Ethical Life, freedom progresses in a linear way. This means that the most complete form of freedom is manifested in the institutions of the modern state.[26] For some, it may seem quite puzzling and worrying. After all, the state as an institution having the monopoly on violence seems to contrast sharply with the idea of freedom. In fact, there is much literature on the dark side of Hegel's political theory, where the aim of Ethical Life is depicted as subsuming the individual to the power of the state.[27] Such an interpretation also finds textual support in the Philosophy of Right. But this approach, as Fine comments, runs in contrast with how Hegel views the relationship between the state and freedom.[28]

'The state', Hegel writes, 'is the actuality of concrete freedom'. Yet, he adds, 'concrete freedom requires that personal individuality and its particular interests should reach their full development'.[29] Hegel's main interest here is to do with how to preserve the fundamental structure of the modern state without disrespecting the inviolable rights of individuals. This shows, at least, that there is an attempt in Hegel's system to provide a synthesis of individual freedom and political authority. Once understood this way, the shift from Morality to Ethical Life can entail an emancipatory transition from which emerges a satisfying moral life, expressing both individuals' independence from and dependence upon each other. In other words, one is fully and *concretely* free in Hegel's theory when one is in harmony with the terms of Ethical Life.[30]

3. The boundaries of subjective freedom in Ethical Life

Nonetheless, the harmony in the practices of socio-political life is achieved at the expense of either shrinking subjective freedom or losing depth and richness in the way individuals lead their moral life. This is not simply to say that moral subjectivity and conscience are totally crushed for the sake of maintaining a public order. By contrast, as many Hegelian commentators argue, individual freedom is often preserved and supported by the laws and institutions of Ethical

26 Taylor, *Hegel* p.438.

27 For a famous critic of Hegel see: Bertrand Russell, *History of Western Philosophy* (Routledge 2004) p.670. Hegel's Philosophy of Right 'justifies every internal tyranny and every external aggression that can possibly be imagined.' For a criticism of this reading see: Robert Fine, *Political Investigations: Hegel, Marx and Arendt* (Routledge 2005) p.15.

28 Fine, *Political Investigations: Hegel, Marx and Arendt*; there has been a growing group commentators in recent years criticising the notorious charge against Hegel that he advocates an authoritarian political state. Houlgate, *Freedom, Truth, and History: An Introduction to Hegel's Philosophy*; Paul Franco, *Hegel's Philosophy of Freedom* (Yale University Press 1999); Alan Patten, *Hegel's Idea of Freedom* (Oxford University Press 1999).

29 Hegel, *Outlines of the Philosophy of Right* para.260.

30 Dudley Knowles, *Routledge Philosophy Guidebook to Hegel and the Philosophy of Right* (Routledge 2004) p.238.

Life.[31] But when subjective freedom operates within a formal framework, it is confined and sometimes undermined by the boundaries of the established order.

Consider, for example, the freedom of those who, according to Hegel, have lost their 'sense of right and wrong' due to the dim social conditions that befall them: the case of the rabble.[32] In Hegel's system, poverty 'is a structural phenomenon, the result of the operation of civil society when it is in a state of unimpeded activity and not the result of some personal failing on the part of the poor'.[33] For this reason, Hegel says, it is 'a wrong done to one class by another', undermining the freedom of those who live below the level of subsistence. But the structural inequalities and failings of modern societies go further than this. If we are led to see 'the rabble' in Hegel's world as 'a state of mind, a mentality', rather than a certain class defined by economic relations, the society he describes becomes more fragmented and a less secure place for the flourishing of freedom than it is claimed to be. In this view, the rabble is made up of the sort of people who believe that they are dissociated from others. 'This disassociation', as Brooks notes, 'is based upon a sense of injustice: that they lack in some significant share of right, legitimacy, and honour'. They are 'divorced from lawful society; that the rules applying to all somehow do not relate to them because of this sense of political otherness'.[34] How should we then solve the tension or contradiction between freedom and state authority that maintains this social (im)balance?

One way to overcome this impasse is to suggest that the feelings of outrage and resentment expressed against the order are the rightful manifestation of individuals' freedom. In other words, we could grant the rabble the right to resist the political authority. But Hegel has not pursued that path. The dialectic, as it were, stops here. Instead, he has left this problem unsolved, while having 'nothing more to say than that it is one of the disturbing problems which agitate modern societies'.[35] In fact, when forced to confront this conflict in the *Philosophy of Right*, Hegel implies the priority of state authority over individual freedom.[36] For him, freedom is always dependent on the existence

31 See for example: Christian Hofmann, 'Autonomy and the concrete universal: Moral subjectivity and its function in Hegel's Philosophy of Right' (2014) 35 *Hegel Bulletin* 252; Frederick Neuhouser, 'Ethical life and the demands of conscience' (1998) 19 *Hegel Bulletin* 35; Houlgate, *Freedom, Truth, and History: An Introduction to Hegel's Philosophy* p.185.

32 Hegel, *Outlines of the Philosophy of Right* para.244.

33 Raymond Plant, 'Hegel on identity and legitimation' in Zbigniew Andrzej Pelczynski (ed), *The State and Civil Society: Studies in Hegel's Political Philosophy* (Cambridge University Press 1984) p.242.

34 Brooks, *Punishment* p.144.

35 Shlomo Avineri, *Hegel's Theory of the Modern State* (Cambridge University Press 2003) p.154. Against this view: see: Houlgate, *Freedom, Truth, and History: An Introduction to Hegel's Philosophy* p.203–204.

36 Here are two quotes 'The right of the state therefore stands above the preceding stages'... 'it is the actuality of the ethical idea.' Hegel, *Outlines of the Philosophy of Right* p.52 and para.257;

of social and political structures unless they are totally corrupt and weaken the subjectivity of individuals. 'It is only in times when the world of actuality is hollow, spiritless, and unstable', says Hegel, 'that an individual may be allowed to take refuge from actuality in his inner life'. Socrates, for example, he goes on, 'lived at the time of the ruin of the Athenian democracy, where he was right to 'withdraw into himself to search there for the right and the good'.[37] The main assumption here is that at the core of modern conditions lies a normative and emancipatory base that fosters individual freedom.[38]

Be that as it may, the way subjective freedom is expressed in Abstract Right and Morality is often curtailed by the terms of Ethical Life. When writing of the ethical experiences of individuals, for example, Hegel views them as having no active role to play in the social world. For him, to act with 'the law of heart' is to act within the contingent realm of subjective feelings and therefore produce a morally deficient behaviour. It lacks normative guidelines provided by a rationally constructed normative order.[39] Remarking on the experience of guilt, for example, Hegel argues that the acceptance of crime with a confession of guilt is necessary for the compatibility of individual freedom with penal force. But if 'the interest of justice is jeopardised' by the criminal's denial, we would have nothing but to accept that the declaration of guilt by the jury springs from the soul of the criminal.[40] The underlying implication here is that 'moral guilt' is contingent, but 'legal guilt' is not. Similarly, in Hegel's world, forgiveness is a valuable moral experience, a way of 'making undone what has been done and wiping out a crime'.[41] But forgiveness cannot have a 'cleansing' power when granted by ordinary human beings. The only person who can be in the business of forgiveness is the sovereign monarch, a self-standing individual occupying a central place in Ethical Life.[42] In other words, forgiveness operates only where it is concretised and objectified by a political normative framework.

There is not the scope here to discuss whether Hegel is successful when reconciling subjective freedom with the terms of Ethical Life, but what is most clear is that the manifestations of subjective freedom shrink in the shift from Morality to Ethical Life, particularly in cases of experiences that point us towards a broader and deeper ethical realm. Even if subjective freedom is harmonised with the authority of law, the harmony comes at a cost: a narrower and shallower conception of freedom, limited by the normative authority of Ethical Life. In the next section, I will explain how Hegel's ethical outlook bears on his conception of punishment.

for a similar view: Norrie, *Law, Ideology and Punishment* p.87–88.

37 Hegel, *Outlines of the Philosophy of Right* para.13.

38 Honneth, *The Pathologies of Individual Freedom: Hegel's Social Theory* p.41.

39 Hegel, *Outlines of the Philosophy of Right* para.282.

40 Hegel, *Outlines of the Philosophy of Right* para.227.

41 Hegel, *Outlines of the Philosophy of Right* para.282.

42 Hegel, *Outlines of the Philosophy of Right* para.282.

4. Punishment in dialectical forms: retaliation, self-punishment and legal punishment

What does this brief and yet hopefully accurate analysis of Hegel's moral and political theory tell us about his account of punishment? As is shown in the second section, his moral and political insights consist in the idea of freedom and its development. For Hegel, like his ethical and political theory, punishment has a distinctive role to play in the social world insofar as it is linked up with the freedom of individuals. When freedom is in jeopardy or destroyed by criminal violation, punishment comes on the scene and takes the role of negation. In Hegel, because crime is the *negation* of law, punishment is portrayed as *the negation of the negation*. Logically, punishment follows (or should follow) criminal violation in order to be at the service of the development of human freedom.[43] As a response to the past wrong, punishment is an institution that is morally good and necessary in Hegel's system, and thereby it can be seen as retributive.

Nonetheless, the form of punishment depends on the level of freedom from which it is generated. Punishment at the most basic level of human interaction (Abstract Right) is simply a painful response directed at the wrongdoer in retaliation for the wrong. It becomes self-punishment at the level of subjective freedom (Morality), in which individuals acquire moral autonomy and confront the (internal) consequences of their behaviour. Finally, the most complete form of punishment is the state's penal coercion, through which retaliation and self-punishment are synthetised (Ethical Life). Each form of freedom in Hegel's system generates its own conception of punishment. Let me explain each form of punishment in more detail.

As is widely accepted in the literature on Hegel, punishment as a reaction to crime at the level of Abstract Right is based upon the principles of interpersonal morality and does not involve a public authority.[44] For Hegel, in principle, it is morally right for someone to retaliate against another who has violated their rights. In his own words, 'as the criminal has done, so should it be done to him'.[45] The criminal deserves to be punished not only because they deserve it but also because it is their own act that makes them due for punishment. The idea behind this is that violating the rights of another deprives one of the right to complain about being punished or treated in the same way as one treats

43 Note that to say that the circuit of crime and punishment is logical in Hegel's system is also necessarily to accept that it is moral. For a different view on this see: Anthony M Quinton, 'On punishment' (1954) 14 *Analysis* 133.

44 Thom Brooks, 'Hegel and the unified theory of punishment' in Thom Brooks (ed), *Hegel's Philosophy of Right* (Blackwell Publishing 2012) p.111; Antje Du Bois-Pedain, 'Hegal and the justification of real-world penal sanctions' (2016) 29 *Canadian Journal of Law & Jurisprudence* 37; Peter G Stillman, 'Hegel's idea of punishment' (1976) 14 *Journal of the History of Philosophy* 169. For an exception to this interpretation see: David E Cooper, 'Hegel's theory of punishment' (1971) 151 *Hegel's Political Philosophy* 153.

45 Hegel, *Outlines of the Philosophy of Right* para.101.

one's victims. It is the criminal's own behaviour that somehow creates the law that permits their punishment.[46]

Nonetheless, such a practice of punishment cannot escape appearing to be a kind of revenge, in that it involves a subjective goal of getting even with the criminal. Retaliation is usually inflicted with 'a particular emotional tone', followed by a pleasure in the suffering of another.[47] In so doing, it lacks an objective judicial power, and thereby it is a 'defective' form of punishment, expressing the moral voice of private individuals that is likely to turn into a new transgression.[48] Highlighting the contingency of the payback response, Johnson claims, retaliation 'attains justice, if at all, only by chance'.[49] It does not end the cycle of coercive violence; rather, it perpetuates and amplifies it.[50] It should therefore be overcome by another higher form of response to crime that is produced by a more developed conception of freedom.

From a textual reading of the *Philosophy of Right*, there is no mention of punishment at the level of Morality other than thoughts linking the abstract conception of crime to the subjective moral lives of offenders. As Marcuse points out, Morality, as it were, seems 'a mere joint between . . . abstract right and societal life'.[51] This section of Hegel's work may be read as developing a specific form of punishment that is to be the basis for his conception of legal punishment in Ethical Life. As stated earlier, individuals at the Morality stage acquire a conscience through which they engage with what they have done and make a judgement about their actions in their inner world. Once conscience is at work, a peculiar form of punishment is produced at this stage, shaped by an appreciation of the wrong as wrong. This form of punishment arises out of moral reflection over the wrong. It is thus self-willed and likely to be ethically deep and transformative for individuals, even though it does not necessarily result in 'bad conscience' or feelings of guilt.[52] This form of punishment at this stage is what I call 'self-punishment'.

Any moral thinking over the wrong in Hegel's view, however, is disposed to evaporate into radical subjectivism and can become 'something completely powerless and empty' when not supported by an objective normative sphere.[53] Self-punishment must be created by what Hegel calls a 'true conscience', the

46 Knowles, *Routledge Philosophy Guidebook to Hegel and the Philosophy of Right* p.150.

47 Robert Nozick, *Philosophical Explanations* (Harvard University Press 1981) p.367.

48 Hegel, *Outlines of the Philosophy of Right* para.102.

49 Johnson, 'Hegel on punishment: A more sophisticated retributivism' p.161.

50 Williams, *Hegel's Ethics of Recognition* p.166.

51 Herbert Marcuse, *Reason and Revolution Hegel and the Rise of Social Theory* (Routledge & Kegan Paul 1955) p.200.

52 While in *the System of Ethical Life*, Hegel argues that the wrongdoer's bad conscience (feelings of guilt) provides an ideal opposition (Gegenwirkung) to, or reversal (Umkehrung) of, his crime, which calls for completion by an external 'avenging justice', in *the Philosophy of Right* he stresses what he calls 'formal conscience', the universal implications of the criminal's rational will rather than his bad conscience.' Inwood, *A Hegel Dictionary* p.234.

53 Hegel, *Outlines of the Philosophy of Right* para.141.

sort of conscience that is rooted in an ongoing system of social practices.[54] But not all forms of moral engagement automatically entail the true conscience, so what is ethically required for Hegel is an external form of punishment that would intervene in the life of individuals without causing a loss in the ethical 'authenticity' of self-punishment.

What follows from this is legal punishment. Punishment takes a legal form and becomes more nuanced in the institutions of criminal justice when it overcomes the logics of retaliation and self-punishment. Like retaliation, legal punishment is a deserved backlash, in that it is described as the turning back of crime against itself – but through *another's hands*.[55] Unlike retaliation, as Hegel argues, it is 'freed from subjective interest and subjective form and the contingency of power'.[56] It is a public institution that engages with wrongs concerning all in order to preserve the political authority as the guarantor of rights.[57] When so doing, it derives its legitimacy from the consent of offenders and their acceptance of the wrong as wrong.

Consent arises from the principle that has been created by the very act of criminal violation. Crime sets up a law that everyone, like the criminal, is free to act as they please. This causes a self-contradiction for the criminal, as the law created by their action undermines their own freedom.[58] Accordingly, 'the nature of the crime', Hegel writes, 'requires that the injury initiated by the criminal should be annulled'.[59] In this sense, punishment is nothing more than the manifestation of the principle that originates from crime. But, from a moral point of view, punishment also gives a concrete shape to the subjective conscience of the criminal by recognising it at a public level. This is to say that punishment is not only just or the right of the state in a legal sense, but it is also the right of the criminal.[60] In other words, it does not only reconcile the

54 Hegel, *Outlines of the Philosophy of Right* para.137.

55 It would perhaps be interesting to note here Robert Solomon's view on revenge and its legitimatisation at a public level. He argues that despite its powerful and dangerous nature, revenge is 'also a socially constructed emotion that can be cultivated to contain not only its own limits but a full appreciation of the general good and the law as well' p.144. Robert C Solomon, 'Justice v. vengeance' in Susan Bandes (ed), *The Passions of Law* (New York University Press 2000)

56 Hegel, *Outlines of the Philosophy of Right* para.103; If there is something subjective in legal punishment, Nozick comments, it is 'the pleasure of observing justice being done.' Nozick, *Philosophical Explanations* p.367.

57 Hegel, *Outlines of the Philosophy of Right* para.103.

58 Alan Brudner, 'The contraction of crime in Hegel's rechtsphilosophie' in Markus D. Dubber (ed), *Foundational Texts in Modern Criminal Law* (Oxford University Press 2014) p.153–154.

59 Hegel, *Outlines of the Philosophy of Right* para.100.

60 The right to punishment is an interesting thought of legacy from Hegel that has attracted a considerable attention in the literature. Even though the content and precise meaning of it is unclear, what is common to almost all scholars is the idea that punishment respects the moral autonomy and responsibility of the criminal. See for proponents: Morris, 'Persons and punishment'; Thom Brooks, 'The right to be punished: A defense' (2013) 3 *Legal Theory*

criminal with the law, but it also reconciles them with themselves by respecting their subjective freedom and giving them the right to punishment.[61] Even though it may appear as taking a form of constraint on the part of the criminal, it is emancipatory at a deeper level, as it actualises their moral agency. Legal punishment, as it were, is the actualisation of self-punishment with a public involvement where the state reasserts its authority.

All of this gives us a multifaceted and complex theory shaped by both moral and political considerations. The moral part addresses the principles that govern how human beings should interact with each other and themselves, while the political part focuses mainly on whether the state should intervene in the lives of human beings to reassert its challenged authority. I claim that Hegel constructs a 'legal' conception of punishment by reconciling the moral and political and building an important theoretical bridge between Abstract Right and Ethical Life. The next section will be concerned with how Hegel generates a legal conception of punishment and whether the political dimension takes priority over the moral one.

5. Hegel's theory of punishment: legal retributivism

Punishment, as I said earlier, is initially buttressed by certain principles of morality in Abstract Right, in the sense that it is conceived of as a practice that stands as part of an abstract moral framework, setting up the foundations of criminal responsibility: one is responsible for the sorts of actions that violate the freedoms of others and thereby deserve punishment. But responsibility is truly taken up only at the stage of Morality, where the offender turns inward and seeks freedom in their inner world. Once the coercion is voluntarily accepted, it becomes self-punishment. From a moral perspective, punishment becomes a deserved suffering that is internalised by the offender.

But desert and self-punishment are not sufficient for a full conception of punishment, as they are moral concepts that are logically prior to and independent of public institutions and their rules.[62] What makes Hegel's theory distinctive is the emphasis he places upon the need for a political community, in which moral responsibility is embedded.[63] Criminal violation at the stage of Ethical Life becomes public and an injury against not only the

in China 21; Markus Dirk Dubber, 'The right to be punished: Autonomy and its demise in modern penal thought' (1998) 16 *Law and History Review* 113; Antony Duff, *Trials and Punishments* (Cambridge University Press 1991) p.283 see for criticism: Adriana Placani and Stearns Broadhead, 'Right to be punished?' (2020) 16 *European Journal of Analytic Philosophy* 53; John Deigh, 'On the right to be punished: Some doubts' (1984) 94 *Ethics* 191.

61 Hegel, *Outlines of the Philosophy of Right* para.220.

62 Joel Feinberg, *Doing and Deserving: Essays in the Theory of Responsibility* (Princeton University Press 1970) p.87.

63 Markus Dirk Dubber, *Rediscovering Hegel's Theory of Crime and Punishment* (1994) 92 *Mich. L. Rev.* 1577. t c (; Brudner, 'The contraction of crime in Hegel's rechtsphilosophie'.

victim but all members of the society.[64] By challenging the rules or laws set down by the state on behalf of all, crime becomes a sort of 'usurpation' of the state's role in setting the terms under which people interact with each other, thereby 'challenging the state's claim to be the sole authority'.[65] In this sense, punishment is a matter of political governmentality that is primarily engaged with the question of whether the state should use force against individuals in return for their disobedience.[66] From such a perspective, legal punishment for Hegel is a legitimate institution that vindicates the normative authority of the state.

It is noteworthy that the moral part of Hegel's account is not completely discarded by the political part. By contrast, the moral conditions of punishment are the precondition for a legitimate state coercion. For example, it is not just to punish someone in a political normative sense unless they deserve suffering in a moral sense. Desert is, therefore, key to the culpability of offenders at a public level. However, it is inadequate for punishing them.[67] This means that there is a gap between moral desert and the state's right to punish those deserving punishment.[68] For a legitimate punishment, therefore, a public purpose is needed. That purpose in Hegel is to vindicate and restore the system of law by annulling the crime. In this light, punishment is just and legitimate insofar as it is a deserved penal sanction that upholds the challenged authority of the state.[69]

Similarly, legal punishment cannot be seen as a justifiable form of state coercion unless it is derived from the *moral licence* given by offenders. As argued earlier, for Hegel, the licence emanates from the very act of crime. Because crime pushes aside the law and places offenders above others, it involves a claim that there is no such thing as freedom that everyone enjoys. If there is no freedom for anyone, then it would not be wrong to coerce offenders in return for their crime. For this reason, punishment does to offenders nothing more than what has already been implied in their transgression. It 'unmasks' the crime through offenders' *own hands* and brings home to them the consequences of their crime.[70] In so doing, punishment is a sort of respect for the rational choice of offenders, by subjecting them to the consequences they have themselves set into motion. Accordingly, it is not only just from a political perspective

64 Hegel, *Outlines of the Philosophy of Right* para.220.

65 Thorburn, 'Punishment and public authority' p.9.

66 Brudner, 'The contraction of crime in Hegel's rechtsphilosophie' p.160.

67 Alec Walen, 'Retributive Justice' in Zalta EN and Nodelman U (eds), *The Stanford Encyclopedia of Philosophy* (Winter 2023 Edition), https://plato.stanford.edu/entries/justice-retributive/ accessed on 28.04.2025.

68 Fletcher, 'Political theory and criminal law' p.18; see also: David Dolinko, 'Some thoughts about retributivism' (1991) 101 *Ethics* 537.

69 Hegel, *Outlines of the Philosophy of Right* para.99.

70 Timothy C Luther, *Hegel's Critique of Modernity: Reconciling Individual Freedom and the Community* (Lexington Books 2009) p.176.

but also morally desirable, in the sense that it gives offenders their right to punishment and drives them to reconcile with themselves:

> Objectively, this is the reconciliation of the law with itself; through the annulment [Aufheben] of the crime, the law restores itself and thereby actualizes its authority. Subjectively, it is the reconciliation of the criminal with himself, i.e., with the law known by him as his own and as valid for him and his protection; when this law is executed upon him, he himself finds in this process the satisfaction of justice and nothing save his own act.[71]

This is a passage that gives us a dense and succinct summary of how Hegel links the subjective, moral dimension of punishment to its objective, political aspect.[72] For some, embedded deeply within this passage is a truly restorative account of punishment.[73] In this reading, left unpunished, offenders remain divided against themselves because they will not be able to come to recognise that they are dirempted by criminal violation.[74] Offenders ultimately punish themselves in Hegel's theory, says Schild, and 'the justice of punishment can consist only precisely in this'.[75] Likewise, when not punishing, the state ceases to maintain its authority over its members and remains broken and disunified. By righting the wrong, punishment is therefore said to restore both offenders and the state.

Clearly, punishment in Hegel's world is designed as part of a political framework that gives the opportunity for the fulfilment of every single individual's freedom, including offenders.[76] It is therefore not totally unjustified to read punishment as a restorative moral phenomenon that can provide a sound basis to drive offenders to reintegrate into the political community. The passage also gives us some hints of Hegel glorifying punishment in such a manner that is structured to be 'an attempt to elicit soul-saving repentance'.[77] After all, ethical and social cohesion can only be fully maintained in cases of

71 Hegel, *Outlines of the Philosophy of Right* para.220.

72 See for a similar view: Tunick, *Hegel's Political Philosophy: Interpreting the Practice of Legal Punishment* p.36.

73 Philippe Nonet, 'Sanction' (1994) 25 *Cumberland Law Review* 489, 516; J Ellis McTaggart, *Studies in Hegelian Cosmology* (Cambridge 1901) p.114.

74 Nonet, 'Sanction' punishment in Hegel's theory 'is precisely the overcoming of and return from estrangement' p.490.

75 Wolfgang Schild, 'The contemporary relevance of Hegel's concept of punishment' in Robert B Pippin and Otfried Höffe (eds), *Hegel on Ethics and Politics* (Cambridge University Press 2009) p.166.

76 Ossip K Flechtheim, 'Hegel and the problem of punishment' (1947) 8 *Journal of the History of Ideas* 293, 297.

77 Stanley Cavell, *The Claim of Reason: Wittgenstein, Skepticism, Morality, and Tragedy* (Oxford University Press 1999) p.476.

serious violations when it is nurtured or backed up by the remorseful feelings of offenders.

Nonetheless, the restoration of the damaged community ties can easily run against individual freedom such that punishment can become a tyrannical state practice, like 'a soul-destroying attempt to mortify the criminal into bringing peace to those who destroy him'.[78] Punishment takes neither of these roles in Hegel's system. That is, legal punishment is not a form of atonement that repairs the moral integrity of offenders. If that were so, it would have posed a serious threat to individual liberty. Neither is it a sheer violence that is visited upon offenders for the sake of maintaining state authority. If it were so, it would have totally undermined the legitimacy of the political authority that arises within a mutually agreed formal framework that respects the freedom of offenders. Remember that Hegel is the philosopher of mediation and reconciliation. Thus, what he seeks to do is explore ways to justify state coercion without ruining at least the formal kind of individual freedom. The next section will show how Hegel formulates this and then critique it in light of his overall moral and political framework.

6. Legal retributivism: structural and ethical deficiencies

From the concluding part of the previous section, it becomes apparent that Hegel's theory of punishment should be understood in a less ethically vigorous way than its restorative interpretation. His theory of punishment is read here as a version of legal retributivism, which views punishment as a multilayered phenomenon shaped by retaliation, self-punishment and state sanction coming together and making a whole. In this theory, offenders deserve punishment, but they deserve it only for wrongs that are legally prohibited. They see their punishment as self-imposed, but self-punishment is formal in that it is seen simply as the *logical* consequence of their crime. Put differently, a punishment is self-imposed in legal retributivism only because of the implications drawn from the meaning of crime. The assumption is that crime challenges the whole system of rights – rights which benefit everyone, including offenders. For this reason, punishment does not only reaffirm the authority of law, but it also places offenders safely back within the system of rights.

This complex and multilayered theory, however, is ***unevenly compounded*** and ***ethically truncated***. It is unevenly compounded because its various components are not fully coherent or integrated. How does the restoration of rights as a public function of punishment, for example, comply with moral or legal desert as a principle?[79] Even if we accept that they comply with each other, are there not other ways to restore the rule of law, without giving

78 Cavell, *The Claim of Reason*.

79 This is the question that has been satisfactorily answered by neither Hegel nor those who read Hegel's theory as a mixed theory of punishment. Andrew Komasinski, 'Hegel's complete

offenders their just deserts? On the other hand, if we are to see punishment as self-imposed, it is not clear how some offenders (most notably the defiant ones) reconcile with themselves when they clearly view the imposition of punishment as unfair. This question is actually what Hegel excludes as even a pertinent possibility in his discussion of moral conscience in the sphere of Morality. Put otherwise, how self-punishment in Morality is transposed into legal punishment in Ethical Life remains a question that has not been fully resolved. The broader, richer area of moral guilt marked by self-punishment is replaced by a narrow legalistic conception where law ascribes blame and punishment to offenders.[80] The idea of taking responsibility for hurting others with a kind of moral self-introspection is severely impoverished and even made redundant at the institutional level, where offenders are held responsible for their criminal actions.

Perhaps one might ask more fundamentally, is punishment the only method of cancelling crimes and reasserting the authority of law?[81] In fact, every step Hegel takes from Abstract Right to Ethical Life to establish the moral and political foundations of punishment provokes more questions than it answers. It is, therefore, based upon a range of principles that are contested and problematic. It is not possible here to provide a detailed critique of these principles[82] – but even if we accept that Hegel's arguments are convincing enough when developing a legal conception of punishment at the stage of Ethical Life, there is another major deeper problem with his theory. That problem is to do with the assumption that *ethicality* is preserved in the transition to *legality*.

Let us recall that the state's authority to punish for Hegel derives from the message 'you can punish me' inherent in the crime of offenders. In other words, when they commit crime, offenders craft their own fate and create their own punishment from their own world. Violating the freedom of others, they legislate that their freedom can also be violated. In this sense, offenders acknowledge in advance the responses that may be directed to their wrongful behaviour, in that they cannot deny the logical consequences of what they have done: They contradict themselves as a result of their actions and should expect legal intervention to resolve that contradiction.

One could readily react here by questioning whether offenders give a message that their freedom can be violated when they violate others. In

views on crime and punishment' (2018) 4 *Journal of the American Philosophical Association* 525; Thom Brooks, 'Is Hegel a retributivist?' (2004) 25 *Hegel Bulletin* 113.

80 See for how it happens in contemporary penal thought: Amanda Wilson, 'Guilt beyond guilt: From political theory to metaphysics with Herbert Morris' (2021) 84 *The Modern Law Review* 89, 92.

81 Stephen Paul Brown, 'Punishment and the restoration of rights' (2001) 3 *Punishment & Society* 485, 493.

82 For a short and yet concise critique of Hegel's arguments see: Ted Honderich, *Punishment the Supposed Justifications Revisited* (Pluto Press 2006) p.25–42.

other words, it is far from certain that every crime establishes a law granting complete freedom of action. Consider, for example, the offences committed by individuals who are not sufficiently recognised in society and who join a criminal organisation that respects them and recognises their existence. Do these offences convey the message that 'everyone is free to do as they wish'? Or do these offences reveal a kind of 'desire for recognition' of those individuals? Suppose that all offences involve the message 'you can punish me', and the state takes it as a duty to do so. Even so, can we say that legal punishment, as Hegel claims, reconciles offenders with both society and themselves? Or do offenders have the right to resist the state's use of force and see it as mere violence?

Hegel is not particularly concerned with these kinds of questions. Yet he believes that *legal guilt* replaces *moral guilt* in the transition from Morality to Ethical Life. For him, the offender's taking responsibility and desire to repair the harms caused by their crime is, at best, of secondary importance. In fact, Hegel suggests that moral responsibility may not even be necessary from a legal perspective as the offender is already held accountable by the state in a way that moves them to face the consequences of what they have done. This means that dialectics operates well in the sphere of punishment given that state sanction can fulfil the functions of earlier forms of punishment: it can both hold the offender responsible and give them what they deserve at the same time. Alongside that, with its objective and impartial character, legal punishment is also thought to not suffer from the problems associated with retaliation and self-punishment. Unlike retaliation and self-punishment, law guarantees freedom for everyone by not leaving the conflict to the parties to be solved on their own. But does this necessarily lead us to think that the solution presented by law as an 'impartial' arbiter is ethically satisfactory or fulfilling for both parties?

This is, for sure, a rhetorical question that implies its own answer. What is more noteworthy here is the fact that this question seems irrelevant from a legal point of view because what ultimately matters in law, as Hegel expressly argues, is: 'the wrong and the righting of it, that is, *justice*'.[83] It is not that criminal violation is addressed in a way that all the parties involved are morally satisfied. Neither is it the healing of the wounds with an actual substantial reconciliation of human beings. It is, rather, the violation of law and its restoration.

But such a legalistic view brings with it an ethical loss. The parties lose their control over criminal violation.[84] The victim, for example, is sidelined in a legal conception of punishment, when crime is understood primarily as a

83 Hegel, *Outlines of the Philosophy of Right* para.99.

84 See for this famous statement: Nils Christie, 'Conflicts as property' (1977) 17 *The British Journal of Criminology* 1.

public wrong committed against all.[85] At a socio-political level, they not only forfeit their moral power to respond to crime as they would like to do, but they become devoid of any authority over criminal violation. For example, be it conditional or unconditional, they cannot grant forgiveness to the criminal. More precisely, forgiveness has almost no role to play within a legal framework in which the experience of victimhood is reduced to the demand for punishment. Victimhood, however, is more than a desire to get offenders punished. Rather, it is more about finding some meaning in suffering and coming to terms with what has happened through a strenuous process.

Likewise, what it means for the criminal to violate another's freedom becomes narrower and less ethically significant within a legalistic framework. The idea of self-punishment, for example, becomes impoverished when it is only seen as an acknowledgement of the crime as crime. For sure, this might be seen as the confession of guilt, so it may open the door for a deeper engagement with the crime while leaving the criminal weighted down with a sense of having to make amends and repair what has been damaged. But, for Hegel, self-punishment is not an internal moral process that the criminal goes through. Instead, it is at best a realisation of the connection between crime and legal punishment. In so being, the ethical implications of self-punishment for the criminal are seriously blunted.

All of this suggests that punishment in Hegel's legal retributivism is a complex phenomenon that comes at a serious ethical cost. The political part of his theory, with its emphasis on the restoration of the *violated* law, elides a broader ethical area opened up by the moral part. In other words, an engagement with whether state punishment is a legitimate response to the violations of law leaves less room for thinking seriously about questions around whether offenders deserve punishment or how crime calls for punishment from a moral point of view. The ethical questions become useful and relevant only insofar as they are at the service of normative political theory. Once they are drawn upon, they are impoverished. Desert becomes the *exchange* of crime *for* punishment, while self-punishment becomes associated with the acknowledgement that punishment is the *logical* consequence of crime. Punishment becomes legal, but by becoming legal, it loses or compromises the ethical principles and standards from which it is derived.

Conclusion

The reconstruction presented here of Hegel's theory of punishment provides a paradigmatic version of legal retributivism. As such, it operates in a unique space where the ethical, moral and political principles intersect with each other and constitute a legal conception of retributive punishment. Shaped by the

85 Alan Norrie, 'Love in law's shadow: Political theory, moral psychology and Young Hegel's critique of punishment' (2019) 28 *Social & Legal Studies* 10, 15–16.

amalgam of legal right and moral desert, self-punishment and the restoration of legal authority, the formulation can provisionally be defined as follows: punishment is a deserved and self-willed imposition of certain losses upon the legal subject by which the violated law reaffirms its contested authority.

For Hegel, legal punishment is manifested in the socio-political world as a complex and multifaceted institution, according to the dynamic and progressive movement of reason. Nonetheless, the legal is not formed by an evenly integrated set of principles. This section has raised questions particularly over how moral desert complies with self-punishment and whether the function of restoring the law is consistent with moral desert. Moreover, even if Hegel's legal retributivism provides a consistent and coherent account of punishment, the ethical possibilities that may emerge as a result of the full *possession* of violation, such as self-punishment, forgiveness and restorative guilt, are jettisoned in favour of the claims of the restoration of legal authority. The *ethical* in legal retributivism is somehow overshadowed by the *legal*.

That said, what is notable about legal retributivism is the normative potential to produce more vigorous ethical demands. In particular, the idea of self-punishment as an ethical principle can be so central and strong that punishment can be pushed in the direction of moral reconciliation and reparation. We can claim, for example, that legal punishment cannot be seen as justified unless it brings the offender to repent their crime, feel guilty and undertake the state's sanction as a way to redeem themselves and restore the damage they have caused.[86] Such an understanding of punishment, of course, can create too wide a gap between the ideal and the actual that a utopian ethical promise is pitted against the real conditions of social and political life. After all, it is painfully obvious that the present system of trials and punishment is deficient and not well-suited to reflect the principle of self-punishment.

This is not to say that utopian ideals should have no role to play in thinking about our penal practices. By contrast, they direct us towards a different future. But the sharpness of ethicality as a utopian ideal remains limited by the actual conditions of legal practice and the structural constraints of normative theory. What is needed, therefore, is a sense of ethicality that is neither constricted by actual penal practices nor confined by normative theory. It should stay within the actual, but it should also point us beyond the actual. The next chapter concerns a non-normative conception of ethical self-punishment in which is developed *ethical retributivism*.

Bibliography

Avineri S, *Hegel's Theory of the Modern State* (Cambridge University Press 2003)
Beiser FC, *Hegel* (Routledge 2005)

86 See for this conception of punishment: Duff, *Trials and Punishments*.

Brooks T, 'Hegel and the unified theory of punishment' in Brooks T (ed), *Hegel's Philosophy of Right* (Blackwell Publishing 2012)
Brooks T, 'Hegel's ambiguous contribution to legal theory' (2005) 11 *Res Publica* 1
Brooks T, 'Hegel's Social and Political Philosophy' in Zalta EN and Nodelman U (eds), The Stanford Encyclopedia of Philosophy (Summer 2025 Edition), https://plato.stanford.edu/entries/hegel-social-political/
Brooks T, 'Is Hegel a retributivist?' (2004) 25 *Hegel Bulletin* 113
Brooks T, 'The right to be punished: a defense' (2013) 3 *Legal Theory in China* 21
Brown SP, 'Punishment and the restoration of rights' (2001) 3 *Punishment & Society* 485
Brudner A, 'The contraction of crime in hegel's rechtsphilosophie' in Dubber MD (ed), *Foundational Texts in Modern Criminal Law* (OUP 2014)
Cavell S, *The Claim of Reason: Wittgenstein, Skepticism, Morality, and Tragedy* (OUP 1999)
Christie N, 'Conflicts as property' (1977) 17 *The British Journal of Criminology* 1
Conklin W, *Hegel's Laws The Legitimacy of a Modern Legal Order* (Stanford University Press 2008)
Cooper DE, 'Hegel's theory of punishment' (1971) 151 *Hegel's Political Philosophy* 153
De Boer K, 'Beyond recognition? Critical reflections on honneth's reading of hegel's philosophy of right' (2013) 21 *International Journal of Philosophical Studies* 534
Deigh J, 'On the right to be punished: some doubts' (1984) 94 *Ethics* 191
Deligiorgi K, 'Hegel's moral philosophy' in Moyar D (ed), *The Oxford Handbook of Hegel* (OUP 2017)
Dolinko D, 'Some thoughts about retributivism' (1991) 101 *Ethics* 537
Du Bois-Pedain A, 'Hegal and the justification of real-world penal sanctions' (2016) 29 *Canadian Journal of Law & Jurisprudence* 37
Dubber MD, 'Rediscovering Hegel's theory of crime and punishment' (1994) 92 *Mich. L. Rev.* 1577
Dubber MD, 'The right to be punished: autonomy and its demise in modern penal thought' (1998) 16 *Law and History Review* 113
Duff A, *Trials and Punishments* (Cambridge University Press 1991)
Feinberg J, *Doing and Deserving: Essays in the Theory of Responsibility* (Princeton University Press 1970)
Fine R, *Political Investigations: Hegel, Marx and Arendt* (Routledge 2005)
Flechtheim OK, 'Hegel and the problem of punishment' (1947) 8 *Journal of the History of Ideas* 293
Fletcher G, 'Political theory and criminal law' (2006) 25(1) *Criminal Justice Ethics* 18
Franco P, *Hegel's Philosophy of Freedom* (Yale University Press 1999)
Hegel GWF, *Outlines of the Philosophy of Right* (OUP, 2008)
Hegel GWF, *The Encyclopaedia Logic: Part I of the Encyclopaedia of Philosophical Sciences with the Zusätze* (Hackett Publishing 1991)
Hofmann C, 'Autonomy and the concrete universal: moral subjectivity and its function in hegel's philosophy of right' (2014) 35 *Hegel Bulletin* 252
Honderich T, *Punishment The Supposed Justifications Revisited* (Pluto Press 2006)
Honneth A, *The Pathologies of Individual Freedom: Hegel's Social Theory* (Princeton University Press 2021)
Houlgate S, *Freedom, Truth, and History: An Introduction to Hegel's Philosophy* (Blackwell 2005)

Houlgate S, 'G.W.F. Hegel: an introduction to his life and thought' in Houlgate S and Michael B (eds), *A Companion to Hegel* (Blackwell 2011)
Houlgate S, 'Hegel's ethical thought' (1992) 13 *Hegel Bulletin* 1
Houlgate S, *The Opening of Hegel's Logic: From Being to Infinity* (Purdue University Press 2005)
Inwood MJ, *A Hegel Dictionary* (Blackwell 1992)
Johnson J, 'Hegel on punishment: a more sophisticated retributivism' in White MD (ed), *Retributivism: Essays on Theory and Policy* (OUP 2011)
Knowles D, *Routledge Philosophy Guidebook to Hegel and the Philosophy of Right* (Routledge 2004)
Komasinski A, 'Hegel's complete views on crime and punishment' (2018) 4 *Journal of the American Philosophical Association* 525
Luther TC, *Hegel's Critique of Modernity: Reconciling Individual Freedom and the Community* (Lexington Books 2009)
Marcuse H, *Reason and Revolution Hegel and the Rise of Social Theory* (Routledge and Kegan Paul 1955)
McTaggart JE, *Studies in Hegelian Cosmology* (Cambridge University Press 1901)
Morris H, 'Persons and punishment'(1968) 52(4) *The Monist* 475
Neuhouser F, 'Ethical life and the demands of conscience' (1998) 19 *Hegel Bulletin* 35
Nonet P, 'Sanction' (1994) 25 *Cumberland Law Review* 489
Norrie A, *Dialectic and Difference: Dialectical Critical Realism and the Grounds of Justice* (Routledge 2010)
Norrie A, 'Love in law's shadow: political theory, moral psychology and young hegel's critique of punishment' (2019) 28 *Social & Legal Studies* 10
Nozick R, *Philosophical Explanations* (Harvard University Press 1981)
Patten A, *Hegel's Idea of Freedom* (OUP 1999)
Pelczynski ZA, 'An introductory essay' in Hegel GWF and Knox TM (eds), *Hegel's Political Writingstrans* (Clarendon 1964)
Pinkard T, *Hegel: A Biography* (Cambridge University Press 2001)
Pippin RB, 'Hegel on logic as metaphysics' in Moyar D (ed) *The Oxford Handbook of Hegel* (Oxford University Press 2017), 199–218
Placani A and Broadhead S, 'Right to be punished?' (2020) 16 *European Journal of Analytic Philosophy* 53
Plant R, 'Hegel on identity and legitimation' in Pelczynski ZA (ed), *The State and Civil Society: Studies in Hegel's Political Philosophy* (Cambridge University Press 1984)
Quinton AM, 'On punishment' (1954) 14 *Analysis* 133
Redding P, 'Georg Wilhelm Friedrich Hegel' in Zalta EN and Nodelman U (eds), The Stanford Encyclopedia of Philosophy (Fall 2024 Edition), https://plato.stanford.edu/entries/hegel/
Russell B, *History of Western Philosophy* (Routledge 2004)
Schild W, 'The contemporary relevance of hegel's concept of punishment' in Pippin RB and Otfried H (eds), *Hegel on Ethics and Politics* (Cambridge University Press 2009)
Solomon RC, 'Justice v. Vengeance' in Bandes S (ed), *The Passions of Law* (New York University Press 2000)
Steinberger PJ, 'Hegel on crime and punishment' (1983) 77 *American Political Science Review* 858
Stillman PG, 'Hegel's idea of punishment' (1976) 14 *Journal of the History of Philosophy* 169

Taylor C, *Hegel* (Cambridge University Press 2005)
Thorburn M, 'Punishment and public authority' in Ulväng M, Asp P and Du Bois-Pedain A (eds), *Criminal Law and the Authority of the State* (Hart Publishing 2017)
Tunick M, *Hegel's Political Philosophy: Interpreting the Practice of Legal Punishment* (Princeton University Press 2014)
Walen A, 'Retributive justice' in Zalta EN and Nodelman U (eds), The Stanford Encyclopedia of Philosophy (Winter 2023 Edition), https://plato.stanford.edu/entries/justice-retributive/
Williams RR, *Hegel's Ethics of Recognition* (University of California Press 1998)
Wilson A, 'Guilt beyond guilt: From political theory to metaphysics with herbert morris' (2021) 84 *The Modern Law Review* 89
Wood AW, *Hegel's Ethical Thought* (Cambridge University Press 1990)
Wood AW, 'Hegel's ethics' in Beiser C (ed), *The Cambridge Companion to Hegel* (Cambridge University Press 1999)

3 Ethical retributivism

Introduction

The opening chapter concluded with the idea that legal retributivism promises a world it cannot deliver, in that the ethical seeds of punishment cannot flourish within a setting where criminal violation is exclusively understood in formal and legal terms. In this chapter, I want to take the ethical core of retributivism out of its legal ecosystem and pose the following question: what does retributivism look like without legal punishment? To answer this question, the chapter will visit Hegel's early writings, which point towards an unusual and yet ethically promising form of retribution.

At stake in this enquiry is an attempt to understand the idea of retributive punishment in moral psychological terms. What is it like for the offender to come to terms with criminal violation? This will be the grounds on which to introduce a non-legal phenomenological account of retribution. Following Hegel's notion of 'punishment as fate', this work proposes that, for the offender, the distressing realisation of having injured another is a retributive loss in return for their violation. Behind the ethical impulse of this sort of punishment lies the (moral) truth that all human beings are interconnected in the web of shared life: to violate another is to violate oneself. In other words, criminal violation recoils or 'boomerangs' on its offender. From this point of view, punishment is nothing more than a form of (moral) self-destruction.

But the work of retribution does not end here. The suffering of recognising another's suffering drives the offender to amend their wrong and heal the wounds inflicted on their bonds with others. On the part of the offender, the moral task is to restore the dirempted world, the world that inhabits both themselves and others. Once undertaken, punishment as an ethical suffering brings a unity and wholeness to the offender as a moral being. But it also sets the scene for better moral transactions between the offender and victim, ideally opening the way towards forgiveness and genuine reconciliation.

In the current moral and legal outlook, there is, of course, little room for retribution to be expressed in this way. Placing the victim and offender in certain rigid categories, the orthodox legal framework juridifies individuals

DOI: 10.4324/9781003563150-6

and thereby 'deforms' intersubjective relationships.[1] It frames crime and its correction exclusively in a legal vocabulary while also taking state punishment as an unquestionable rational response. For an ethically better form of retribution, there is, thus, a need to move away from the legalist set-up of crime and punishment. Via the young Hegel, this work will suggest that love supplies a better medium through which to view crime as a separation from the ethical union in which one lives. Understood in these terms, the idea of separation in crime also sheds light on how (ethical) punishment is intrinsically linked to the feelings of lack and deficiency that the offender experiences after having injured another.

Such a conception of crime and punishment requires the overcoming of the law and justice discourse in favour of relationships of love and mutual care. As deployed by the young Hegel, love locates the individual within a harmonious social whole, in which one feels at one with oneself and others. Unlike the legal field, where rights compete with each other for the satisfaction of justice, love is concerned with the restoration and improvement of intersubjective relationships. To illuminate further the settled dichotomy between law and love, this chapter opens with the young Hegel's critique of rationality and law alongside a sketch of his ethics of love, from which he introduces a model of ethical life superior to law. The second section explains the notion of criminal violation informed by love; the third section establishes the unique place the young Hegel occupies in relation to restorative justice and retributivism. Having examined Hegel's account of "punishment as fate", the fourth section provides the nub of ethical retributivism. This chapter concludes by exploring the practical implications of the young Hegel's theory, especially highlighting the connections and disconnections between ethical retributivism and transformative justice.

1. In praise of love: the dismissal of reason

It is commonly thought that what makes Hegel a self-contained philosopher is his first radical divergence from the Kantian position in *The Spirit of Christianity and Its Fate,* written in what Kroner calls 'the years of discovery'.[2] It is in this essay, and under the influence of the Romantic movement, that Hegel begins to come to grips with the difficulty of understanding human

1 Here are the words of a rape victim describing concisely the way the law approaches her: 'I believe we are all multi-dimensional beings, and in court, it felt harmful being flattened, characterized, mislabelled, and vilified.' Chanel Miller, *Know My Name: A Memoir* (Penguin Books 2020) p.1.

2 Richard Kroner, *Introduction to Hegel's Early Theological Writings. Translated by TM Knox. With an Introduction and Fragments,* trans. by Richard Kroner (Chicago, IL: The University of Chicago Press 1948) p.8; H. S Harris, *Hegel's Development: Toward the Sunlight 1770-1801* (Oxford University Press 1972) p.xxvii.

freedom within social, legal and political relations.[3] In contrast to his later thoughts, where modern institutions are conceived of as providing a basis for free ethical life, his early thinking is more concerned with the limitations of loose communal ties shaped by modernity. The young Hegel, thus, wrote at a peculiar phase of history marked by 'the shattering of the bonds of trust upon which traditional community depended, the undermining of the security and stability of that world, and the condition of alienation, insecurity, and war into which moderns have thrust themselves in their struggle for individual freedom'.[4] What is particularly visible in this period of Hegel's life is the idea that legal morality or legalism stands in the way of the full flourishing of human beings.[5] This idea takes its departure point from a critique of Enlightenment reason, and its particular conception of morality and law.[6]

For the young Hegel, reason operates by a process of breaking something into its component parts. Infamously, in human moral interactions, it does so in three senses. Reason breaks down one's unity of life with oneself, with others and with nature.[7] First, reason distorts the inner life of the individual by dividing the integrated self into rationality and inclination (emotionality). In the second sense, it damages societal unity by considering the parts (individuals) as detached from the whole (socio-political order). Finally, perhaps at a more fundamental level, it misrepresents nature, by demonstrating it as a mechanical and an alien being, rather than a living spirit that is part of the human experience. Given our threefold fragmentations, the primary goal, says Hegel, should be to see the world as a whole and as part of ourselves so that we can

3 Marcuse, *Reason and Revolution Hegel and the Rise of Social Theory* p.33; Franz Gabriel Nauen, *Revolution, Idealism and Human Freedom: Schelling Hölderlin and Hegel and the Crisis of Early German Idealism* (Springer Science & Business Media 2012) p.69–86.

4 Alice Ormiston, *Love and Politics: Re-interpreting Hegel* (New York University Press 2012) p.2.

5 María del Rosario Acosta López, 'On the violence of positivity in Hegel's early theological writings' in Evangelia Sembou (ed), *The Young Hegel and Religion* (Peter Lang 2017); W. Clark Wolf, 'The weakness of the law: The opposition of concept and life in Hegel's early ethics' in Evangelia Sembou (ed), *The Young Hegel and Religion* (2017).

6 It is significant to note that Hegel in his early writings struggles with the 'splits' of Kant, so what he talks about reason and law makes more sense when it is understood within the context of Kantian philosophy. In other words, his critique of reason is to a large extent the critique of 'Kantian' reason. In fact, he keeps a critical distance to this form of rationality in the later period, where he views 'negative reason' as a thinking process that need to be overcome by 'speculative reason'. For some Hegelians scholars, the best way to see Hegel's critical take on reason in the *Spirit* essay is to view it as part of the developmental process of his later dialectical thinking. Accordingly, love in the early period constitutes the kernel of his later dialectics. I cannot get into the details of this discussion. But here my point is that the early concept of love provides a radically different conception of ethical life to the one generated by speculative reason even though it seems an undeveloped version of speculative reason. Georg Lukács, *The Young Hegel: Studies in the Relations between Dialectics and Economics* (Merlin Press 1975) p.101–105; for a similar view see: Todd McGowan, *Emancipation after Hegel: Achieving a Contradictory Revolution* (Columbia University Press 2019) p.99.

7 Evangelia Sembou, *The Young Hegel and Religion* (Peter Lang 2017) p.6; Taylor, *Hegel* p.60.

overcome the alienation in and between ourselves and the world and 'restore humanity in its entirety'.[8] This section and those following will think through the first two sets of fragmentations Hegel identifies as the problems of reason in the modern period.

At the basic moral realm, Hegel's view of reason directs us in the light of the division between 'what is' and 'what ought to be'. While the former (what is) is supposed to surrender to the necessities of nature, the latter (what ought to be) is taken as belonging to the higher realm of human reason, where moral commands are produced. Reason in this sense has a direct bearing on the idea of emancipation from external powers, either being an outgrowth of human freedom or a source of autonomy because of its absolute power and guardianship in the moral world of the individual. But for Hegel, the ethics and law that derive from reason are at the same time the creator of human bondage.[9] This is in large part because the antagonistic image of the human self (reason versus inclination) presupposes an imbalanced moral structure in which the ethical disposition is exclusively determined by the sense of duty.

In Hegel's view, having and considering only a set of moral commandments when pursuing a life is 'a direct slavery, an obedience without joy, without pleasure or love'.[10] The lord who is to be served may not be 'the Shaman of the Tungus', as a ruler outside human agency, but human rationality, acting as an internal authority, pushing sensual inclinations and motives to the background. The only difference between listening to the command of duty and being subject to a tyrannical ruler is that while the former leads one to 'carry his lord [reason] in himself', the latter makes the subject surrender to an outside lord.[11] In sum, human beings qua rational agents, Hegel thinks, are not really free and autonomous, as the Enlightenment envisages. Rather, they are restricted by the sense of duty which 'excludes or dominates all other relations'.[12]

For Hegel, at a social level, reason also moves us to take a divisive view of the relationship between the individual and political community.[13] In a rational framework, law as the regulation of social relations becomes nothing to do with the internal bonds connecting the joys and woes of human beings to the lives of others.[14] Instead, it consists in the production of moral and political duties by an external power, setting limits to the desires of the individual that are

8 Hegel, *Early Theological Writings* p.212.
9 Hegel, *Early Theological Writings* p.222.
10 Hegel, *Early Theological Writings* p.206.
11 Hegel, *Early Theological Writings* p.211.
12 Hegel, *Early Theological Writings* p.212.
13 Hegel, *Early Theological Writings* p.260.
14 Georgios Tsagdis, 'Love and the apparatus: On a hegelian fragment' in C Zeiher and T McGowann (eds), *Can Philosophy Love? Reflections and Encounters* (Rowman & Littlefield 2017) p.127.

supposed to be inimical to the unity of the political community.[15] Where the individual is taken as an isolatable unit and standing against the society, thinks Hegel, his relations to legal authority are prone to be characterised by either domination or subjection. And, for Hegel, this sort of asymmetrical relationship with the law is not something resolvable under a formal structure of ethical life. It may provide some sort of stability and security for individuals, but it is far from building connections with the full richness of ethical relations.[16]

In place of the divisions of reason, the young Hegel proposes *love* as a harmonious and peaceful mode of living. First, at an individual level, his notion of love promises to reconcile the individual with themselves by taking them in their wholeness as a rational loving being. Love – in this sense, as many commentators point out – is inspired by the figure of Jesus,[17] a real man carrying both the divine and human elements in himself and representing the possibility in the here and now of attaining a morally good life, as 'the most profound expression of human moral existence'.[18] Presenting par excellence how contradictions are perfectly preserved in a harmonious whole (the beautiful soul), the life of Jesus for the early Hegel expresses a concrete manifestation of love against the fragmented, 'ugly' conception of the modern self.[19]

By combining the impersonal and universal demands of reason, and the claims of the emotions in finding one's uniqueness in the world, love provides a mysterious experience. It embraces contraries and supersedes them in a way that brings about a unity in the sensing of life. In the realm of love, Hegel writes, 'the separate does still remain, but as something united and no longer as something separate'.[20] Seen in this light, love is the source of moral purity and unity that is present in this world and embedded in the very nature of ethical beings, the mystery of which cannot be grasped by rational thought.[21]

On the other hand, at a social level, love views the individual as standing in harmony with others and takes the community as a therapeutic unit that is defined by mutual care and support. 'Is there an idea', asks Hegel rhetorically, 'more beautiful than that of a nation of men related to one another by love'? He continues, 'the individual is not simply a part of the whole. The whole does not lie outside him; he himself is just the whole'.[22] In such a community of

15 Jay M Bernstein, 'Love and law: Hegel's critique of morality' (2003) 70 *Social Research: An International Quarterly* 393; Shannon Hoff, *The Laws of the Spirit: A Hegelian Theory of Justice* (SUNY Press 2014) p.16.

16 Hegel, *Early Theological Writings* p.210–211.

17 Raymond Plant, *Hegel* (London: Allen & Unwin 1973) p.58; Harris, *Hegel's Development: Toward the Sunlight 1770-1801* p.xxvii.

18 Norrie, *Law and the Beautiful Soul* p.2; Robert Norton, *The Beautiful Soul* (Ithaca, NY: Cornell University Press 1995) p.211.

19 Pinkard, *Hegel: A Biography* p.215.

20 Hegel, *Early Theological Writings* p.305.

21 Beiser, *Hegel* p.119.

22 Hegel, *Early Theological Writings* p.260.

love, as Taylor highlights, 'the citizens' fullest moral and spiritual aspirations are answered in the common life of the society'.[23] In this sense, love sets up a harmonious blend of individuality and sociality in which intersubjective relationships are both inclusionary and emancipatory.

In other words, when love is substituted for reason, it also brings with it a new way of communal living or ethics (loving ethics). It denies the ***vertical*** structure of law, in which 'the universal becomes the master and the particular mastered',[24] replacing it with an ethical framework that is ***horizontally*** shaped. Through love, Hegel comments, the law 'ceases to be the universal, opposed to inclination (the individual subjective act), and inclination ceases to be particular, opposed to the law'.[25] 'This correspondence of law and inclination ... as the relation of difference to one another' fulfils law, and becomes 'a unified sense of life'.[26] Mediating the opposition between the universal and the particular (the individual), love takes legal relations as necessary and yet as something that must be overcome. So doing, love locates itself beyond law, in which social relations are driven by mutual care and solidarity.

Law generates a space to live in basic peace and order – but it is inadequate for the moral fulfilment of human beings. Love, says Hegel, 'exhibits that which fulfils the law but annuls it as law and so is something higher than obedience to law and makes law superfluous'.[27] In other words, individuals' moral and legal relations to fellow beings are part of their ethical life, but it is only one part which should be superseded by more substantial and respectful interactions between human beings: love. Proceeding with the young Hegel's critique, the next section will move on to discuss how law limits the ways human beings interact with each other; it will then explain how the concept of crime informed by love uncovers a new ethical domain in which we think about punishment afresh.

2. Beyond the law: rethinking criminal violation

To live exclusively under the law in Hegel's world is to occlude other forms of living. If human beings cannot go beyond legal relations and become stuck at the formal level of right and wrong, particularly when they are in dispute, says Hegel, they 'would let something alien, a law on the judge's lips, pass sentence on them. Hence, they submit to a treatment against which both parties had [initially] protested'.[28] In other words, where violation hits human beings, law often stands as an alien power by taking up the conflict and placing

23 Taylor, *Hegel* p.51.
24 Hegel, *Early Theological Writings* p.214.
25 Hegel, *Early Theological Writings* p.213.
26 Hegel, *Early Theological Writings* p.215.
27 Hegel, *Early Theological Writings* p.212.
28 Hegel, *Early Theological Writings* p.234.

it within a formal sphere.[29] It 'colonises' the way in which human beings relate to each other, whereby intersubjective relationships are 'deformed, distorted, or made deficient' by a 'who is right?' approach.[30] In so doing, law speaks its own language and applies its own formulation: crime plus punishment equals justice.[31]

Love, however, works above law and justice, requiring human beings to come to grips with violation in a way that improves themselves under the rubric of their relationships:

> [It] makes a general demand on [human beings] to surrender their rights, to lift themselves above the whole sphere of justice or injustice by love, for in love there vanish not only rights but also the feeling of inequality and the hatred of enemies which this feeling's imperative demand for equality implies.[32]

Moved by love, a forgiving attitude in the legal realm is what Hegel suggests in response to violation. But if one goes above the ties of law and rights, he argues, there would be then nothing left to forgive the offender, since they have done no injury to any right.[33] What matters in the sphere of friendship and love is thus reconciliation and the restoration of human relations. But before demanding moral change and transformation, and a move beyond law and justice through forgiveness and reconciliation, love requires a process of breaking the habit of seeing violation in legal terms.

Under a legalistic vocabulary, crime, as is well-known, is simply what is defined as such by the law. But a non-legal account of violation generated by love takes this deeper by concerning itself with the damage done to the relationship based on affection, care and trust.[34] In this sense, criminal violation can be defined as a sort of 'departure' from the ethical union within which people are joined or an act of rupturing one's ties with others.[35] Within equal relations of reciprocal respect and care, crime is somehow a sort of destruction of life. But because there is only one (shared) life, Hegel thinks, 'there is as much destruction in what destroys as in what is destroyed'.[36] In other words,

29 See: Christie, 'Conflicts as property'.

30 Daniel Loick, 'Terribly upright: The young Hegel's Critique of Juridicism' (2014) 40 *Philosophy & Social Criticism* 933, 934.

31 Norrie, *Law and the Beautiful Soul* p.75.

32 Hegel, *Early Theological Writings* p.218.

33 Hegel, *Early Theological Writings* p.236.

34 According to this conception, for Hegel, being a 'quick reaction of feeling to an oppression, the uprush of the desire to oppress in turn, which is a kind of blind justice, 'even anger is a crime.' Hegel, *Early Theological Writings* p.216.

35 Hegel, *Early Theological Writings* p.229; For a similar definition see: Herbert Morris, 'Guilt and suffering' (1971) 21 *Philosophy East and West* 419.

36 Hegel, *Early Theological Writings* p.225.

crime should not only be seen as an act of violence against another and the community, but it is also an act of self-harm from the perspective of the offender. 'A human life', in Hegel's world, 'relates to another as a part of an organism to another part, such that the failure of one part is effectively the failure of all parts'.'[37]

When violation is understood in such ethical terms, law becomes insignificant – or sometimes worse, an insurmountable obstacle to exploring better ways of dealing with post-violation. As Norrie argues, law may even act 'as a further aggressor', with no role to play 'in dealing with grief and reconciliation in the face of violation'.[38] That being said, it is often taken as a legitimate default mechanism for dealing with terrible violations.[39] This is mainly because the law, with its own logic and moral discourse, stands in the way of a wide range of unacceptable practices that may arise in the conflict: revenge, denial, cover-up, and so on. Drawing on rational calculations in the balancing of rights against rights, law usually appeals to punishment in the name of doing justice and blocks off morally undesirable outcomes. But, when so doing, as stated earlier, it also dismisses developing better ways of coming to terms with criminal violation and a more insightful understanding of the aftermath of violation. Law blocks off what is morally desirable in the name of excluding practices that are morally undesirable.

From a relational ethical perspective, however, it is not only that forgiveness and other acts of love may come to the scene as better forms of response to criminal violation. It is also that the analysis of the *disordered* conditions of post-violation may reveal something ethically significant for the maintenance and restructuring of relationships. By reference to Hegel's Jena writings, Honneth maintains that within the uncertainties arising during the post-violation period lies the possibility of exploring whether crime is a result of the offender's experience of not being fully satisfied with the current form of mutual recognition.[40] In that light, crime is not seen as a pure blind destruction of the law, but rather it is taken as an act that can be driven or motivated by prior *broken* ethical relations. Put differently, even though crime appears as an action transgressive of law, it has, in fact, more to do with what Honneth calls 'conditions of incomplete recognition'.[41] From this approach, criminal

37 Loick, 'Terribly upright: The Young Hegel's critique of juridicism' p.942.

38 Norrie, 'Love in law's shadow: Political theory, moral psychology and Young Hegel's critique of punishment' p.11.

39 Norrie, 'Love in law's shadow: Political theory, moral psychology and Young Hegel's critique of punishment' p.16.

40 Axel Honneth, *The Struggle for Recognition: The Moral Grammar of Social Conflicts* (MIT Press 1996) p.20; Georg Wilhelm Friedrich Hegel, *Hegel's System of Ethical Life and First Philosophy of Spirit* (SUNY Press 1979).

41 Honneth, *The Struggle for Recognition: The Moral Grammar of Social Conflicts* p.20.

violation is a sign for the offender of not being in a 'good enough' and loving interaction.[42]

This does not tell us that crime is lawful or ethically neutral. Neither does it say that, because crime is a natural consequence of an already corrupt relationship, it is ethically valid, completely excused or justified. But it does show us that a legalistic vision misses two fundamental points about criminal violation and punishment. First, violation is at bottom more about relationships between human beings than it is about law-breaking, as it has substantially to do with being cut off from others. Second, following from the first is the idea that, precisely because the violation that manifests as crime is more about relationships, there is a need to review the existing framework of moral and legal relations in terms of whether it is shaped by an inherently corrosive structure. In this light, it may be that the legal processing of relationships as aspects of crime and punishment misses those relationships that are unjust and criminogenic and therefore need revision when they are violated and challenged.

That said, even in morally distorted or flawed interactions, violation for the offender remains an experience of being separated from the ethical relationship. The offender feels guilty at what they have done and may be pained by another's being pained.[43] At the core of this 'phenomenological development of [moral] experience' lies the idea that violation necessarily brings the depth of detachment and estrangement to the offender's notice and gives birth to their own loss and suffering.[44] This form of suffering arises spontaneously, flowing from recognising the commonality of everyone's life, and drives the offender to restore the breached ties of interconnectedness and perhaps also urges them to ask for forgiveness.

To sum up, love in Hegel's early writings takes us in the direction of intersubjective relationships that go beyond law, where criminal violation is defined by the ideas of rupture and repair. The main thought is to rise above right and wrong and to deal with violation at the level of respectful interactions between individuals. From the perspective of the victim and community, giving up on the rigid claims of law and justice is key to reconciliation and a better way of coming to terms with injurious violation; it is the feelings of separation and disconnection that define the offender's moral status and move them to return to the unity and wholeness of moral existence. After a brief

42 Donald Woods Winnicott, *Playing and Reality* (Routledge 2012) p.187. The idea that a moral critique of post-violation urges us to revise our framework of ethical relations is in fact based more on the theory of mutual recognition, rather than an ethics of love. In fact, for Honneth, mutual recognition at a social level repudiates the principle of love in intimate relations. But for the purpose of this work, I take love as a triggering force to renew the relationships at intimate, interpersonal, and public levels.

43 Reeves, Norrie and Carvalho, 'Between persecution and reconciliation: Criminal justice, legal form and human emancipation' p.381.

44 Richard Beardsworth, *Derrida and the Political* (Routledge 2013) p.83.

discussion of how Hegel's loving ethics sits in relation to restorative justice, the next section will set up the basis for his conception of retribution.

3. From restoration to retribution: Hegel's early conception of punishment

It is noteworthy that the young Hegel's emphasis on love and its moral power to repair relationships chimes in today with what is broadly called 'restorative justice'.[45] Long before many restorative scholars, Hegel promoted love as governing our relations against a cold abstract form of legality and penal justice.[46] Likewise, he stressed the need to understand criminal violation as a threat to the bonds of a cooperative community and prioritised forgiveness and reconciliation over legal intervention. In this regard, Hegel's early writings come out of a 'restorative' impulse to provide a set of ethical ideas about how human beings should relate to each other.[47]

Alongside drawing attention to the non-punitive ways of dealing with criminal violation, the young Hegel also highlights the reparative feelings of the offender that flow from the realisation of another having been injured. These feelings of concern for another, coupled with a sense of responsibility, orient the offender towards corrective action.[48] In other words, being fostered by the painful and illuminating journey of introspection around crime, for Hegel, the offender seeks to undo what they have done and opens the path towards ethical reconciliation and reunion. In fact, by not instrumentalising these feelings for the service of restoration, and having a full-fledged account of what it means to violate another, Hegel's early works can also be viewed as providing a broader and deeper theory of restorative justice.[49]

Nonetheless, his writings differ from restorative justice scholarship in at least two respects. Firstly, the community is not taken for granted as providing a stable balanced unity that is to be restored, but rather it is viewed as a form of reciprocal relations that are imperfect and thereby open to improvement

45 For a similar reading of the young Hegel see: Norrie, 'Love in law's shadow: Political theory, moral psychology and Young Hegel's critique of punishment'.

46 It is notable that many restorative scholars see love as the primary source to be appealed to deal with the problems of the orthodox conception of justice. see for example: Howard Zehr, *Changing Lenses: A New Focus for Crime and Justice* (Herald Press 2015) p.139; Daniel Van Ness and Karen Heetderks Strong, *Restoring Justice: An Introduction to Restorative Justice* (Routledge 2014) p.175; John Braithwaite, *Restorative Justice & Responsive Regulation* (Oxford University Press on Demand 2002) p.218. For Braithwaite, restorative justice is 'a ritual of love.' For a critique of the 'loving' restorative justice approach see: Annalise E Acorn, *Compulsory Compassion: A Critique of Restorative Justice* (UBC Press 2004) p.27–45.

47 Gerry Johnstone, *A Restorative Justice Reader: Texts, Sources and Context* (Willan Publishing 2003) p.6.

48 Hegel, *Early Theological Writings* p.231–232.

49 For a critique of the moral feelings in restorative justice, see: Wilson, 'Guilt beyond guilt: From political theory to metaphysics with Herbert Morris' p.113.

and enrichment. In Hegel's understanding, love is not taken to be an idea of restoring a harmonious social world but rather as an ethical source that reorganises or renews the building blocks of relationships that cause violation in the first place. In other words, unlike the restorative justice vision, where the normative validity of a 'just' status quo is maintained,[50] what Hegel suggests is perhaps more akin to what is called 'transformative justice'.[51] It can be taken as pointing in the direction of more informal and intimate ethical arrangements, beyond criminal justice, in a way that excludes all kinds of formal justice procedures. I will talk more about Hegel's loving ethics and transformative justice in the last part of this work.

Secondly, and what is more relevant for the purpose of this work, is the fact that the young Hegel suggests a dialectical understanding of restorative and retributive justice. Despite his emphasis on the ideas of guilt and reconciliation, his restorative world is built from the very structure of retribution.[52] In Hegel's description of violation and punishment, the way the offender suffers is *part* of the moral cycle of retribution. Crime is necessarily followed by punishment. Indeed, it *creates* its own punishment. The painful realisation of the wrongness of crime, according to Hegel, springs from 'the equal reaction of the trespasser's own deed, of a power which he himself has armed, of an enemy made an enemy by himself'. It is the trespasser's own violation that 'has created a law' in which the trespasser is maltreated 'as he has maltreated the other'.[53]

Plainly, this is more like the operation of the principle of retribution than restoration. Inspired by the Greek tragedies,[54] Hegel calls this 'punishment as fate'. Fate in the Ancient Greeks is interpreted as the path of life that is allotted and bound to someone either as reward or punishment. It is 'the law-like necessity' of connection between violation and punishment that creates someone's fate by virtue of his guilt 'through the inexorable will of a punishing deity'.[55] Punishment by fate is retributive, as it is only because of crime that fate's unpleasant touch is exerted upon the offender. But it is also restorative, in the sense that the punishment befalling the offender moves

50 Acorn, *Compulsory Compassion: A Critique of Restorative Justice.*

51 Anastasia Chamberlen and Henrique Carvalho, 'Feeling the absence of justice: Notes on our pathological reliance on punitive justice' (2022) 61 *The Howard Journal of Crime and Justice* 87, 98.

52 For similar views:, see: Harris, *Hegel's Development: Toward the Sunlight 1770-1801* p.349; Williams, *Hegel's Ethics of Recognition* p.162.

53 Hegel, *Early Theological Writings* p.229–230.

54 Joshua Billings, *Genealogy of the Tragic* (Princeton University Press 2014) p.143.

55 Hans Kelsen, *Essays in Legal and Moral Philosophy* (Springer 1973) p.173. Kelsen's work is in fact based on a strong criticism of the emergence of the principle of retribution. I cannot discuss his arguments here, but I find it useful in terms of Kelsen's detailed account of how the notion of fate is linked up with the idea of retribution.

them to repair the wounds in their own life, the life that is also shared by the victim and others.

The 'punishment' of fate is natural, internal and extra-legal. It arises spontaneously, as a peculiar form of suffering brought about by the violation itself without any intervention from a legal apparatus. Having injured another's life, a person's fate necessarily faces up to a punishment that must be completed according to the natural order of things. That punishment is self-triggered and turned back from the offender's own crime.[56] This means that crime and punishment are the two successive stages of the same (retributive and restorative) process within the moral world of the offender. Because retribution opens up a space to heal the wounds created by criminal violation, it is also deeply restorative for both the offender and victim. For this reason, I take this as a form of ethical retributivism, the sort of retributivism that works within the 'restorative' interconnected world of human beings.

Yet, as Hegel realises, this is not the most visible image of retribution in the modern moral and legal outlook. Comparing 'punishment as fate' with what he calls 'punishment as law' (legal punishment), Hegel states that legal punishment, like fate, is 'inevitably deserved; that is inescapable'.[57] In fact, 'retribution and its equivalence with crime is the sacred principle of all justice, the principle on which any political order must rest'.[58] In other words, the functioning of both penal law and the 'natural law' of fate is fundamentally shaped by the principle of retribution, but for Hegel, they nonetheless belong to entirely distinct domains.[59]

Unlike the retribution of fate, the punishment of law is artificial, external and institutional. It is imposed by a juridical machine where every crime is followed by an external sanction. In a legal setting, retribution is necessarily impersonal, automatic and unbending.[60] Where violation occurs, punishment is inevitably deserved and visited upon the offender. Like punishment as fate, it is generated by the very act of crime. But unlike fate's punishment, the

56 Robert R Williams, *Tragedy, Recognition, and the Geath of God: Studies in Hegel and Nietzsche* (Oxford University Press 2012) p.122. 'The individual creates his own fate by asserting himself against and violating the whole of which he is a member, dividing it and bringing it down upon himself.'

57 Hegel, *Early Theological Writings* p.226.

58 Hegel, *Early Theological Writings* p.218.

59 It is noteworthy that the way the young Hegel contrasts legal punishment with 'punishment as fate' seems to flow from Kant's distinction between 'juridical punishment' and 'natural punishment'. Kant in *Metaphysical Elements of Justice* takes 'natural punishment as a principle of 'vice punishes itself' in the inner world of the offender and finds this sort of punishment irrelevant within the realm of criminal justice. It seems that the young Hegel with his notion of 'punishment as fate' presents an account of natural punishment that is both relevant to and higher than legal punishment. Kant, *Metaphysical Elements of Justice: Part I of the Metaphysics of Morals* p.138.

60 Hegel, *Early Theological Writings* p.226; Lewis P Hinchman, 'Hegel's theory of crime and punishment' (1982) 44 *The Review of Politics* 523 p.533.

punisher is not same as the punished. It is, as it were, not self-punishment but hetero-punishment. Therefore, punishment as law produces a 'passive' suffering for the offender that does no good to them or their relationships.[61] This punishment shall be termed 'legal retributivism': the sort of retributivism that works within the realm of rights, law and justice.

It becomes apparent that Hegel's early thinking is built around a binary dichotomy where stands, on the one side, the cold face of law and punishment and, on the other, the natural ethical experiences of human beings, both moulded by the idea of retribution. For Hegel, a world shaped by subtle loving relationships is more likely to produce an ethically desirable form of retribution than one framed by a simple one-sided legalistic approach. Accordingly, the former is certainly superior to the latter in terms of its ethical depth and soundness. After the overall critique of the legalist approach provided in the previous chapter and earlier, the remainder of this chapter will clarify the young Hegel's notion of fate in more detail, and present the core of ethical retributivism.

4. Punishment as fate

As has already been shown in the division between legal punishment and ethical suffering, 'punishment as fate' consists of a distinct account of retributivism, operating beyond the boundaries of the legal territory. Contrasted with the normative necessity of legal retributivism, fate connotes a *phenomenological* theory of punishment, with a particular focus on the question of what it means for the offender to violate their fellow beings.[62] It tries to grasp the experience of criminal violation from a wider perspective than that of law, where the notions of blame, guilt and responsibility are systematically taken in their 'limited and impoverished' forms.[63] Under *punishment as fate*, the offender is not viewed as a legal subject, regarded only as an object of blame and guilt, and as one who must be held accountable for their crime. Instead, they are portrayed as an ethical being capable of actively undertaking guilt and blame and disposed to take productive responsibility for their misdeeds. With this shift of orientation, Hegel calls our attention to the ongoing moral struggle of the offender in relation to themselves and others.

Hegel dramatically describes how, when violation occurs, a terrifying ghost appears as a force and 'vindicates every branch of life and lets loose its

61 Hegel, *Early Theological Writings* p.231.

62 I draw on phenomenology here along the lines of Merleau Ponty as a term that provides 'a direct description of our experience such as it is.' Merleau-Ponty, *Phenomenology of perception* p.xx. for the similar terminology see: Beardsworth, 'Tragedy, world politics and ethical community'p.130.; Rajan and Plotnitsky describe it as 'experiential': Rajan and Plotnitsky, *Idealism without Absolutes: Philosophy and Romantic Culture* p.221.

63 Alan Norrie, 'Animals who think and love: Law, identification and the moral psychology of guilt' (2019) 13 *Criminal Law and Philosophy* 515, 516.

Eumenides'.[64] That 'ghost' haunts the offender and carries out the retribution not as the lord of law standing *above* him but rather as an enemy standing *against* him on an equal plane.[65] Illustrating how the offender ruins the harmony of life and its 'warmth' and 'friendliness', Hegel writes:

> The disembodied spirit of the injured life comes on the scene against the trespass just as Banquo who came as a friend to Macbeth was not blotted out when he was murdered but immediately thereafter took his seat, not as a guest at the feast, but as an evil spirit.[66]

Plagued by the intangible power of his own 'evil spirit', the offender gets into a moral turmoil, where he is forced to live a fractured and distorted life. To use Erving Goffman's terms, violation causes a 'splitting of the [offender's] self into a blameworthy part and a part that stands back and sympathizes with the blame giving'.[67] Having broken selves fighting against each other, the offender inflicts an injury on themselves. The offender, writes Hegel, 'intended to have to do with another's life, but he has only destroyed his own'.[68] What the offender has done 'sets in motion' the process of the (retributive) fate which 'strikes back' and generates a loss of unity and wholeness in their own life:[69] the rebounding of crime. For Hegel, punishment is precisely derived from this loss of moral unity and integrity and the offender's own alienation from themselves:

> When the trespasser feels the disruption of his own life, … the working of his fate commences, and this feeling of a life disrupted must become a longing for what has been lost. The deficiency is recognized as a part

64 Interestingly, for many commentators, the Eumenides (The Kindly Ones) in Greek mythology is the transformed and *legalised* version of the Furies, the goddesses of revenge. For this reason, it seems to represent 'legal retribution' rather than 'ethical retribution'. But, to my mind, Hegel here does not mean to give a legalistic character to fate's punishment. He only wants to make the reality of the psychological experience of the offender more tangible. Martha C Nussbaum, *Anger and Forgiveness: Resentment, Generosity, Justice* (Oxford University Press 2016) p.3. For an interesting reading of the Eumenides along the lines of restorative justice see: Eric Dugdale and Loramy Gerstbauer, 'Forms of justice in Aeschylus' Eumenides' (2017) 34 *Polis: The Journal for Ancient Greek and Roman Political Thought* 226.

65 Peter Wake, *Tragedy in Hegel's Early Theological Writings* (Indiana University Press 2014) p.187; Martin Thibodeau, 'Tragedy and ethical agency: Remarks on Hegel's early essay on the spirit of Christianity and its fate' (2016) 10 *Revista Eletrônica Estudos Hegelianos* p.44.

66 Hegel, *Early Theological Writings* p.229.

67 Erving Goffman, *Relations in Public: Microstudies of the Public Order* (Routledge 2017) p.144.

68 Hegel, *Early Theological Writings* p.229.

69 Jurgen Habermas, *Theory and Practice*, trans. J Biertel (London: Beacon Press 1988) p.148.

> of himself, as what was to have been in him and is not. This lack is not a not-being but is life known and felt as not-being.[70]

Entangled in this passage is the fact that fate consists of the feelings of loss and deficiency that happen to the offender, as well as an urge to fulfil that loss and deficiency. When fate begins to work, 'life becomes but a walking shadow', a painful sequence of moments that interrupts the sense of wholeness and harmony.[71] But the moments in the tragic unfolding of fate are also followed by a sense of discovery and recognition with an 'awareness of the hurt and damage that has been caused to others', marked by 'a degree of empathetic pain on the part of the one who has caused the fracture.'[72] Driven by an awakening that the ties binding them to others are the very ties that make up their moral integrity, the offender seeks to undo the harm they have caused.[73]

Put differently, the offender is caught up in the toils of fate and loses the friendliness of life when faced with the bitter truth that they are part of the very life they intended to destroy. But within the uneasiness of the offender having to come to terms with fate for themselves also lies an endeavour to make things right for the victim. Here is the point where, Hegel notes, 'life can heal its wounds again' and return to its original wholeness and unity.[74] What the offender has to do in the troubled moral atmosphere of post-violation is then to express a recommitment to the fundamental unity of life. If they do so, they can gain the power to restore life in its totality and take steps to achieve reconciliation.

This is certainly not the sort of reconciliation we can identify in law, where punishment is employed as a way of bringing closure to conflict and reaching some peace between individuals. Reconciliation in law is largely to do with the reaffirmation of legal norms in the face of their denial and repairing a disrupted public order. In legal reconciliation, there is less concern with how individuals make transition from a violent past to a better future world and coexist in a peace of mind without being disturbed by the violation.[75] When reconciliation is brought about by an ethically oriented punishment (fate), however, as Hegel comments, crime's 'evil spirit has been chased away' and there stands 'no longer anything hostile in the man'. It 'remains at most as a

70 Hegel, *Early Theological Writings* p.231.

71 William Shakespeare, *Macbeth* (Open Road Integrated Media, Inc. 2018) p.107.

72 Harvey Cox, 'Repentance and forgiveness: A Christian perspective' in Amitai Etzioni (ed), *Repentance: A Comparative Perspective* (Rowman & Littlefield Publishers 1997) p.25.

73 Herman W Siemens, 'Punishment by fate' as a cypher for genealogy: Hegel and Nietzsche on immanent law' in dos Santos Katia and Leonel R Hay (eds), *Nietzsche, German Idealism and Its Critics*, vol. 4 (De Gruyter 2015) p.60.

74 Hegel, *Early Theological Writings* p.230.

75 Alan Norrie, 'Love and justice: Can we flourish without addressing the past?' (2018) 17 *Journal of Critical Realism* 17, 31.

soulless carcass lying in the charnel-house of actualities, in memories'.[76] This, then, says Hegel, 'betters' the criminal and gives to them 'an enjoyment of life'.[77] Fate means *more* than closure and norm affirmation. It also means moral healing and transformation. In other words, it does not simply produce a backlash that besets the offender. Rather, it also generates the inner pain of lack and longing that orients towards spiritual growth.

Therefore, the punishment of fate also sets the stage for the resolution of the unsettled relations between offender and victim. The refusal of judgement and conviction sparked by legal righteousness strengthens the capacity of both to come to terms with violation – on the same track, but each within their own dialectic.[78] While the offender is driven to take responsibility to re-unite with the world which they share with the victim and others, the victim is given time to recover within a reliable ethical setting, in which to engage in dialogue without losing their moral position. Unlike legal punishment – where penal suffering is delivered top-down, with almost no meaningful moral transactions between the conflicting parties – an ethically retributivist punishment is bottom-up, produced 'from within the offender towards the victim'.[79] It emanates from an ethical zone where violation is addressed retributively without necessarily recourse to law. The upshot is that retributivism, in its standard form, can be broken down and reassembled with a fresh look but needs new soil to thrive. As pointed out earlier, I take love as the new soil for retributivism to develop an ethically mature conception of punishment. Yet I have said little about how the young Hegel's theoretical reflections are related to contemporary conceptions of justice and punishment.

5. Ethical retributivism: practical implications

If ethical retributivism is derived from a kind of intersubjectivity that exists in an organic, religious loving community (*Gemeinshaft*), as indicated in Hegel's early writings, then there is little doubt that the nostalgic return to a lost ideal is doomed to failure. In other words, reaching a peaceful and harmonious union of individuals in modern fragmented societies is unlikely where the bonds are notably loose or at times even dissociative. In this sense, the functioning of contemporary societies can hardly enable the production of punishments that promote a sense of unity, harmony and healing. Thus, a conception of punishment driven by this kind of communitarian ethical retributivism is an impossible vision to achieve.

76 Hegel, *Early Theological Writings* p.232.

77 Hegel, *Early Theological Writings* p.231.

78 Austin Sarat, 'Remorse, responsibility, and criminal punishment: An analysis of popular culture' in Susan Bandes (ed), *The Passions of Law* (NYU Press 1999) p.169.

79 Norrie, 'Taking guilt seriously: Towards mature retributivism' p.141.

At this point, it is worth noting that some of the main struggles faced by restorative justice today are to do with the failure of awareness of the sharp incongruence between traditional communities and contemporary societies. Like small-scale transparent pre-modern communities, the community of restorative justice, as briefly mentioned earlier, is a static, cosy, social organisation that is directly disrupted or damaged by criminal violation. It is often viewed as intrinsically good, constituted by a caring structure that is flourishing and emancipatory for all its members.[80] As such, it is rightly criticised by several scholars, as 'it refutes a proper engagement with the context and root-causes of harm' that pervade modern societies with their structural inequalities, criminogenic features and internal conflicts and thus 'denies a proper community-based opportunity to take collective responsibility for injustice'.[81]

Certainly, the longing for the sense of an immediate being together can also provide us with a sharp critical analysis of contemporary societies and their penal practices. But the idea that we have lost something essential that was previously present is neither useful nor accurate, particularly because it derives from an insufficient appreciation of the present. We may have lost the strong ties of an intimate community based on love, where punishment is typically and ideally practised in an ethically retributivist tone. And we should regretfully acknowledge that love is neither the defining nor the operating principle of modern societies. Perhaps quite the reverse. Yet, seeking to redress unjust and unequal relations, there are also sub-communities or networks within modern societies that can foster a loving and caring space in which alternative non-punitive ways are sought when responding to criminal violation.[82] In other words, love is still at work, even where it seems it is absent or far away.

In this sense, this work's account of ethical retributivism echoes, in particular, the values and aims of what today is called 'transformative justice'.[83] Striving to use conflict as an opportunity to come to terms with larger problems of inequities, injustices, oppression and domination in society, transformative justice works to connect incidences of criminal violation to the conditions that create and perpetuate them. It seeks to explore, like ethical retributivism, the liberating bonds within the community that can both address the immediate violence inflicted upon the victim and heal the ongoing trauma of past violence

80 Chamberlen and Carvalho, 'Feeling the absence of justice: Notes on our pathological reliance on punitive justice' p.15.

81 Chamberlen and Carvalho, 'Feeling the absence of justice: Notes on our pathological reliance on punitive justice' p.15.

82 Ruth Morris, *Stories of Transformative Justice* (Canadian Scholars' Press 2000) p.14–23. See also Ching-In Chen, Jai Dulani and Leah Lakshmi Piepzna-Samarasinha, *The Revolution Starts at Home: Confronting Intimate Violence within Activist Communities* (AK Press 2016).

83 Mia Mingus, 'Transformative justice: A brief description' (2022) 84 *Fellowship* 17; Erin Daly, 'Transformative justice: Charting a path to reconciliation' (2001) 12 *International Legal Perspectives* 73.

by creating individual and collective resilience.[84] In transformative justice, 'individual justice and collective liberation are equally important, mutually supportive, and fundamentally intertwined' such that 'the achievement of one is impossible without the achievement of the other'.[85] It is, therefore, more than an alternative to punishment-based criminal justice systems but a holistic social justice philosophy that offers collective healing and safety within meaningful communal connections and engagement.

Transformative justice proposes a strong aversion to the legalist set-up of crime and punishment, and like ethical retributivism, it complains that the state relies heavily on individual responsibility with no regard to community accountability.[86] Positioning itself as a 'protector' and 'promoter' of safety, the state draws on coercive interventions to maintain power and control in society. But doing so creates more harm and violence and perpetuates the previous oppressive conditions. Thus, the state does not have a vested interest in sustainably ending violence and providing safety and support to community members. In fact, the state is poorly equipped to do so in its current strategies and mechanisms, in which offenders and victims are over-individualised and have few options when dealing with crimes in a constructive manner. Though not directly expressed, behind the force of transformative justice lies a loving relational ethos, which introduces a novel way of approaching crimes through informal, non-institutional arrangements in civil society settings.[87] As such, it has much in common with ethical retributivism, being an approach that sets the ground for a better kind of both criminal and social justice.

Nonetheless, there is also a notable incongruence between the two which sets them apart. It seems that transformative justice is mainly initiated by local mechanisms that are more practically oriented. Its strength lies in its ability to confront the violence and injuries that plague societies in a direct manner. The intuitive loving impulse is so strong that it makes a difference in practical terms. It heals the wounds and traumas of the living community and rebuilds it in an ongoing process in order to make it more inclusive, less unequal and more just. That is, it does not only 'interpret the world' in an enlightening way, as Marx once said – it seeks to change it.[88] To this end, it draws on various mechanisms from circle sentencing, family group conferencing, reparation programmes and participatory processes that address structural violence

84 Chen, Dulani and Piepzna-Samarasinha, *The Revolution Starts at Home: Confronting Intimate Violence within Activist Communities* p.104.

85 Anthony J Nocella and J Anthony, 'An overview of the history and theory of transformative justice' (2011) 6 *Peace & Conflict Review* 1, 6.

86 Mimi E Kim, 'Moving beyond critique: Creative interventions and reconstructions of community accountability' (2011) 37 *Social Justice* 14, 17.

87 Alisa Bierria, *Community Accountability: Emerging Movements to Transform Violence* (Social Justice 2012).

88 Karl Marx, 'Theses on Feuerbach' in Frederick Engels (ed), *Ludwig Feuerbach and the End of Classical German Philosophy* (Foreign Languages Press 1976) p.65.

and socio-economic conditions.[89] In collaboration with non-governmental organisations (NGOs), trade unions and social movements, it also promotes existing tools designed for combating poverty, inequality or corruption.[90] In other words, transformative justice seeks to operate in a broad area in which to develop the measures aimed at promoting both social and criminal justice in a holistic way.

Nevertheless, despite its practical strength and broad scope, as some critics claim, transformative justice remains 'inadequately theorised'.[91] It seems that it is a blend of values and principles of restorative and transitional justice, but it is not sufficiently clear how it brings restoration, healing and reconciliation together. The structural critique of the legalistic paradigm, alongside the promotion of informal collective actions to address background injustices, would appear to place it in a unique space. But there is not much clarity with regard to how local mechanisms should be structured and operate when dealing with both individual and social injustice.

On the other hand, like transformative justice, an ethically retributivist form of justice also aims to bring restoration, healing, and reconciliation together, without losing focus on forms of underlying structural violence that cause criminal violation. In this sense, it is relational, intersubjective and even transformational, in that it transforms the way we see social relations and address violation. Nonetheless, operating in a relatively narrow scope, it is mainly theoretical in its nature, investigating the ethical core of how human beings experience violation and how they respond to it in moral psychological terms. Its depth lies in the peculiar way it engages with the moral and psychological aspects of criminal justice and punishment. As such, it is also unavoidably more oriented towards criminal justice than transformative justice.

There is, however, a more significant difference between transformative justice and ethical retributivism. As noted earlier, both approaches have a strong aversion to the legalist paradigm, viewing the law and punishment approach as structurally problematic. Nevertheless, ethical retributivism, unlike transformative justice, does not propose a strict abolitionist strategy that must immediately be pursued. In fact, as highlighted in the previous chapter, we could say that there is also something to the idea that legal punishment appears to do something special or unique that other non-penal mechanisms cannot, however effective and sustainable they may sometimes seem. For it is often taken to be very deeply linked to the maintenance and restoration of the moral and political values that form the bedrock of the community.

89 Morris, *Stories of Transformative Justice*; Chen, Dulani and Piepzna-Samarasinha, *The Revolution Starts at Home: Confronting Intimate Violence within Activist Communities.*

90 Matthew Evans, 'Structural violence, socioeconomic rights, and transformative justice' (2016) 15 *Journal of Human Rights* 1, 2.

91 Paul Gready and others, 'Transformative justice – A concept note' (2010) Unpublished manuscript <http://www.wun.ac.uk/sites/default/files/transformative_justice_-_concept_note_web_version pdf> p.1.

It is also viewed as functioning to promote a sense of order that cannot be easily provided by other means. It may even be said that there may be a virtue in the legalist paradigm that the alternative approaches have not sufficiently addressed and brought to light, at least in the public's eyes. In turn, we may have a solid grounding to challenge the whole criminal justice system and unmask the hidden, deep problems of orthodox penal thinking while also suggesting alternative forms of doing justice. But our strategies may not be welcome, unless they are convincingly designed to address the normative harms that crimes visit on the community.

This is certainly not to say that ethical retributivism does not propose an abolitionist framework. In fact, it does so by debunking the orthodox paradigm, emphasising its ethical incompleteness or insufficiency. However, it seeks to challenge this paradigm without dismissing its possible virtues – perhaps the most notable being respect for rational agency. In his early writings, the young Hegel does not explicitly stress the notion of respect for rational agency when discussing what I call ethical retributivism. Nonetheless, ethical retributivism endorses the principle that legal retributivism paradigmatically advocates: the respect for individuals' rational choices. Certainly, this respect need not translate into an unwavering commitment to punishment. That said, ethical retributivism can be seen as endorsing a form of suffering – though the nature of this suffering differs from the traditional punitive infliction of pain on offenders. It is the suffering that arises empathetically from witnessing the harm endured by the victim.

Concluding with a new start

By reference to Hegel's early works, this chapter began with an analysis of how love can hint at a new and more compelling form of ethical relations than that provided by the legal vision. In relations of love, crime is defined by an act of rupturing and breaking the union within which human beings relate to each other. Arising within and against the existing framework of mutual trust and respect, it is intrinsically relational. It upsets everyone in different ways. Crime is as much injurious to the offender as to the victim and community. The offender suffers a kind of rebound of their own crime upon themselves: the suffering of being cut off from others, the sort of suffering that emerges from the mental revisiting of the scene of crime. By coming back from the initial violation, the offender's suffering is truly retributive. But it is also intrinsically restorative by giving the offender an opportunity to remake their world, the world they share with others. This chapter drew attention to how the young Hegel's metaphysics could ground and inspire modern restorative justice practices.

Hegel calls the 'boomerang' of crime 'punishment as fate'. I name it 'ethical retributivism'. Perhaps most view it as an account of self-punishment or natural punishment. Leaving aside the terminological perplexity, what is notable here is the chasm that has been created between legal punishment and the sort of punishment identified in the moral world of the offender. It seems that they have nothing to do with each other. The young Hegel leaves us with two contrasting worlds: those of legal and ethical retributivism. We know that he seeks to reconcile these two worlds in his later period, where legal punishment is taken as being born out of self-punishment through a dialectical process. But, as stated in the previous chapter, that reconciliation comes at a cost. The ethical voice of 'loving punishment' is silenced or blunted, while legal punishment is largely shaped by a formal political structure. In truth, the strictures placed upon self-punishment there do not permit reconciliation.

Is it possible to align ethical retributivism with legal retributivism, without substantially undermining the *sui generis* character of both approaches? Departing from the idea that much of what has been written about legal retributivism in recent decades is moved by a revisionist and reconciliatory narrative, the rest of this work will be concerned with this question. The main argument will be that legal punishment is made *relational* within three perspectives: the victim, the offender, the state. From the perspective of the victim, punishment is portrayed as a mode of recognition, an expression of solidarity with those who are morally vulnerable. For the offender, it is taken as the delivery of a burden that gives them an opportunity to apologise and restore the harms they have caused. Finally, from the perspective of the state, it is structured as a way of reaffirming the normative validity of mutual recognition. The next chapter will take the question of what punishment means for the victim.

Bibliography

Acorn AE, *Compulsory Compassion: A Critique of Restorative Justice* (UBC Press 2004)
Beardsworth R, *Derrida and the Political* (Routledge 2013)
Beardsworth R, 'Tragedy, world politics and ethical community' (2008) 22 *International Relations* 127
Beiser F, *Hegel* (Routledge 2005)
Bernstein JM, 'Love and law: hegel's critique of morality' (2003) 70 *Social Research: An International Quarterly* 393
Bierria A, *Community Accountability: Emerging Movements to Transform Violence* (Social Justice 2012)
Billings J, *Genealogy of the Tragic, Genealogy of the Tragic* (Princeton University Press 2014)
Braithwaite J, *Restorative Justice & Responsive Regulation* (OUP 2002)
Chamberlen A and Carvalho H, 'Feeling the absence of justice: notes on our pathological reliance on punitive justice' (2022) 61 *The Howard Journal of Crime and Justice* 87
Chen C, Dulani J and Piepzna-Samarasinha LL, *The Revolution Starts at Home: Confronting Intimate Violence within Activist Communities* (AK Press 2016)
Christie N, 'Conflicts as property' (1977) 17 *The British Journal of Criminology* 1
Cox H, 'Repentance and forgiveness: a Christian perspective' in Etzioni A (ed), *Repentance: A Comparative Perspective* (Rowman & Littlefield Publishers 1997)

Daly E, 'Transformative justice: charting a path to reconciliation' (2001) 12 *International Legal Personality* 73

Dugdale E and Gerstbauer L, 'Forms of justice in Aeschylus Eumenides' (2017) 34 *Polis: The Journal for Ancient Greek and Roman Political Thought* 226

Evans M, 'Structural violence, socioeconomic rights, and transformative justice' (2016) 15 *Journal of Human Rights* 1

Goffman E, *Relations in Public: Microstudies of the Public Order* (Routledge 2017)

Gready P and others, 'Transformative justice–a concept note' (2010) Unpublished manuscript <http://www.wun.ac.uk/sites/default/files/transformative_justice_-_concept_note_web_version pdf>

Habermas J, *Theory and Practice*. Translated by Biertel J (Beacon Press 1988)

Harris HS, *Hegel's Development: Toward the Sunlight 1770–1801* (OUP 1972)

Hegel GWF, *Early Theological Writings* (University of Pennsylvania Press 1971)

Hegel GWF, *Hegel's System of Ethical Life and First Philosophy of Spirit* (Suny Press 1979)

Hinchman LP, 'Hegel's theory of crime and punishment' (1982) 44 *The Review of Politics* 523

Hoff S, *The Laws of the Spirit: A Hegelian Theory of Justice* (Suny Press 2014)

Honneth A, *The Struggle for Recognition: The Moral Grammar of Social Conflicts* (MIT Press 1996)

Johnstone G, *A Restorative Justice Reader: Texts, Sources and Context* (Willan Publishing 2003)

Kant I, *Metaphysical Elements of Justice: Part I of the Metaphysics of Morals*. Translated by Ladd J (Hackett Publishing 1999)

Kelsen H, *Essays in Legal and Moral Philosophy* (Springer 1973)

Kim ME, 'Moving beyond critique: creative interventions and reconstructions of community accountability' (2011) 37 *Social Justice* 14

Kroner R, *Introduction to Hegel's Early Theological Writings*. Translated by Knox T M. With an Introduction and Fragments translated by Kroner R (University of Chicago Press 1948)

Loick D, 'Terribly upright: the young Hegel's Critique of Juridicism' (2014) 40 *Philosophy & Social Criticism* 933

López MRA , 'On the violence of positivity in hegel's early theological writings' in Sembou E (ed), *The Young Hegel and Religion* (Peter Lang AG 2017)

Lukács G, *The Young Hegel: Studies in the Relations between Dialectics and Economics* (Merlin Press 1975)

Marcuse H, *Reason and Revolution Hegel and the Rise of Social Theory* (Beacon Press 1960)

Marx K, 'Theses on feuerbach' in Frederick Engels (ed), *Ludwig Feuerbach and the End of Classical German Philosophy* (Foreign Languages Press 1976)

McGowan T, *Emancipation after Hegel: Achieving a Contradictory Revolution* (Columbia University Press 2019)

Merleau-Ponty M, *Phenomenology of Perception* (Routledge 2012)

Miller C, *Know My Name: A Memoir* (Penguin 2020)

Mingus M, 'Transformative justice: A brief description' (2022) 84 *Fellowship* 17

Morris H, 'Guilt and suffering' (1971) 21 *Philosophy East and West* 419

Morris R, *Stories of Transformative Justice* (Canadian Scholars' Press 2000)

Nauen FG, *Revolution, Idealism and Human Freedom: Schelling Hölderlin and Hegel and the Crisis of Early German Idealism* (Springer Science & Business Media 2012)

Nocella AJ and Anthony J, 'An overview of the history and theory of transformative justice' (2011) 6 *Peace & Conflict Review* 1

Norrie A, *Law and the Beautiful Soul* (Glasshouse Press 2005)

Norrie A, 'Love and justice: can we flourish without addressing the past?' (2018) 17 *Journal of Critical Realism* 17

Norrie A, 'Love in law's shadow: political theory, moral psychology and young hegel's critique of punishment' (2019) 28 *Social & Legal Studies* 10

Norrie A, 'Taking guilt seriously: towards mature retributivism' in Solanke I (ed), *On Crime, Society, and Responsibility in the Work of Nicola Lacey* (OUP 2021)

Norrie N, 'Animals who think and love: law, identification and the moral psychology of guilt' (2019) 13 *Criminal Law and Philosophy* 515

Norton R, *The Beautiful Soul* (Cornell University Press 1995)

Nussbaum MC, *Anger and Forgiveness: Resentment, Generosity, Justice* (OUP 2016)

Ormiston A, *Love and Politics: Re-interpreting Hegel* (New York Press 2012)

Pinkard T, *Hegel: A Biography* (Cambridge University Press 2001)

Plant R, *Hegel* (Allen & Unwin 1973)

Rajan T and Plotnitsky A, *Idealism Without Absolutes: Philosophy and Romantic Culture* (SUNY Press 2012)

Reeves C, Norrie A and Carvalho H, 'Between persecution and reconciliation: criminal justice, legal form and human emancipation' in Christodoulidis E, Dukes R and Goldoni M (eds), *Research Handbook on Critical Legal Theory* (Edward Elgar Publishing 2019)

Sarat A, 'Remorse, responsibility, and criminal punishment: an analysis of popular culture' in Susan Bandes (ed), *The Passions of Law* (NYU Press 1999)

Sembou E, *The Young Hegel and Religion* (Peter Lang 2017)

Shakespeare W, *Macbeth* (Open Road Integrated Media, Inc. 2018)

Siemens HW, 'Punishment by fate'as a cypher for genealogy: hegel and nietzsche on immanent law' in Hay K and dos Santos LR (eds), *Nietzsche, German Idealism and Its Critics*, vol. 4 (De Gruyter 2015)

Taylor C, *Hegel* (Cambridge University Press 2012)

Thibodeau M, 'Tragedy and ethical agency: remarks on hegel's early essay on the spirit of christianity and its fate' (2016) 10 *Revista Eletrônica Estudos Hegelianos*

Tsagdis G, 'Love and the apparatus: on a hegelian fragment' in Zeiher C and McGowann T (eds), *Can Philosophy Love? Reflections and Encounters* (Rowman & Littlefield 2017)

Van Ness D and Strong KH, *Restoring Justice: An Introduction to Restorative Justice* (Routledge 2014)

Wake P, *Tragedy in Hegel's Early Theological Writings* (Indiana University Press 2014)

Williams RR, *Hegel's Ethics of Recognition* (University of California Press 1998)

Williams RR, *Tragedy, Recognition, and the Death of God: Studies in Hegel and Nietzsche* (OUP 2012)

Wilson A, 'Guilt beyond guilt: from political theory to metaphysics with Herbert Morris' (2021) 84 *The Modern Law Review* 89

Winnicott DW, *Playing and Reality* (Routledge 2012)

Wolf WC, 'The weakness of the law: the opposition of concept and life in hegel's early ethics' in Sembou E (ed), *The Young Hegel and Religion* (Peter Lang 2017)

Zehr H, *Changing Lenses: A New Focus for Crime and Justice* (Herald Press 2015)

Part III

Revival

4 Punishment

Between vindication and healing

Introduction

The first part of this work has presented and juxtaposed two models of retributivism.[1] The first one is based on a state-centric legalistic paradigm; the latter consists in an intersubjective framework. Both provide a different image of punishment. The first part concluded with the question of whether the two models can be reconciled within a broader vision; the rest of this work will be dedicated to the analysis of this question from three perspectives: those of the victim, the offender and the state. This chapter moves on to explore how legal retributivism can be ethically enriched by a victim-oriented approach.

One straightforward way of linking retributive punishment to the victim is through the principle that the state owes to them a duty to take crime seriously and respond to it appropriately. From this approach, by punishing perpetrators of crimes, the state expresses solidarity with victims and rejects the dominance acquired over them by offenders. It counteracts the disruption of an equal relationship between victims and their perpetrators and reaffirms the former's value and dignity. In this sense, punishment restores victims to the position they occupied prior to criminal violation. It is restorative of their subjectivity in their relationship with offenders and others. In this work, this approach may be seen as a *legalistic form of restoration*. By way of punishment, legal restoration recognises the injustice that victims suffer from and affirms their moral or normative standing in the face of criminal violation.[2]

The suffering of injustice, however, is different from the sense of loss and grief that victims experience. The latter requires more than punishment. In other words, the recognition of crime as an injustice against victims does not

1 H Cesur, Retributive Punishment: Between Vindication and Healing' (2025) 0(0) Intl Rev Victimology https://doi.org/10.1177/02697580241309352.

2 Hampton, 'Correcting harms versus righting wrongs: The goal of retribution'; Adam J MacLeod, 'All for one: A review of victim-centric justifications for criminal punishment' (2008) 13 Berkeley Journal of Criminal Law 31; Fletcher, 'The place of victims in the theory of retribution'; Lippke, 'Victim-centered retributivism'; Diane Whiteley, 'The victim and the justification of punishment' (1998) 17 Criminal Justice Ethics 42.

DOI: 10.4324/9781003563150-8

sufficiently address their losses and sufferings. From this perspective, victims do need recognition – but of an ethical kind, where their grief at what has happened are genuinely shared by others. Unlike legal recognition, where the state declares crime as a public wrong through punishment, ethical recognition addresses crime as an ethical wound, with an awareness of or sensitivity to the deeper harms and injuries related to how victims subsequently move on with their lives. Ethical recognition does not only seek to re-locate victims in relation to their offenders by repairing the normative harm they suffer. It also becomes more attuned to the losses and vulnerability of victims and looks for ways to improve their wellbeing and restore their trust in the world.

To spell out the twofold nature of restoration, the first section will begin with a brief analysis of the impact statement of a rape victim, Chanel Miller, in particular in light of the needs of victims. I will discuss what it means to be victimised, with a particular emphasis on the ideas of vulnerability and resilience. Most of the time, at the heart of the swinging feelings of vulnerability and resilience in victims, there is a demand for punishment. I will question whether that demand ***necessarily includes a desire for the punitive suffering of the offender***. This discussion will then set the stage for a theoretical debate about how retributive punishment is linked to victim restoration.

The departure point for this discussion will be based on the idea that there is a shared ethical zone between the victim and offender, where the restoration and healing of the former is closely linked with whether the latter suffers. This is not to say that the victim's call for punishment should be immediately echoed or met in the legal order – this would make the justice system an institutionalised or 'tamed' version of revenge.[3] Rather, the discussion starts with the idea that there seems something morally significant in the punishing of offenders, that facilitates the healing and recovery of victims.

To expand this thought, the second section will examine Hampton's theory of punishment, wherein retributive punishment is presented as a principal way of standing up for victims. Punishment, for Hampton, is designed to restore the value and dignity of victims – value and dignity which have been put into question by criminal violation. It does this by humbling the will of offenders. The third section challenges Hampton's theory, arguing that it provides an insufficient conception of the moral psychology of offenders; legal punishment may misdirect the victim's attention towards their healing and recovery and even lock them into a state of vulnerability. The fourth section analyses some of the retributive practices Hampton suggests, where both legal and ethical restoration are at stake. The chapter concludes by suggesting that retributive punishment can be both legally and ethically restorative as long as it fosters a genuine concern and compassion in offenders towards victims, followed by the full recognition of their loss and grief.

3 For this view see: Solomon, 'Justice v. vengeance';

1. Victimhood: two levels of harms

> *I have become a little barnacle always needing to be at someone's side … It is embarrassing how feeble I feel, how timidly I move through life, always guarded, ready to defend myself, ready to be angry … I have to relearn that I am not fragile, I am capable, I am wholesome, not just livid and weak.*
>
> *The damage is done, no one can undo it. And now we both have a choice. We can let this destroy us, I can remain angry and hurt and you can be in denial, or we can face it head on, I accept the pain, you accept the punishment, and we move on.*
>
> *Had Brock admitted guilt and remorse and offered to settle early on, I would have considered a lighter sentence, respecting his honesty, grateful to be able to move our lives forward. Instead, he took the risk of going to trial, added insult to injury and forced me to relive the hurt … [He] should face the consequences of challenging his crime, of putting my pain into question, of making us wait so long for justice.*[4]

After having 'a year of anger, anguish, and uncertainty', during which the rape trial had been searching for the legal truth, Chanel Miller gave a strong statement that tells her story of what it feels like to be a victim. It may not be 'universal', describing the internal tribulations of every single human being who has been violated. Neither is it a fully completed emotional journey for the victim in question. But veering between the various forms of anger and the feelings of distrust and fear, it provides vivid hints about the dynamic nature of victimhood with its struggles and pains, as well as its subsequent process of recovery and healing.

Driven initially by an injurious violation, this story starts with feelings of frailty and disappointment along with hidden bitter emotions of rage and frustration. Here perhaps, the most dominant theme that pervades the inner world of the victim is an uncontrolled anger at the offender, presumably accompanied by a powerful desire for punitive payback. It then moves on to the acknowledgement stage, where the victim gains some acceptance towards the assault. At this stage, the narrative strikingly shifts from the 'I' to the 'We': 'We can face it head on, I accept the pain, you accept the punishment'. Here comes the moment of realisation: that the two lives can be related to each other in a more positive and constructive manner.[5] The wish for payback, along with a relatively more moderate form of anger remains, and yet it notably diminishes within a quasi-reconciliatory spirit.[6] Finally, the story goes

4 J.m Katie Baker, 'Here's the powerful letter the Stanford victim read to her attacker' *BuzzFeed News* <https://www.buzzfeednews.com/article/katiejmbaker/heres-the-powerful-letter-the-stanford-victim-read-to-her-ra> accessed 3 February 2023.

5 Lorraine S Amstutz, *The Little Book of Victim Offender Conferencing: Bringing Victims and Offenders Together in Dialogue* (Simon and Schuster 2009) p.12.

6 Nussbaum, *Anger and Forgiveness: Resentment, Generosity, Justice* p.6.

on with the feelings of further anger and resentment, sparked by the denial of responsibility on the part of the offender. This stage is somehow diverted from the previous stage where reconciliation has failed.

This short narrative of victimhood provides an interesting emotional map that discloses the victim's two related, yet distinct needs. On the one hand, it shows that the victim wants to see that justice is done when the offender is punished. We may call this the need for vindication: the victim's sense of injustice should be addressed and redressed. On the other hand, the narrative also shows that the victim needs healing and recovery alongside the desire to see the offender suffer. We may call this the need for healing: the victim's injury should be acknowledged and treated. Vindication and healing are separate, as they require two different responses. While vindication requires holding the offender accountable, healing involves providing therapeutic support to the victim. Yet they are also connected, as vindication can pave the way for healing. Consider, for instance, Miller's words: 'Had Brock admitted guilt and remorse and offered to settle early on, I would have [been] grateful to be able to move our lives forward'. What is remarkable is that vindication is demanded from the offender, not solely from the state. It is the offender's apologetic response that seems to help the victim 'move forward', not the state's punitive actions, which bypass the offender's soul. In fact, the state is portrayed as a party that causes her to 'relive the hurt' through the penal process, not one that soothes her pain.

To express my thoughts in a clearer way, I now want to draw your attention to the second stage of victimhood, in which both the desire for justice and recovery are mingled. The wounds are not unbearably fresh at this point and yet not entirely healed either. This stage marks the moment of awareness that the victim's life is in some way connected to that of the offender. Adam Towler, a victim of serious physical violence, describes that moment, perhaps in a quite unusual way for many, as 'a sense of connection', where two individuals are linked in an event.[7] Likewise, Paul Kohler, a victim of a violent attack, which causes a serious trauma within a family, says that his daughter was 'hugely helped' by meeting with their attacker because it 'demythologised' him.[8] Not all victims would phrase the sense of interrelatedness with a sense of connection or be helped by being physically together with their offender. But in a typical form of victimhood there comes a period where two lives are joined and mingled together, and the victim realises that his or her healing might be to do with the offender's taking responsibility.

7 Jamie Grierson, 'Doctor stabbed nine times tells attacker: 'I am not angry with you'' *The Guardian* <https://www.theguardian.com/uk-news/2022/feb/18/doctor-stabbed-nine-times-tells-attacker-i-am-not-angry-with-you> accessed 3 February 2023.

8 Paul Kohler, <https://www.theforgivenessproject.com/stories-library/paulkohler/> accessed 9 September 2024.

Note, however, that there is no complete withdrawal from the demand for retribution at this stage. In this sense, legal punishment is usually thought to bring a sort of relief to the victim, a legitimate moral need to be met, deriving naturally from their rightful status as someone seeking justice.[9] The most common way to understand the linkage between punishment and the victim is based on the assumption that the victim is morally satisfied by seeing the offender suffer, in that the victim's 'pain of injustice' is soothed with the pain of the offender. In this line of thinking, the victim is severely disturbed by the affective imbalance between themselves and the offender in the aftermath of criminal violation: 'He walks in pleasure and I in suffering'.[10] This moves them to look for ways to reduce this imbalance, either by exacting a retribution or just by wishing the offender to suffer.[11] In score-keeping mode, legal punishment provides a sense of gratification to the victim by inflicting an appropriate amount of harm upon the offender. That is, it helps them to satisfy their sense of reciprocity and view the world again as balanced and fair, a perspective which has been disturbed by the commission of crime. I take this to mean that punishment restores victims to the position they were in before their right was infringed, at least in their own eyes.[12] This is what I call 'normative restoration', the sort of restoration that can be provided by retributive punishment.

Nevertheless, there is another – less dangerous – emotional layer in the second phase of victimhood, from which emerges an active and a more enduring form of restoration and recovery. Here the wish for things to go badly for the offender starts to fade while also being infected with a willingness to work through the pains of violation in a non-punitive way. In this transitional process, the victim is more inclined to ask their offender to admit the crime than to have a blind desire to retaliate. 'I do not want Brock to rot away in prison', says Miller, for example. 'What I truly wanted was for Brock to get it, to understand and admit to his wrongdoing'. At this ambivalent stage, Miller explores that there are other ways of asserting herself against the wrongful behaviour without being exclusively directed by vengeful anger. At the heart of

9 Jean Hampton, 'An expressive theory of retribution' in Wesley Cragg (ed), *Retributivism and its Critics* (Franz Steiner Verlag Stuttgart 1992); Antony Duff, 'Punishment, communication and community' in Matt Matravers (ed), *Punishment and Political Theory* (Hart Publishing 1998) p.114; Jaime Malamud Goti, 'Equality, punishment, and self-respect' (2001) 5 *Buffalo Criminal Law Review* 497; Paul Butler, 'Retribution, for liberals' (1998) 46 *UCLA Law Review* 1873.

10 Nico H Frijda, *The Laws of Emotion* (Psychology Press 2017) p.267.

11 Margaret R Holmgren, *Forgiveness and Retribution: Responding to Wrongdoing* (Cambridge University Press 2012) p.30.

12 Heather Strang and Lawrence W Sherman, 'Repairing the harm: Victims and restorative justice' (2003) 1 Utah Law Review 15, 24; Karsten J Struhl, 'Retributive punishment and revenge' in Karsten J Struhl and Kimora (eds), *When Young People Break the Law* (Idea Publications 2015); Jonathan Jacobs, 'The retributive theory of punishment' in Karsten J Struhl and Kimora (eds), *When Young People Break the Law* (Idea Publications 2015).

her concern lies the offender's taking responsibility for his crime and changing his moral standing in relation to her.

In other words, the victim wants the offender to be engaged in an effort of rearranging their 'mental furniture' about what has happened and acknowledge the injustice the victim suffers. What is typically expected or demanded from the offender is a genuine apology or similar form of rectifying response, perhaps, but not necessarily concretised by an act of restitution. Inherent in the victim's mental state is the need to be confirmed by the offender about their wrongful loss and suffering.[13] This is an important juncture for the victim, in that they come to realise that their healing is not solely concerned with a punitive sanction imposed on the offender. In fact, they may even reckon that their immediate desire to hurt back is part of a more fundamental need for the recognition of their loss and suffering.[14]

One might react here by claiming that the state's punitive action against the offender operates well if the aim is to recognise the wrong and harm done to the victim, since by punishing the state publicly declares that it is on the side of the victim.[15] That said, we should distinguish the mere recognition of the wrong from the therapeutic healing of pain and loss. While the former has most of the time to do with a normative stance towards the offender, the latter requires a deeper set of vindicatory responses that address the victim's harms and injuries. Legal punishment does recognise the wrong in an abstract sense; but it does little to provide a meaningful opportunity to deal with the ambiguities and unaddressed wounds that haunt the victim.[16] It may give the victim a sense of closure, and yet this happens often unsatisfactorily, leaving a variety of injuries unhealed.[17] It may even sometimes cause the victim, as stated earlier to 'relive the hurt' rather than to heal it. There is, therefore, often a deep crevasse between formal justice and true healing.

An apology or a similar kind of response, however, is better suited than the law to address and recognise both the sense of injustice and the pains of victimhood. In other words, it has the power or capacity to both 'right the wrong' and 'repair the harms' caused by the criminal violation. Certainly, as

13 Mark Umbreit, 'Restorative justice through victim-offender mediation: A multi-site assessment' (1998) 1 *Western Criminology Review* 1; Stephanos Bibas and Richard A Bierschbach, 'Integrating remorse and apology into criminal procedure' (2004) 114 *The Yale Law Journal* 85 Friederike Funk, Victoria McGeer and Mario Gollwitzer, 'Get the message: Punishment is satisfying if the transgressor responds to its communicative intent' (2014) 40 *Personality and Social Psychology Bulletin* 986.

14 Howard Zehr, *Transcending: Reflections of Crime Victims* (Simon and Schuster 2001). Even though retalitation is 'one among a number of ways that one can seek vindication', says Walgrave, 'the need for vindication is more basic and instinctual.' p.191.

15 Joshua Kleinfeld, 'Reconstructivism: The place of criminal law in ethical life' (2015) 129 *Harvard Law Review* 1485 p.1509.

16 Linda G Mills, 'The justice of recovery: How the state can heal the violence of crime' (2005) 57 *Hastings Law Journal* 457, 507.

17 Bandes, 'When victims seek closure: Forgiveness, vengeance and the role of government'.

with legal punishment, the offender's vindication involves an arduous process where they come to terms with their past behaviour and its consequences. In this sense, the offender is burdened with a peculiar form of suffering that results from their realisation of the victim being unjustly treated by themselves. In apologetic recognition, the offender, in a sense, participates in the suffering of the victim while seeking ways to relieve it. Being punished by the boomerang of their own behaviour, the offender suffers a retributive loss. But the punishment they undertake does not simply restore the victim to their former pre-injury status in a normative sense. That is, it does not simply vindicate the equal status of both offender and victim. Rather, it sets the ground for a deeper therapeutic recovery of the victim by recognising or sharing in their suffering. In other words, the aim is not merely to acknowledge that a wrong has been done but also to seek ways to mend the victim's wounds and support the process of healing and recovery.

If apologetic response is successful, it helps the victim to view the world again as unified and whole, in which their personal insecurity or vulnerability gradually dissipates. This is what I call 'ethical restoration', the sort of restoration that might be provided by apologetic recognition. I do not, of course, argue that an apologetic response by the offender is always sufficient for complete healing and recovery. I do, however, argue that an apology is better than a legal response at recognizing both the wrong and the suffering of the victim. We should, therefore, reform our criminal justice systems more in the direction of apology and away from retributive punishment, which simply recognises crimes as wrongs without concern for the victim's healing.

To highlight, my aim in this chapter is not to map out a comprehensive account of victimhood but rather to explore how retributive punishment relates to the victim's various needs. In this regard, it must so far become clear that from the perspective of the victim, there are two layers or levels of need. At the first level, the victim seeks moral balance and normative vindication. At this level, legal punishment can be taken as restoring the asymmetry between the victim and offender by bringing the latter down from an ill-gotten position and reaffirming the former's moral status. At the second and more fundamental level, however, the victim needs a more substantial recognition that would help them take active steps to facilitate their own recovery and healing. Apologetic recognition can operate at this level, seeking to vindicate the victim and repair their relationship with themselves and the world.

Some might question whether my analysis applies only to certain types of crimes or to all crimes in general. They could argue that each crime has its own specifics and therefore requires a tailored approach. I agree that different crimes can have varying effects on victims, but I believe that all victims, regardless of the crime, share two core needs: vindication and healing. First, victims should be recognised and acknowledged as individuals who have been wronged. Second, they should receive actions that make amends and provide therapeutic support. While minor offenses may not necessitate the same depth of restorative and therapeutic intervention as more severe crimes, even in cases of relatively minor violations, such as battery or trespassing, victims still need healing and reassurance that their environment is secure. This reassurance is an integral part of their therapeutic recovery. My argument is that retributive punishment vindicates victims, but it does little to facilitate their healing and recovery. In contrast, an apology or a similar response is more effective at recognizing both the wrongs and the harms done to victims, and offers more support in their healing process. The question is then whether retributive punishment can be transformed into a form that incorporates apologetic elements. The aim is to pursue a victim-oriented (legal) punishment that not only acknowledges the wrong done (vindication) but also sets the ground for the victim's healing (therapeutic recovery). To this end, I will now analyse Hampton's theory of punishment, which takes the victim's world, needs, and interests seriously.

2. The moral psychology of the victim: resentment

In the first section, I have supplied an analysis of victimhood around the feelings of vulnerability and fragility mixed with a desire for justice and punishment, arguing that the victim needs both normative vindication and therapeutic healing. Yet, I have said little about how and why victims need vindication and support. In this section, by focusing on Hampton's account of resentment, more light will be shed on victimhood in a theoretical way, particularly connecting it to the normative foundation of retributive punishment.

For Hampton, what bothers victims about being wronged is, at bottom, a peculiar form of moral sentiment that is combined of various emotions, including resentment. 'Frequently linked with a verbal rebuke, reprimand or complaint directed at the insulter', Hampton says, resentment is generally viewed as a protest declaring that what has been done is not morally acceptable.[18] Involved in this mental state is a perception of unfairness along with the feeling of anger. So being, it has fundamentally to do with the disapproval of certain sorts of behaviour, and reaffirming a particular moral norm or principle that the victim finds valuable in the face of its violation.

But Hampton also thinks that resentment is not only concerned with a sort of aversion about the failure of moral or normative expectations. For crime is not a mere violation of a law or moral rule. It is rather also an expressive act that conveys certain messages about the value of individuals. At its heart, though not always expressed unequivocally, for Hampton, crime involves a message that the victim is 'not valuable enough to require better treatment'.[19] In other words, crime is an intentional attitude of disrespect and disregard for the victim, and an attack against his dignity and self-image.

18 Jean Hampton, 'Forgiveness, resentment and hatred' in Jeffrie Murphy and Jean Hampton (eds), *Forgiveness and Mercy* (Cambridge University Press 1988) p.55.

19 Hampton, 'Forgiveness, resentment and hatred' p.44

In Hampton's view, therefore, there is something more in the build-up of resentment that moves beyond the annoyance that results from the violation of law. In this regard, resentment is firmly to do with an emotional challenge against the moral-meaning that is implicit in the offender's disrespectful or demeaning behaviour. It is somehow a self-defensive resistance, seeking to communicate a counter message that refutes the initial (moral) message of the crime. But when someone is slighted or insulted, Hampton emphasises, defensiveness comes with the feelings of suspicion and uncertainty:

> *There are (at least) the following two ways a victim can respond to this message: She can reject it as wrong and hence regard the action as inappropriate given what she believes to be her true (high) worth, or she can worry (or even believe) that the wrongdoer is right, that she really isn't worth enough to warrant better treatment, so that his action is permissible given her lower worth.*[20]

For Hampton, what is at stake in most cases of resentment is the mixture of these two responses. The victim is generally stuck in a psychological vacuum, in which they try to vindicate their moral value while also being influenced by the false implication given by the crime. The message of the crime, which raises a doubt about the value of the victim, can tenaciously be rebuffed by those who are what Hampton calls 'beyond resentment'. Yet, those who resent the wrongful act have usually some degree of fear of the fact that their status is either low enough to be treated this way, or that it can be lowered by the offender, even though they would challenge that.[21] Put differently, manipulated by the affront to their dignity, the victim is somehow disposed to engage in a kind of self-questioning, where they come to doubt whether their suffering is deserved or permissible.[22]

Grave criminal offences, such as physical assault or rape, are obvious examples where victims come to question their own dignity. But for Hampton, even a petty act of wrongfulness, like sneaking a book out of a university library without checking it out, can 'inflict' a demeaning message upon the victim.[23] When sneaking, the wrongdoer's action 'means (or is evidence of) the superiority of his needs over those of the rest of the university community'. Standing in the way of the victims' realisation of their real value, Hampton thinks this trivial wrong is an attempt to diminish the victim by making circumstances such that they cannot benefit from the services of the library

20 Hampton, 'Forgiveness, resentment and hatred' p.44

21 Hampton, 'Forgiveness, resentment and hatred' p.57–58.

22 Hampton does not draw explicitly on the term 'self-questioning', but the term is not uncommon in the literature on victimhood. See for example: Ronnie Janoff-Bulman, *Shattered Assumptions* (Simon and Schuster 2010) p.80.

23 Hampton, 'A new theory of retribution' p.397.

as much as the wrongdoer.[24] The victims are, therefore, injured by the wrong in both material and moral senses and rightly become resentful, asking 'why should she get exclusive enjoyment of the book while the rest of us can't use it at all? Who does she think she is?' and thus 'who does she think I am?'[25]

I do not think that victims typically question their own value in cases of petty wrongs or some crimes that do not affect their self-esteem. In some crimes, such as theft or battery, victims usually feel anger toward the offender but remain confident that the offender's actions do not diminish their own worth. It may, thus, be useful to differentiate between wrongs that lead victims to question their value and those that merely provoke anger without impacting their self-esteem.

Nonetheless, I agree that the acts of defiance in most of the serious wrongs can involve an unstable emotional state, in which the victim alternates between the feelings of fear and low self-esteem, and those of courage and restored self-respect. In the grip of this psychological uncertainty, the victim can search for evidence to be assured that they are not as low in rank and value as the wrongdoer's action assumes to be, and to fight against the wrong. But Hampton is not full of hope about this fight:

> *No matter how much we applaud resenters, there is something worrying about their defensive response. How can one succeed in defying the truth of something that one half believes? Resenters are vulnerable, … their defiant act requires buttressing if they are going to be able to gain a high degree of belief in what they wish to believe.*[26]

When faced with a denial of their value, this passage stresses, the victim goes in pursuit of validation and reaffirmation. But because they are vulnerable, Hampton thinks, we should be in careful and attentive engagement with the victim's painful experience of having been wronged. We should have a decent compassion for their distress and stand in (moral) solidarity with them. In other words, to be wronged is somehow to be misrecognised by another, and to fall into a flawed pattern of thinking, in which one becomes susceptible to having a demeaning or contemptible picture of oneself. And the non-recognition of this misrecognition, to use Charles Taylor's terms, can inflict further harm: 'can be a form of oppression, imprisoning someone in a false, distorted, and reduced mode of being'.[27] We should, therefore, confirm the victim's sense of injustice and 'offer some forms of solace, safety, and relief' to them.[28]

24 Hampton, 'Correcting harms versus righting wrongs: The goal of retribution' p.1679.
25 Hampton, 'Correcting harms versus righting wrongs: The goal of retribution' p.1681.
26 Hampton, 'Forgiveness, resentment and hatred' p.58.
27 Charles Taylor, 'The politics of recognition' in John Arthur and Amy Shapiro (eds), *Campus Wars: Multiculturalism and the Politics of Difference* (Routledge 2021) p.25.
28 Margaret Urban Walker, 'The cycle of violence' (2006) 5 *Journal of Human Rights* 81, 20.

Here is where resentment in Hampton's theory is linked to retributive punishment. For Hampton, punishment denies the false claim procured by crime, and repairs the damage to self-respect entailed by the resentful feelings of the victim. It expresses solidarity with the victim by reaffirming the equality of relationship that precedes the crime. Even in cases where the crime does not alter the victim's self-perception but only causes anger, punishment validates the victim's position and asserts that what has been done is unacceptable. This can be termed as legal restoration.

Yet, for Hampton, punishment as a form of retribution must also "repair the damages" caused by crime, constructing a moral situation in which the victim's injustice and loss is recognised by the offender. As Hampton puts it, 'to vindicate the victim, a retributive response must strive first to re-establish the acknowledgement of the victim's worth damaged by the wrongdoing, and second, to repair the damage done to the victim's ability to realize her value.'[29] As suggested by Hampton, retributive punishment should not only help the victim recognise their own value but also address the harms and injuries caused by the crime. This may require additional support from the state to ensure the victim's full recovery and healing, which I referred to earlier as apologetic recognition.

To clarify, resentment is backed up and followed by retributive punishment in Hampton's theory – not because it manifests the rightful retributive anger of the victim.[30] In other words, Hampton does not believe that resentment is an appropriate reaction to criminal wrongdoing. Rather, she argues that we should support those who have been violated and reaffirm their value in the face of its denial. There seems less controversy about the fact that legal punishment, at least symbolically, restores victims by standing by them when it publicly declares that they have been wronged.[31] But it is not clear how retributive punishment bears centrally on their coming to terms with their injured past and their healing. Equally debatable is whether legal punishment is the only way to vindicate the victim's value and whether this would pose the risk of degrading the offender's value.[32] In the light of these misgivings, the discussion now moves on to the role that punishment plays in Hampton's theory, analysing it in terms of the restoration of the victim. In the light of these misgivings, the discussion now moves on to the role that punishment plays in Hampton's theory, analysing it in terms of whether it can take an apologetic form.

29 Hampton, 'Correcting harms versus righting wrongs: The goal of retribution' p.1686.

30 Joel Feinberg, 'The expressive function of punishment' (1965) 49 *The Monist* 397.

31 Daniel Farnham, 'A Hegelian theory of retribution' (2008) 39 *Journal of Social Philosophy* 606; Lippke, 'Victim-centered retributivism' For an opposing view; Brown, 'Punishment and the restoration of rights'; Arthur Ripstein, *Equality, Responsibility, and the Law* (Cambridge University Press 2001); Robert Nozick, *Anarchy, State and Utopia* (Basic Books 2013) p.138;

32 Ripstein, *Equality, Responsibility, and the Law* p.146.

3. Linking resentment to retribution: punishment as defeat

What has been evident from the previous section's analysis of Hampton's conception of violation is that crime is a wrongful act, and one that not only causes some harm in its ordinary sense, where the victim suffers some sorts of physical or material harm. It is also an act that generates what Hampton calls a moral injury, an injury that is to do with the damage to the realisation of the victim's value.[33] Crime, on the other hand, is also an expressive act, from the perspective of the offender, involving a claim about the moral position of the offender. It reveals that the offender holds themselves to be superior to the victim, or that their needs are more important than those of the victim. Whether or not the offender intends their act to be demeaning, Hampton says we can read crime, 'as defeating the victim and elevating the offender'.[34] At the hands of the offender, the victim 'is humbled and made to look inferior'. Crime somehow creates evidence that the victim is less valuable than the offender. But because all human beings are of equal and immutable worth, in Hampton's theory, legal punishment performs to nullify the evidence produced by crime with the new evidence effected through punishment.[35]

As with criminal wrong, punishment is a communication about the values of individuals.[36] It represents 'the defeat of the wrongdoer at the hands of the victim (either directly or indirectly through an agent of the victim's, e.g., the state) that symbolizes the correct relative value of wrongdoer and victim'.[37] By conveying the message that the political community is committed to the equal dignity of all persons, punishment clears the offender's *hubris* asserted in the criminal wrong.[38] It 'masters the offender in the way that he mastered the victim', writes Hampton, so that 'the score is even'.[39] In other words, punishment is retributive in a moral sense, 'the victim's value 'striking back' and in this way proving itself'.[40] It is typically and conventionally unpleasant or painful for Hampton, aiming to cause the offender to suffer so that their wrongful elevation is decisively rejected. For the suffering in punishment is a useful medium that incorporates the ideas of defeat and submission to the punisher.[41]

There are, however, a couple of major problems with the way Hampton formulates crime and punishment from the perspective of the offender. First,

33 Hampton, 'Correcting harms versus righting wrongs: The goal of retribution' p.1666.
34 Hampton, 'An expressive theory of retribution' p.13.
35 Hampton, 'An expressive theory of retribution'.
36 Hampton, 'A new theory of retribution' p.397.
37 Hampton, 'A new theory of retribution' p.397; Hampton, 'The retributive idea' p.125.
38 It is interesting to note that the idea of retribution in Ancient Greece is associated with clearing up the hubris of transgressors. Folake Onayemi, 'Sin, punishment and forgiveness in ancient Greek religion: A Yoruba assessment' (2006) 3 *Journal of Philosophy and Culture* 72, 85.
39 Hampton, 'The retributive idea' p.128.
40 Hampton, 'A new theory of retribution' p.396.
41 Hampton, 'The retributive idea' p.143.

Hampton is not as scrupulous about the world of the offender as that of the victim's world. Unlike the meticulous construction of the victim's ambivalent mental state, her account of the moral psychology of the offender is largely based on an unclear metaphor, that seems barely supported by serious reflection: the idea of superiority (crime) and the symbolic message of 'getting someone down' (punishment). There is perhaps a sort of disregard for the value of the victim in most cases of violation, but does this always include a superiority claim?[42] Even if it does, is that not sometimes mixed with or resulting from the *inferior* self-image of offenders that has been caused, for example, by social injustice or insufficient recognition?[43] After all, the lack of due respect and the wounds that accompany it are often part of an offender's mental life, that may set the conditions for criminal violation. Thus, Hampton's account can be seen as a form of what Bernard Williams calls *moralised* psychology, in which a given moral, legal, or political theory dominates and shapes the understanding of human psychology.[44]

Second, it is doubtful whether the intentional infliction of pain upon someone necessarily connctes their defeat or surrender to the punisher. When suffering, one is usually forced to endure a kind of hardship that is outside of one's control. Human beings are disposed to accept the hardship with the hope of preserving a kind of peace and harmony in their lives, but they are also inclined to keep resisting it, if they view it as unfair or pointless. In this sense, the suffering of punishment may sometimes imply the defeat of the offender, but it can also be an indication of a continuous battle or struggle, if the suffering is rejected and seen to be unjustified. In fact, even if punishment *is* experienced as a kind of defeat, it is not clear why that should happen through force and hard treatment.

Hampton acknowledges that punishment does not have to involve harsh treatment, but it does have to involve an unpleasant experience that is designed to humble the offender. She says:

> *If one considers the wide variety of experiences which count as punishment in our society but which are not inherently painful (e.g., requiring public service), one realizes that what makes any experience the suffering of punishment is not the objective painfulness of the experience, but the fact*

42 For a sharper criticism see Heather J Gert, Linda Radzik and Michael Hand, 'Hampton on the expressive power of punishment' (2004) 35 *Journal of Social Philosophy* 79, 81.

43 There is a large body of scholarship focusing on the relationship between social injustice and criminal justice. Honneth, *The Struggle for Recognition: The Moral Grammar of Social Conflicts*; Wojciech Sadurski, 'Social justice and the problem of punishment' (1991) 25 *Israel Law Review* 302; Roberto Gargarella, 'Penal coercion in contexts of social injustice' (2011) 5 *Criminal Law and Philosophy* 21; Göran Duus-Otterström and Erin I Kelly, 'Injustice and the right to punish' (2019) 14 *Philosophy Compass* e12565.

44 Bernard Williams, *Shame and Necessity* (University of California Press 1993) p.160–162.

> *that it is one the wrongdoer is made to suffer and one which represents his submission to the punisher.*[45]

I am dubious about the way inherently painful punishments are separated from the other types of practices.[46] But the underlying thought in this passage is that punishment is in essence 'the infliction of defeat' on the offender, not the imposition of certain sorts of pain or harm. The idea of punishment as a means of defeating the offender resonates with the sentiment expressed by many victims of crime, particularly those who have been physically harmed or sexually assaulted, who often feel a strong desire to assert: 'I won't let you win.'

When understood in this light, the suffering caused by punishment becomes instrumental, or a means to the aim of a moral goal, i.e., representing the offender as the equal of their victim. But this is not to say that punishment is used to produce social goods in a utilitarian sense. Rather, as Hampton puts it, punishment exists to 'establish goodness' by revealing the moral truth that every human being is equal in value.[47] In this line of thinking, the offender deserves punishment, not because they deserve the right amount of suffering; but because they deserve 'a kind of subjugating experience' that would remove the appearance of their superiority and make the equal status of the victim manifest.[48] To sum up, the real motive behind punishment in Hampton is not mere pain delivery; but rather the repair of the moral injury caused by crime through the subjugation of the offender and elevation of the victim. For this reason, any experience that can humble the offender and raise the victim up can be classified as a justified form of retributive punishment or perhaps an apology extracted from the offender to validate the victim's real value.

Some would perhaps find this an interesting and yet pernicious way of side-lining the problem of suffering in legal punishment. I am also uneasy about the idea of defeat, particularly when cast as a way of justifying punitive forms of punishment like imprisonment.[49] Suffice it to say, for the purpose of this discussion, the main concern is the question of how legal punishment is related to the victim's restoration. From that point of view, certainly, the defeat of the offender may be thought of as shoring up the victim's sense of worth or their moral standing in their own eyes. Legal punishment is a way of expressing that the message – implicitly or explicitly claimed by crime – is denied: the offender is not superior in value to their victim.

45 Hampton, 'A new theory of retribution' p.399.

46 Antony Duff, 'Alternatives to punishment–or alternative punishments?' in W. Cragg (ed), *Retributivism and Its Critics* (Franz Steiner Verlag 1992); Dan M Kahan, 'What do alternative sanctions mean?' (1996) 63 *The University of Chicago Law Review* 591.

47 Hampton, 'A new theory of retribution' p.399.

48 Hampton, 'An expressive theory of retribution' p.15.

49 Ben Crewe, 'Depth, weight, tightness: Revisiting the pains of imprisonment' (2011) 13 *Punishment & Society* 509.

Nonetheless, by visiting harm on the offender as they did on their victim, punishment can also feed the logic of revenge into the victim's moral psychology, making them susceptible to the deceptive thought that they are elevated directly in proportion to the suffering of the offender. Because of its 'violent' or 'painful' nature, such punishment may seem to lower the offender to the level to which the victim has been reduced.[50] Doing so, it may give the victim a message as misleading as the message involved in crime. Punishment, however, elevates the victim not because the offender is made to suffer and look inferior to the victim and others but because the unjust treatment of the victim is addressed and clearly announced. Accordingly, punishment may be viewed as a suitable public tool for the recognition of the wrong, but it may also misdirect the victim about the moral meaning of punishment, by leading to the view that hurting another is adequate compensation for being violated.

Related to this is the worry that, with its sole focus on blaming and placing fault on the other, punishment may reinforce the victim's negative moral position and sense of vulnerability.[51] It can divert the victim's attention from their responsibility to heal and deal with the other significant issues of mourning, such as finding the meaning in suffering, working through the wound, and reconnecting with others. In this regard, the Glasgow rape case of 1982 serves as a notable example. In this case, the victim sought justice and vindication by bringing a private prosecution against the offenders, aiming to ensure that others would not endure similar suffering.[52] Her fight against the injustice and her altruistic actions vindicate both her own rights and those of others. Nevertheless, it also masks the significance, for the victim, of undertaking a process of self-rehabilitation, as the focus is placed solely on punitive measures, rather than on a more constructive approach that incorporates healing and personal growth. Perhaps, more concerningly, an intense focus on punishment may lock the victim into a repressive kind of relationship with their offender, in which there remains a continuing control exercised over themselves.[53] Thus, while punishment can vindicate the victim, it can also lead to ongoing and regressive suffering if it does not help the victim rebuild their sense of self and restore their life.[54]

That being said, Hampton claims that the poor instances of punishment in contemporary societies should not blind us to the moral potential of the principle of retribution. For her, the idea of defeating the offender – despite its

50 Zehr, *Changing Lenses: A New Focus for Crime and Justice* p.193.

51 As succinctly put by Judith Herman, 'if one set out intentionally to design a system for provoking symptoms of posttraumatic stress disorder, it might look very much like a court of law.' Judith Herman, *Trauma and Recovery* (Basic Books 1992).

52 R Harper and A McWhinnie, *The Glasgow Rape Case* (Hutchinson, 1983).

53 L Henderson, 'Commentary-co-opting compassion: The Federal Victim's Rights Amendment' (1997) 10 *St. Thomas Law Review* 579.

54 JM Wheatcroft, GF Wagstaff and A Moran, 'Revictimizing the victim? How rape victims experience the UK legal system' (2009) 4(3) *Victims and Offenders* 265–284.

negative connotations – can also facilitate the healing and recovery process for the victim, or at least help address the harms caused by the criminal violation. It can bring the offender to acknowledge the victim's value, and thereby set the stage for a full recognition of the position of the victim by addressing their losses and suffering. In other words, retributive punishment for Hampton can turn into what I call 'apologetic recognition', where the suffering of the offender might be more closely tied up with the recovery and healing of the victim. In the final section, I will expand upon the restorative effects of retributive punishment.

4. Between defeat and correction: punishment as restorative retribution

Once we start conceiving of punishment primarily as restoring the victim's value and correcting the offender's inflated sense of self, rather than the infliction of suffering, any type of moral response to Hampton's theory may have a penal character. In this sense, surprisingly, Hampton says the most common and successful practice of retributive punishment is 'the one that all of us, when we commit a wrong, standardly inflict upon ourselves when we come to understand ourselves as guilty of an offense': apology.[55] What is crucial in our performance of apology is the idea that we express regret, and humble ourselves in front of the one whose value we have failed to respect. We accept our wrong as behaviour that harms and disrespects the person we hurt and acknowledge their real value by attempting to make amends or set the things right. In Hampton's words, 'by apologizing, we deny the diminishment of the victim, and our relative elevation, expressed by our wrongful action'.[56] The practice of apology is, thus, retributive – not because it causes us an unpleasant experience – rather, it reaffirms the value of the wronged person or rights the wrong by repairing the moral injury.[57]

Exploring a retributive rationale in the most common type of restoration (apology), Hampton draws an interesting parallel between restoration and retribution. For her, just because vindication of the victim 'requires among other things, repairing the wrongdoer's damage to the victim's entitlements (generated by her value)', the demand for a wrongdoer to apologise and make amends to their victim is essentially a retributive idea. Thus, a punishment can incorporate 'actions or services that constitute such amends and remedies' which may express the offender's apologetic reaction and efforts to help the victim to recover from their injuries.[58] But, in Hampton's view, even where

55 Hampton, 'Correcting harms versus righting wrongs: The goal of retribution' p.1697–1698.
56 Hampton, 'Correcting harms versus righting wrongs: The goal of retribution' p.1697–1698.
57 Hampton, 'Correcting harms versus righting wrongs: The goal of retribution'.
58 Hampton, 'Correcting harms versus righting wrongs: The goal of retribution' p.1697–1698.

our response has an implicit demand from the wrongdoer, retribution can be tied up with restoration.[59]

Consider, for example, the passive and loving response of 'turning the other cheek' when faced with a wrongdoing. Hampton posits that 'acting benevolently toward one's enemy cannot be said to be a way of inflicting punishment' in its usual sense.[60] Neither does it encompass an explicit moral demand from the wrongdoer. It might even, for some, be seen as a sort of unconditional forgiving and condoning. But Hampton views the kindness of the victim's response as enabling the triggering of 'emotions of humiliation and shame' in the wrongdoer, leading them to rethink their actions as 'so much uglier than his victim's behaviour towards him'.[61] Though not being punished in the ordinary sense, Hampton thinks the wrongdoer in this instance undergoes a retributive experience that humbles and corrects them. When defeated by such a loving response, as Murphy says incisively, shame in the wrongdoer 'creeps through guilt and feels like retribution'.[62]

If unconditional forgiveness is constructed as some sort of dishing out of pain or humiliation, rather than restoration, then ironically it may become a form of payback and punitive retribution.[63] It may even be viewed as a kind of revenge in Hampton's sense, establishing the forgiver's superiority over the wrongdoer.[64] For sure, this is the darkest way of thinking about the good behaviour and forgiving demeanour of human beings. Neither is it the only way. Unconditional forgiveness is usually produced to place a tacit demand on the offender, inviting them to embrace 'the good' and cultivating a kind of moral growth within themselves, often done with the awareness of the painful process that must be endured.[65]

59 Hampton, 'An expressive theory of retribution' p.16.

60 Hampton, 'Correcting harms versus righting wrongs: The goal of retribution' p.1695.

61 Hampton, 'Correcting harms versus righting wrongs: The goal of retribution' p.1695.

62 Jeffrie G Murphy, 'Shame creeps through guilt and feels like retribution' (1999) 18 *Law and Philosophy* 327; for other people who see shame as a kind of retribution see: Toni M Massaro, 'Shame, culture, and American criminal law' (1990) 89 *Michigan Law Review* 1880; James Q Whitman, 'What is wrong with inflicting shame sanctions' (1997) 107 *The Yale Law Journal* 1055; for the criticism of this view see: Dan Markel, 'Are shaming punishments beautifully retributive: Retributivism and the implications for the alternative sanctions debate' (2001) 54 *Vanderbilt Law Review* 2157.

63 Nussbaum, *Anger and Forgiveness: Resentment, Generosity, Justice* p.77.

64 Reflect, for example, on the following conversations in von Trier's film DogVille: 'Grace: So I'm arrogant. I'm arrogant because I forgive people? The Big Man: My God. Can't you see how condescending you are when you say that? You have this preconceived notion that nobody, listen, that nobody can't possibly attain the same high ethical standards as you, so you exonerate them. I cannot think of anything more arrogant than that. You... you forgive others with excuses that you would never in the world permit for yourself.'

65 I cannot defend my reading of unconditional forgiveness here in detail. I am also aware of some of the debates around it. But here I take it that it can also be viewed as a retributive demand. Jacques Derrida, *On Cosmopolitanism and Forgiveness* (Routledge 2003); Garrard and McNaughton, 'In defence of unconditional forgiveness'.

No doubt, here one would not be too wrong to challenge that acts of benevolence are effective only on offenders who are remorseful or who possess some measure of 'goodness'. After all, one might go on, some offenders are simply not receptive to 'loving' or 'compassionate' responses, as they take pleasure in causing others pain rather than reflecting on their actions or seeking to make amends. In such cases, it may seem more appropriate to impose penal measures that send a clear message to offenders, ideally causing them significant discomfort and distress and prompting an apologetic response that addresses the wrong and harm done to the victims.

Nevertheless, as Hampton puts it, it is sometimes too hard to construct 'right responses that succeed in vindicating the victim's value without compromising the wrongdoer's value as a person', particularly in a legal context. But she claims that retribution is still often the best and normatively most appropriate method that can function as a mechanism of restoration.[66] Having stressed the necessity to be creative and flexible about retributive responses in criminal justice, Hampton remarks on an alternative and thought-provoking practice: confrontational programmes. In programmes of this kind, 'convicted sex offenders are forced to listen to the words and accusations of rape victims', with a role play where they take the role of the women they raped. Undergoing an experience that is more or less similar to the feelings of anger, hurt, and frustration they caused in their victims, offenders are challenged to admit their wrong in a retaliatory tone. Commenting on these practices, Hampton argues:

> They must confront what they did to other human beings, and appreciate how badly their actions affected them. Thus, these programs are intended as an experience in retribution, not rehabilitation. ... By doing so, not only does the state confirm the victim's importance, but it also defeats the rapist's claim to mastery by putting him in a position where he must, through his imagination, become her, and suffer as if he were her.[67]

There seems a peculiar form of pain delivery in this sort of victim empathy role play that is oriented towards a particular moral goal. It drives offenders to recognise the substantive harm they have done by making them *identify with* their victims, through a process in which they are expected to feel their victims' pains and distress.[68] It requires offenders to enter into the world of their victims, or to mould their identity into that of victims, in order to be

66 Hampton, 'Correcting harms versus righting wrongs: The goal of retribution' p.1689.

67 Hampton, 'Correcting harms versus righting wrongs: The goal of retribution' p.1659.

68 There is a growing number of works on these practices in which both retributive and restorative elements are explored. Here is a quote from the result of these works: 'Interestingly, the most helpful part of the programme seemed to be the whole victim empathy block (of which role plays are a part). It seems that parts of the programme which direct participants to gauge how others feel evokes the most negative affect, but yet these parts also appear to be rated as the most useful by the participants.' Helen C Wakeling, Stephen D Webster and Ruth E Mann,

atone – or as Norrie phrases it, to be 'at one with' their victims.[69] More directly, it seeks repentance from offenders, ideally expressed through an apology and proportionate reparation, moving them to do what they can to make amends.

Taking a form of retribution, the process of identification seems surprisingly like a rehearsal of the archaic notion of *lex talionis*: an eye for an eye, a tooth for a tooth and a life for a life. It is so, however, not in the sense that it does to offenders what they did to their victims or that they suffer losses equal to the losses of their victims. Delivering to offenders what they delivered to their victims is a futile and impossible endeavour as the common criticism goes. The process of identification is, however, a civilised and 'phenomenological' form of *lex talionis* because it inflicts hardship on offenders that mirrors the crime in a moral psychological sense, calling for a kind of suffering that echoes that of victims. But in Hampton's view, in this form of *lex talionis*, the discomfort imposed on offenders does not automatically cause the kind of suffering we normally find in punishment. Rather, the suffering in offenders is internally generated, bringing offenders to recognise the wrongfulness of their crime in a deeper way and make reparation for what they have done.

From the perspective of offenders, there is certainly a sense of being punished and humbled by the process of facing truth and understanding their victims' feelings. Their distress and negative emotional experiences may represent their vulnerability and equal standing with their victims. In this sense, victims can be said to be restored by the penal suffering of offenders in a normative sense, as offenders, through their remorse and the pain of realising they have wronged another, reaffirm the victims' normative status. On the other hand, the distressing sense of humility in offenders also comes with a genuine concern and compassion for victims, followed by the full recognition of their loss and grief. It enables offenders to accept responsibility for their crimes and take steps to enhance the well-being of victims. In so doing, it is driven by the logic of a full apologetic response that may facilitate a deeper form of recovery and healing for victims, which I previously referred to as ethical restoration.

Thus, there are two kinds of restoration that are due to the victim in retributive punishments, tuned more toward apology, such as confrontational programmes. The first one, termed here as "normative restoration", springs from the compulsory subjection of offenders to a particular (restorative) practice in a legal setting. Offenders are required to bear a burden in response to their wrongful behaviour. They owe a (forced) apology to their victims to acknowledge their wrongdoing and reaffirm their victims' equal standing. The aim is to persuade offenders to withdraw the insult to the dignity of their victims that was expressed by their wrongful act. The second kind of

'Sexual offenders' treatment experience: A qualitative and quantitative investigation' (2005) 11 *Journal of Sexual Aggression* 171, 184.

69 Alan Norrie, 'Identification, atonement and the moral psychology of violation: On Patricio Guzman's nostalgia for the light' (2019) 18 *Journal of Critical Realism* 383, 389.

restoration, termed "ethical restoration", involves whether offenders take positive or constructive actions to make amends for the harm they caused. In ethical restoration, offenders are obligated to bear the costs of their wrongful behaviour in a way that lays the foundation for deeper and more substantial reparation to the victims. Ethical restoration, in other words, goes beyond mere compensation or material restitution. It involves a kind of emphatic pain in offenders, compelling them to share in the suffering of their victims. The aim is to vindicate the suffering of the victims and help them recover from the injuries or deeper harm caused by the crime.

Nevertheless, punishments, even reformed in the way of apology, are typically imposed within an uncaring, unresponsive, or punitive environment, where offenders are expected to pay their debt through non-constructive suffering. This suggests that these forms of punishment are at significant risk of being overshadowed or seriously undermined by a broader retributive mechanism that is solely concerned with a status adjustment between victims and offenders. There is also a general consensus that standard criminal justice systems not only fail to encourage deeper forms of restoration but often actively prevent them.[70] Ethical restoration is, therefore, deemed to be incomplete if punishments aim to restore victims solely by imposing requirements and restrictions on offenders or by subjecting them to sanctions. After all, the healing and recovery of victims is not simply about whether offenders have an obligation to bear a cost or suffer in response to their crime. Rather, it is also about whether victims can rebuild trust in the world after offenders apologise and seek ways to alleviate their suffering so that they restore their sense of self in order to fully recover from what happened.

That said, one might still insist that punishments that are of a restorative nature can still provide ethical restoration even in a punitive setting if they successfully demand offenders to show due recognition to the losses and sufferings experienced by the victim. On this view, when asked to develop empathy or the capacity to care about others, the offender can identify a profound lack of concern involved in their crime and recognises the normative or moral stance of the victim. And this 'normative' awareness can also be accompanied by an opening of their mind and soul towards the victim's experience. By adopting a more caring attitude towards the victim, the offender can take active steps to eliminate or diminish their suffering. In other words, the victim-offender interaction can take place within the offender's mind or moral psychology through which ethical restoration paves the way for both normative vindication and recovery. In other words, the victim-offender interaction can take place not physically but in the offender's mental world through which ethical restoration paves the way for both normative vindication and therapeutic recovery.

70 H Zehr, *Changing Lenses* (Scottdale, PA: Herald Press 1990) p.51–52.

I do not categorically reject restorative practices in legal settings and find them ethically invalid. It is worth noting, however, that two kinds of punishments are at stake here. The main one is the sort of punishment inflicted on offenders in response to crime on the basis of what they deserve. The other one is the sort of punishment that is designed to create meaningful relationships between victims and offenders. If the latter can do what the former does - status adjustment or normative vindication-, then we would not need the former. In other words, legal punishment would become pointless in so far as legal restoration is achieved by non-punitive ethical caring interventions.

In fact, because legal punishment is automatic, unbending, and impersonal, it can stand in the way of ethical restoration. For it produces a 'passive' suffering for the offender that does no good to them, nor their relationships with their victims. Concerned exclusively with what offenders deserve with no regard to the needs and interests of victims in an ethical sense, its "cold" face is prone to undermine the possible warm bonds that may be developed between victims and offenders. This is to say that ethical restoration somehow seeks to "flourish on a soil that is eroded" by the terms of legal justice.

Conclusion

This chapter started with a brief analysis of Miller's victim statement, arguing that retributive punishment can be linked to the restoration of victims in a closer and more complex way than is commonly held. In contrast to the tendency to associate legal retribution with the institutionalised form of vengeful feelings, I emphasised that punishment could address the victim's moral vulnerability and restore their sense of injustice. By recognising the crime as a wrong done to the victim, it can serve a restorative function: legal restoration. However, the public recognition of crime should also be followed by the recognition of further and deeper sufferings that befall the victim. The emphasis on the idea of ethical recognition set the stage for a more theoretical investigation of the connections between the victim and punishment in the following sections.

To shed more light on the moral vulnerability of the victim, in the second section, Hampton's account of resentment was analysed, where the victim's loss of self-respect caused by criminal violation is fused intricately with their moral anger. Resentment is a form of self-defence for Hampton, seeking to suppress the diminishment in the victim's self-respect. But this is the form of defence that should be backed by others. In Hampton's theory, punishment serves as a legal means of supporting victims, and reaffirming the equal relationship that existed between victims and offenders *before* the crime. Imposing punishment on offenders aims to humble their will and remind them that committing a crime does not make them superior to their victims. In other words, punishment expresses solidarity with victims and helps to restore the balance that was disrupted by the crime.

Doubts were raised over whether Hampton provides a sufficient conception of the moral psychology of violation from the perspective of offenders, and whether punishment can be seen as a kind of defeat for them. It was also argued that legal punishment may divert victims' attention away from their healing and recovery, ultimately leaving them in a state of vulnerability. Hampton accepts that there can be poor instances of retribution that destroy the will of offenders when they seek to uphold victims. Yet, in her view, retributive punishment can also be practised in a restorative mood for both victims and offenders.

By drawing on the examples she gives, I finally claimed that apology, and practices that stem from the spirit of apology, are the kinds of retributive punishment that might be restorative in both legal and ethical sense. These kinds of punishment may cultivate a sincere sense of care and empathy within offenders towards their victims, which is then accompanied by a complete acknowledgement of the harm and suffering inflicted upon them. Underlying this argument is the idea that the desire for victims to be heard is rooted in their need to establish a safe and meaningful connection with their offenders, or to continue living peacefully within the same shared ethical world. Nonetheless, this chapter came to question whether ethical restoration is fully achievable in a setting where the infliction of suffering on offenders is seen as justified and sufficient for legal justice. The next section will consider the restoration of offenders.

Bibliography

Alm D, 'Crime victims and the right to punishment' (2019) 13(1) *Criminal Law and Philosophy* 63

Amstutz LS, *The Little Book of Victim Offender Conferencing: Bringing Victims and Offenders Together in Dialogue* (Simon and Schuster 2009)

Baker JMK, 'Here's the powerful letter the stanford victim read to her attacker' (*BuzzFeedNews*, 3 June 2016) <https://www.buzzfeednews.com/article/katiejmbaker/heres-the-powerful-letter-the-stanford-victim-read-to-her-ra> accessed 3 February 2023

Bandes S, 'When victims seek closure: forgiveness, vengeance and the role of government' (1999) 27 *Fordham Urban Law Journal* 1599

Bibas S and Bierschbach RA, 'Integrating remorse and apology into criminal procedure' (2004) 114 *Yale Law Journal* 85

Butler P, 'Retribution, for liberals' (1998) 46 *UCLA Law Review* 1873

Crewe B, 'Depth, weight, tightness: revisiting the pains of imprisonment' (2011) 13(5) *Punishment & Society* 509

Derrida J, *On Cosmopolitanism and Forgiveness* (Routledge 2003)

Dubber MD, 'The victim in American penal law: a systematic overview' (1999) 3(1) *Buffalo Criminal Law Review* 3

Duff RA, 'Alternatives to punishment–or alternative punishments?' in Cragg W (ed), *Retributivism and Its Critics* (Franz Steiner Verlag 1992) 44

Duff RA, 'Punishment, communication and community' in Matravers M (ed), *Punishment and Political Theory* (Hart Publishing 1998)

Duff RA, 'Review essay/justice, mercy, and forgiveness' (1990) 9(2) *Criminal Justice Ethics* 51

Duus-Otterström G and Kelly EI, 'Injustice and the right to punish' (2019) 14(2) *Philosophy Compass* e12565

Farnham D, 'A hegelian theory of retribution' (2008) 39(4) *Journal of Social Philosophy* 606

Feinberg J, 'The expressive function of punishment' (1965) 49(3) *Monist* 397

Fletcher GP, 'The place of victims in the theory of retribution' (1999) 3(1) *Buffalo Criminal Law Review* 51

Frijda NH, *The Laws of Emotion* (Psychology Press 2017)

Funk F, McGeer V and Gollwitzer M, 'Get the message: punishment is satisfying if the transgressor responds to its communicative intent' (2014) 40(8) *Personality and Social Psychology Bulletin* 986

Gargarella R, 'Penal coercion in contexts of social injustice' (2011) 5 *Criminal Law and Philosophy* 21

Garrard E and McNaughton D, 'In defence of unconditional forgiveness' (2003) 102(1) *Proceedings of the Aristotelian Society*

Gert HJ, Radzik L and Hand M, 'Hampton on the expressive power of punishment' (2004) 35(1) *Journal of Social Philosophy* 79

Goti JM, 'Equality, punishment, and self-respect' (2001) 5 *Buffalo Criminal Law Review* 497

Grierson J, 'Doctor stabbed nine times tells attacker: "I am not angry with you"' (*The Guardian*, 18 February 2022) <https://www.theguardian.com/uk-news/2022/feb/18/doctor-stabbed-nine-times-tells-attacker-i-am-not-angry-with-you> accessed 7 February 2025

Haldemann F, 'Another kind of justice: transitional justice as recognition' (2008) 41 *Cornell International Law Journal* 675

Hampton J, 'An expressive theory of retribution' in Cragg W (ed), *Retributivism and Its Critics* (Franz Steiner Verlag Stuttgart 1992)

Hampton J, 'Correcting harms versus righting wrongs: the goal of retribution' (1992) 39 *UCLA Law Review* 1238–1267

Hampton J, 'Forgiveness, resentment and hatred' in Murphy J and Hampton J (eds), *Forgiveness and Mercy* (Cambridge University Press 1988) 35

Hampton J, 'A new theory of retribution' in Frey RG and Postema G (eds), *Liability and Responsibility: Essays in Law and Morals* (Cambridge University Press 1991)

Hampton J, 'The retributive idea' in Murphy J and Hampton J (eds), *Forgiveness and Mercy* (Cambridge University Press 1988) 111

Harper R and McWhinnie A, *The Glasgow Rape Case* (Hutchinson 1983)

Henderson L, 'Commentary—co-opting compassion: the federal victim's rights amendment' (1997) 10 *Thomas Law Review* 579

Herman J, *Trauma and Recovery* (Basic Books 1992)

Hershenov DB, 'Punishment and restitution' in Ryberg J and Corlett JA (eds), *Punishment and Ethics: New Perspectives* (Palgrave Macmillan 2010) 33

Holmgren MR, *Forgiveness and Retribution: Responding to Wrongdoing* (Cambridge University Press 2012)

Honneth A, *The Struggle for Recognition: The Moral Grammar of Social Conflicts* (MIT Press 1996)

Janoff-Bulman R, *Shattered Assumptions* (Simon and Schuster 2010)

Kahan DM, 'What do alternative sanctions mean?' (1996) 63(2) *University of Chicago Law Review* 591

Kleinfeld J, 'Reconstructivism: the place of criminal law in ethical life' (2015) 129 *Harvard Law Review* 1485

Kohler P, 'Paul Kohler' (*The Forgiveness Project*, 2024) <https://www.theforgivenessproject.com/stories-library/paulkohler/> accessed 9 September 2024

Lippke RL, 'Victim-centered retributivism' (2003) 84(2) *Pacific Philosophical Quarterly* 127

MacLeod AJ, 'All for one: a review of victim-centric justifications for criminal punishment' (2008) 13 *Berkeley Journal of Criminal Law* 31

McEwan I, 'Only love and then oblivion: love was all they had to set against their murderers' (*The Guardian*, 2001)

Miller C, *Know My Name: A Memoir* (Penguin 2020)

Mills LG, 'The justice of recovery: how the state can heal the violence of crime' (2005) 57 *Hastings Law Review* 457

Murphy JG, 'Shame creeps through guilt and feels like retribution' (1999) 18 *Law and Philosophy* 327

Norrie A, 'Identification, atonement and the moral psychology of violation: on patricio guzmán's *nostalgia for the light*' (2019) 18(4) *Journal of Critical Realism* 383

Nussbaum MC, *Anger and Forgiveness: Resentment, Generosity, Justice* (OUP 2016)

Onayemi F, 'Sin, punishment and forgiveness in ancient greek religion: a yoruba assessment' (2006) 3(1) *Journal of Philosophy and Culture* 72

Ripstein A, *Equality, Responsibility, and the Law* (Cambridge University Press 2001)

Sadurski W, 'Social justice and the problem of punishment' (1991) 25(3–4) *Israel Law Review* 302

Sarat A, 'Putting a square peg in a round hole: victims, retribution, and George Ryan's clemency' (2003) 82 *North Carolina Law Review* 1345

Strang H and Sherman LW, 'Repairing the harm: victims and restorative justice' (2003) 1 *Utah Law Review* 15

Taylor C, 'The politics of recognition' in Arthur J and Shapiro A (eds), *Campus Wars: Multiculturalism and the Politics of Difference* (Routledge 2021) 249

Umbreit M, 'Restorative justice through victim-offender mediation: a multi-site assessment' (1998) 1(1) *Western Criminology Review* 1

Wakeling HC, Webster SD and Mann RE, 'Sexual offenders' treatment experience: a qualitative and quantitative investigation' (2005) 11(2) *Journal of Sexual Aggression* 171

Walker MU, 'The cycle of violence' (2006) 5(1) *Journal of Human Rights* 81

Wheatcroft JM, Wagstaff GF and Moran A, 'Revictimizing the victim? How rape victims experience the UK legal system' (2009) 4(3) *Victims & Offenders* 265

Whiteley D, 'The victim and the justification of punishment' (1998) 17(2) *Criminal Justice Ethics* 42

Zehr H, *Changing Lenses* (Herald Press 1990)

Zehr H, *Changing Lenses: A New Focus for Crime and Justice* (Herald Press 2015)

Zehr H, *Transcending: Reflections of Crime Victims* (Simon and Schuster 2001)

5 Restorative retributivism

Introduction

The previous chapter focused on victims and how they are restored by retributive punishment. In this chapter, the focus is on the restorative dimension of punishment from the perspective of offenders. At first glance, it appears too difficult to connect the retributive act of punishing with the idea of restoration. After all, punishment is usually viewed as a 'just' response to criminal behaviour, in light of what offenders deserve – regardless of whether it does any good to offenders. Nonetheless, recent theories of retributive justice have opened up ample room to think otherwise.

The prominent ethical impulse in the renaissance of restorative retributivism is the idea that retribution is too tightly, and wrongly, fixed to the ideas of desert and payback. In this approach, retributive punishment can be seen as a deserved response to past wrongful conduct. But it is morally meaningful only when it involves a restorative suffering for offenders and paves the way for moral change and growth. That is, the principle of retribution can (and should) go hand in hand with the ideas of restoration, reparation, and reconciliation. Understood this way, punishment is not simply characterised as deserved pain but also a burden or requirement that offenders undertake to restore relationships with other fellow citizens and to reform themselves. This function of punishment is defined here as ethical restoration.

Nevertheless, there is an unavoidable tension between the core values of retributivism (desert and payback) and the revised ones (restoration and reconciliation). Not all punishments are both deserved and restorative. Some punishments are simply seen as deserved and just, and yet they are far from being reparative. From a revisionist retributive perspective, the emergence of conflicting values is not theoretically worrisome so long as punishment is designed as an appropriate legal that seeks restoration, reconciliation and reform. In other words, the restorative function of punishment in neo-classical retributivism is secondary to its retributive moral ground.

This should not, however, readily lead us to conclude that retributive punishment is theoretically cut off from the idea of restoration altogether. Underlying the insistence on legal punishment, regardless of its restorative

DOI: 10.4324/9781003563150-9

outcome, is the idea that the normative harm caused by crime should be addressed and repaired. In this approach, while crime puts into question the citizenship status of offenders and damages their relationships with others in a normative sense, punishment as a kind of civic duty seeks to amend it. In other words, once offenders are punished, they should be seen as being released from their 'debt' to the society. Their rights should be given back in such a way that they are regarded as full members of the political community. This function of punishment is legal restoration.

This work argues that neo-classical retributivism carves out a new space within penal thinking in which legal punishment as deserved suffering can be joined to restorative intervention as moral reform. But that space, however progressive, also marks an inconsistency or a conflict within the theory. The understanding of punishment driven by desert and payback – despite its significance in terms of its symbolic normative function – stands firmly in the way of moral reform and rehabilitation. Thus, there is a need for radical new thinking that will transform the way retributivism is structured.

To fully flesh out the two dimensions of retributive punishment, and how ethical restoration becomes impoverished in the 'neo-classical' literature, this chapter opens with an analysis of blame as a basis upon which to gain insights into the moral psychology of punishing. It will present a wide spectrum of blaming, from punitive scapegoating to restorative intervention. This will then set the scene for exploring the connection between blame and legal punishment. I will argue that the route from interpersonal blame to state sanction, albeit dangerous and potentially punitive, is a natural part of the process of holding others responsible in the public realm. By reference to Duff's theory, retributive punishment can be considered as being motivated by a moral psychology of blame, where the attribution of responsibility is shaped by both backward-looking and forward-looking (restoration) considerations. This argument will be followed in the second section by a more detailed examination of Duff's communicative theory, where punishment is portrayed as a restorative public blame concretised by certain burdens imposed on offenders. This section will end with an articulation of Duff's ambivalent position with regard to the purely retributive, non-restorative, nature of legal punishment. The final section will shed light on the revised form of retributivism in the light of the ideas of legal and ethical restoration, concluding that it is now in a theoretical impasse.

1. Spectrum of blame

> *You are undoubtedly a dangerous young man, whose history … shows a really worrying defect in your personality.*[1]

1 "'You are undoubtedly a dangerous young man' – What the judge told murderer Kai Nazir' <https://www.cambridge-news.co.uk/news/cambridge-news/kai-nazir-murder-sentence-west-15133047>.

> *It is important to emphasise, so that you and the public can understand the position, that this 20-year minimum term is just that – a minimum period which cannot be reduced in any way.*[2]
>
> *Taking all this into account I have decided that culpability falls within Cat B. Lauren's death was caused in the course of an unlawful act … Jake Notman, please stand up. The sentence for the offence of unlawful act manslaughter is one of 8 years and 8 months imprisonment.*[3]
>
> *It breaks my heart to see someone of your age who has committed so many offences in your short life … I am not entirely confident, but it seems to me that it is worth trying an alternative to immediate prison, which I would suspect would not give any long-term benefit at all.*[4]
>
> *I am going to give you a chance. You must understand it is a chance and don't go back again.*[5]
>
> *His behaviour certainly merits imprisonment to give the public a rest from him. But he has been punished enough, and the time is due to bite the bullet and do something with him.*[6]

Sentencing remarks provide the final version of what happened in a criminal trial, explaining the rationale behind the decision to punish offenders with reference to the factors that have been taken into account in determining how much they 'deserve'. As such, they play an expressive role while targeting more than one audience: offenders, victims and society. They sometimes translate the formalistic narrative of law to a daily life narrative that cannot be easily captured by law with a moral and sentimental load of vocabulary. They are not part of the process in which offenders are found guilty or not guilty, but they speak the voice of law and embody the positioning of society in response to crime and criminals.

The comments quoted earlierconstitute the nub of what has been thought and felt about the offenders, carrying messages that are coloured by the judge's moral stance as an official (supposedly neutral) narrator. They reveal that there is more than one voice to be heard. Perhaps, one might say, there are as many voices as there are crimes, each one reflecting its own unique story, which refers to various sorts of moral experiences and claims. While some of the remarks vividly reflect the ostracizing nature of state punishment in a hostile manner, others display a relatively more compassionate attitude towards offenders. And

2 'Between: Regina -v- TEEKO LE' <https://www.judiciary.uk/judgments/r-v-le-sentencing-remarks/>.

3 in the Crown Court at Stafford Regina v Notman <https://www.judiciary.uk/judgments/r-v-notman-sentencing-remarks/>.

4 https://www.nottinghampost.com/news/drug-addict-mums-criminal-record-294028.

5 https://www.nottinghampost.com/news/nottingham-news/former-royal-marine-given-another-342607.

6 https://www.birminghammail.co.uk/news/local-news/judge-sent-solihull-neighbour-from-hell-159952.

while some are relatively neutral in terms of emotional experience, others give a more intense and immediate expression of negative emotions, like anger and hatred. The addressees are usually offenders, but not necessarily in all cases. The major recipients are sometimes victims or society, depending on the severity or publicity of the crimes that have been committed.

All of this shows that sentencing remarks differ from one another in many respects, particularly in terms of what they tell us about how punishment is delivered. In this sense, it may be thought that law speaks so ambiguously that it is hardly understandable. It creates its own ambiguity and puzzles, which cannot be solved by those who are subject to its messages. But, despite their wide spectrum and variations, there is also a recognisable pattern that is projected into the languages of law and punishment in sentencing remarks. All of them manifest an expression of blame as a moral or emotional component that seems to reflect the mental or psychological bedrock of our punishing experiences.[7]

Firstly: blaming, most of the time, is a response that is related to victims as much as offenders. As discussed in detail in the previous chapter, taking seriously a criminal 'wrong' is often considered to be an act that we owe to its victim(s). Even if it does not necessarily encompass punishment, this perceived responsibility requires us to make an appropriate response to crime and provide a normative support for victims. In this sense, our duty to victims also has a direct bearing on the way we approach offenders. Simply put, when we take notice of criminal violation and address it adequately, we stand on the side of victims and keep a certain distance from those who wrong them. That is, our supportive response to victims marks a shift in our standing in relation to offenders. We somehow see a kind of rupture in our relationship with offenders and modify our attitude towards them in a certain manner.

Though it may be unpleasant for offenders, we often take this response as justified, stipulating that the prior wrongful behaviour of offenders makes it appropriate. In other words, the way we engage with offenders is largely shaped by the normative judgement we make about their behaviour. We come to view what they have done as unacceptable and then re-position or re-orient ourselves towards them accordingly. In serious wrongs, that re-positioning is sometimes so radical that it may set the footing for our infliction of suffering upon offenders, often with certain negative emotions, such as anger and resentment. But we are also usually aware that destructive – non-processed – emotions should not dictate the way we treat each other. Neither should they be followed by a punitive response that does more harm than good. Nonetheless, we are almost always disposed to demand something burdensome from those who do a serious wrong, even though it may not be a kind of penal

7 I do not say that sentencing remarks are the only way of expressing blame at an institutional level. But they provide a good basis to understand the blaming function of legal punishment.

sanction in its usual sense. Our response to offenders is shaped by a kind of moral uneasiness about one who violates another.

This is what it is like to blame others in a moral psychological sense.[8] To reiterate, when we blame others, we react to their actions or approach them in a certain way. This usually starts with an evaluation about their behaviour, or a negative judgement that they are blameworthy and perhaps have a *stain* on their moral self.[9] The judgement is typically followed by an attempt to hold others responsible and an expression of our disapproval towards them. Blame is certainly *only one* among many ways that we respond to wrongdoing and hold others responsible. But in serious wrongs, there is often less room between blaming and the imputation of responsibility. Likewise, the practice of blame does not always come with an emotional expression.[10] That is, we can blame others without feeling negative emotions or directing them towards others. But where someone's conduct is grossly unacceptable or egregious, it is usually marked by a strong affective component. In these cases, blame as a reactive attitude is also inseparably blended with the practice of punishing and sometimes even punitive and vengeful responses.

2. Blame: two kinds of restoration

What has been briefly explained in the previous section provides a broad conception of blame that can account for a wide range of moral sentiments or penal responses. As a corollary of holding others responsible and withdrawing from them in response to their wrong, these acts echo what we may call the 'moral psychology of retributivism'.[11] In other words, blame is retributive, in that it is backward-looking and justified by a past wrong. But it also involves a forward-looking dimension that seeks restoration. The argument presented here is that, from the perspective of offenders, retributive blame can be seen as restorative in two respects. It is legally restorative if it addresses and repairs the damaged normative standing of offenders within the community and gives back them their full citizenship; it is ethically restorative when it is designed as a response that leads to moral growth or transformation for offenders.

8 No doubt, there is much debate about the nature and elements of blame. For the purpose of this work, I will try to give an eclectic or a synthesised account of blame that does due regard to all major theories of blame. We may perhaps call this, like McGeer, a naturalistic account of blame. Victoria McGeer, 'Civilizing blame' in Neal A. Tognazzini and D. Justin Coates (eds), *Blame: Its Nature and Norms* (2013).

9 Michael J Zimmerman, *An Essay on Moral Responsibility* (Rowman & Littlefield 1988) p.38; see also Pamela Hieronymi, 'The force and fairness of blame' (2004) 18 *Philosophical Perspectives* 115.

10 George Sher, *In Praise of Blame* (Oxford University Press 2005) p.80–81.

11 Christopher Bennett, 'The varities of retributivism' (2002) 52 *The Philosophical Quarterly* 150.

At first glance, this may seem counterintuitive, given that blame often takes a punitive form, particularly in the context of criminal justice. Consider, for example, the following statement: 'you are undoubtedly a dangerous young man, whose history . . . shows a really worrying defect in your personality'. This kind of blaming stigmatises and marks out offenders themselves, rather than their actions. It comes with a diagnosis of 'ontological deficit' in the character of offenders, delivering the message that they are morally flawed or have some kind of deficiency in their personality. In this sense, blame targets the 'being' of offenders, which is seen to be 'socially unacceptable and occasions social distancing and othering'.[12] Accordingly, blame in its punitive form is driven by the destructive feelings of resentment and rage towards offenders and has nothing to do with the idea of restoration or any other future-oriented goal.

Nonetheless, albeit punitive, the element of anger inherent in blame is not always as destructive as the above example and may sometimes be relatively mitigated by certain considerations, as present in the following: 'you and the public can understand the position, that this 20-year minimum term is just that – a minimum period which cannot be reduced in any way'. As these words suggest, blame can take a strict face that expresses a reactive anger. At its heart lies a reference to the ideas of desert or fairness through which the infliction of pain, alongside the expression of disapproval, is justified.

It may seem provocative, but this case can provide some room for what may be termed 'legal, formal restoration'. Here, blame is constructed as conveying disapproval in a way that addresses the normative harms caused by the crime: the harm that is inflicted on the status of the offender within formal civic relationships and the harm imposed on the victim and community – even though they are not articulated that way. Behind this kind of blaming lies the thought that it is just to condemn those who have violated laws, not simply because they deserve a condemnatory response, but because our condemnatory response is the only way to maintain the relationship, and restore offenders to their previous position. In this line of thinking, we cannot treat them as if nothing happened, and we should see them as those who violated our shared values so that the alienation caused by crime comes to an end.[13] Blame is restorative because it repairs the damage that crime causes to the lawful status of offenders. By giving an accurate *deserved* reaction to crime, blame repairs the rupture done to the formal bonds between offenders and others and improves the way others see offenders by virtue of crime. In this approach, once blamed, ideally offenders will be able to be restored to their previous (lawful) state and move on their lives without being haunted by the past. Also, they will be seen as being redeemed in others' eyes, at least in a formal way: legal or formal restoration.

12 Graham Scambler, *A Sociology of Shame and Blame: Insiders versus Outsiders* (Springer 2019) p.26.

13 Bennett, 'The varities of retributivism' p.151.

For some, this might be seen as broadening the definition of restoration more than necessary. But formal restoration generated by blame is noteworthy, in particular in terms of transformation of offenders' legal status and public identity – from a criminal to a citizen. It may not be concerned directly with the reform of offenders, but it requires the full acceptance of offenders back into society after they are subject to a kind of withdrawal or alienation. In other words, blame does its work by holding a certain distance from offenders, but it also decrees that this symbolic kind of disconnecting should stop at some point and be replaced by re-recognition of full membership within society.

There is, however, a deeper kind of restoration that blame can provide. Consider, for example, the following comment: 'It breaks my heart to see someone of your age who has committed so many offences in your short life. . . . I am not entirely confident, but it seems to me that it is worth trying an alternative to immediate prison, which I would suspect would not give any long-term benefit at all'. This sort of blame, like others, is part of a process to hold offenders responsible for what they did, at times subjecting them to certain sanctions, and yet in this instance, it is shaped by a more compassionate, caring approach. The motivation is to find ways to change the offender's patterns of recidivism for a more substantial kind of reconciliation with the community and repair the damage they have done to their 'inner self' as well as to others. I call this 'ethical restoration'.

Blame is restorative in an ethical sense when it comes to terms with crime in a manner that repairs the ***damaged agency*** of offenders in their own eyes. By giving an appropriate reformative response to crime, blame restores the ***ethical*** self-harm that has been caused by the crime, the harm that is to do with the way offenders see themselves as well as the world. Blame invites offenders to partake of a kind of moral self-inspection, in which they confront the consequences of their conduct and accept it as wrong with a careful consideration of their past life. In this approach, offenders are given an opportunity to take responsibility and change, as well as to rebuild their lives in light of what has happened. Once blamed, they will not only be restored to their previous state in a legalistic sense but also be able to be in a renewed position, in which they change the way they relate to themselves as well as others.

At this point, it is worth noting that neo-classical retributivists believe that their conception of retributivism can provide both formal and ethical restoration. For them, punishment as public blame is restorative at both levels, in that it can repair both offenders' relationship with their fellow citizens (formal reconciliation) and their relationship with themselves (ethical reconciliation).[14] There are, however, two problems with the double-sense conception of restorative blame that stands in conjunction with retributive

14 Duff, *Punishment, Communication, and Community*; Bennett, *The Apology Ritual: A Philosophical Theory of Punishment*; Brenda M Baker, 'Penance as a model for punishment' (1992) 18 *Social Theory and Practice* 311.

punishment. The first is concerned with whether blame takes an inherently punitive form when concretised by a certain kind of sanction. In other words, does blame cause an engagement with offenders that is too punitive such that it is unlikely to achieve even a formal kind of restoration? The second is whether blame is in essence an interpersonal practice that does not fit with the overall public image of legal punishment. Put otherwise, is blame an essential part of state punishment? Both questions will be addressed, in order, in the following section.

3. Objections to blame

For some scholars, blame is an unusual starting point for talking about the connection between state punishment and the restoration of offenders. After all, too often, they argue, to be blamed is to be subject to another's hostile attitudes and thereby 'detrimental to one's sense of self-worth, one's relationships with others, and one's hopes for the future and motivation to change aspects of oneself that are difficult to face'.[15] As such, the practice of blame, particularly in the context of criminal justice, stands in the way of establishing constructive relationships – for it concretises 'feelings of mistrust, diminishing interest in friendship or intimacy, and prompting feelings of anger and resentment or a desire to meet injury with injury'.[16] For this reason, it frequently lends fundamental support to the infliction of suffering and exacerbates the stigma and deprivations that accompany punitive sanction. Lacey and Pickard call this 'affective blame'.

On the other hand, for other 'blame sceptics', it is unusual to associate blame with the idea of restoration in a legal context, not merely because it feeds into punitiveness, but because all punishment is *contingently* linked to blame.[17] From this perspective, blame is essentially an interpersonal moral practice that fits very uneasily with the political image of state punishment.[18] For example, to punish someone, says Matravers, is 'to respond to a criminal wrong in a way that characteristically marks the harm done to the victim and accords respect to the offender as an agent'[19] – not to find those who are blameworthy and approach them in a particularly negative manner. Accordingly, Matravers

15 Lacey and Pickard, 'From the consulting room to the court room? Taking the clinical model of responsibility without blame into the legal realm' p.14.

16 Erin I Kelly, *The Limits of Blame* (Harvard University Press 2018) p.116.

17 Matt Matravers, 'De-moralising retributivism: Agency, blame, and humanity in criminal law theory and practice' in Jonathan Jackson Jonathan Jacobs (ed), *The Routledge Handbook of Criminal Justice Ethics* (Routledge 2016); Peter Ramsay, 'The dialogic community at dusk' (2014) 1 *Critical Analysis of Law* 332.

18 David Shoemaker, 'Blame and punishment' in Neal A. Tognazzini and D. Justin Coates (eds), *Blame: Its Nature and Norms* (Oxford University Press 2013) p.118.

19 Matravers, 'De-moralising retributivism: Agency, blame, and humanity in criminal law theory and practice' p.158.

writes, we ought to punish people in ways that resist moral blame and other related detrimental passions.[20]

This is not to deny that blame is, at least partly, disposed to buttress the desire to hurt others and pave the way for harsher penal practices, particularly if not expressed in a way that fosters a constructive dialogue with offenders. Neither is this work unaware of the distinct narratives of interpersonal blame and legal punishment, and possible normative problems of relying on an institution that may – under particular social circumstances – lose standing to blame.[21] Nonetheless, I do believe that there are still good reasons for not cutting off punishment from blame and thinking about them in tandem. First, the practice of blame, despite its initial connection with primitive emotions, can be 'recalibrated' into an ethically acceptable form where a more compassionate and constructive response is produced, even within current penal practices, however limited this may be.[22] As the popular phrase goes: hate the sin, love the sinner. In this sense, blame can be 'detached' from its destructive components and exercised in a supportive mood, even though it may sometimes be followed by an imposition of requirement on offenders.[23]

With regard to the worry about the marriage of 'interpersonal' blame with 'public' sanction, it may be agreed that it is significant to separate the ***non-legal*** parts of punishment from the parts that make it 'legal'. However, this chapter would argue that we cannot reach a distinctively 'legal' form of punishment when removing its social and moral psychological component (blaming) from its political or public facet. After all, the 'legal' character of punishment is constituted by the regulation of moral and social relations alongside its political dimension.[24] We must, therefore, keep both the social function and the psychological aspect of punishment in view. Certainly, we must also note that the social function of punishment as public blaming is disposed to generate a repressive kind of order and solidarity that evokes hostile feelings and aggression towards offenders.[25] But this does not mean that public blame cannot have an ethically more promising function that promotes an inclusionary set of penal practices.

20 Matravers, 'De-moralising retributivism: Agency, blame, and humanity in criminal law theory and practice'.

21 Gustavo A Beade, 'Who can blame whom? Moral standing to blame and punish deprived citizens' (2019) 13 *Criminal Law and Philosophy* 271; Antony Duff, 'Blame, moral standing and the legitimacy of the criminal trial' (2010) 23 *Ratio* 123; Lacey and Pickard, 'Why standing to blame may be lost but authority to hold accountable retained: Criminal law as a regulative public institution'.

22 McGeer, 'Civilizing blame' p.162.

23 Hanna Pickard, 'Irrational blame' (2013) 73 *Analysis* 613, 621.

24 Alan Norrie, *Justice and the Slaughter Bench: Essays on Law's Broken Dialectic* (Routledge 2016) p.4.

25 Henrique Carvalho and Anastasia Chamberlen, 'Why punishment pleases: Punitive feelings in a world of hostile solidarity' (2018) 20 *Punishment & Society* 217 p.2.

It has now become relatively clear that blame can be seen as a moral response to criminal wrong that is associated with legal punishment and the restoration of offenders. But it is still not clear yet whether blame materialised by legal punishment (i.e., the infliction of suffering) is restorative, either at a formal or an ethical level. To address this, there follows a brief analysis of Duff's account of moral psychology of blame, from which he sets up a retributive theory that combines restoration and punishment in a unique way.

4. The moral psychology of blame: a restorative account

In Duff's view, to blame someone is at bottom to criticise them, accuse them of an immoral behaviour and then finally to hold them responsible for that behaviour.[26] It is not a simple judgement, decreeing that certain kinds of conduct are unacceptable and require moral disapproval. It is, rather, a special type of moral engagement with those who are perceived to have committed a wrong; a process through which they are held accountable, and Duff adds, 'perhaps' punished for that wrong'.[27] To blame others is also to communicate that the wrong is serious enough that it should be responded to with criticism, disapproval, or condemnation.

In this light, the practice of blame is an attempt at moral dialogue that takes place between the blamer and blamed, where the former calls the latter to account for a wrongdoing, and tries to persuade them to understand the moral implications of what they have done.[28] From the perspective of the blamed, to acknowledge the wrong and work through its moral consequences is a painful psychological process, typically marked by feelings of guilt and remorse. But that process in Duff's account also involves a desire to expiate the harm caused by the wrong, by way of undertaking a burdensome task, enduring some hardship, or a painful set of moral duties.[29] In other words, internal suffering is naturally followed by a further set of moral actions that repair the injuries caused by the wrong. Blame, in its restorative form, is then not only about the blamed person addressing their wrong and purifying themselves of that wrong, but it is also about an 'acting out' of the purification in the eyes of the blamer.

Central to the first element of blame is the fact that wrongdoers get what they deserve when they listen to the criticism of their past transgressive behaviour. That is, the expression of blame is backward-looking and retributive at its heart. From a moral psychological point of view, Duff thinks, we cannot first blame wrongdoers and *then* decide whether they should suffer thus. To

26 Duff, *Trials and Punishments* p.123.
27 Duff, *Trials and Punishments* p.39.
28 Duff, 'Blame, moral standing and the legitimacy of the criminal trial' p.125.
29 Duff, *Punishment, Communication, and Community* p.99

blame others is already to try to induce such suffering.[30] Duff also writes, in upholding the normative force of blame, there might be some questions about the principle that 'crimes deserve punishment', 'but there is surely nothing puzzling about the idea that wrongdoing deserves censure'.[31] From this view, wrongdoers receive an appropriate payback when they are blamed.

But within the moral voice of blame also lies a constructive message, that moves beyond simple disapproval. Wrongdoers are expected to address the message inherent in blame and internalise the moral judgement so that it becomes what we can call self-blame. Self-blame, guilt and remorse are part of the moral process for wrongdoers who come to 'own' their misconduct where they recognise their crime as wrong. But that process is also a process of 'disowning' where they try to renounce their conduct and reform the 'personality' that was in charge at the time of wrong.[32]

When blaming, in Duff's account, we do not simply criticise wrongdoers by inducing some distress in them. Instead, we seek their 'participation' – since the sort of suffering we intend to make them experience is the one that only they can impose on themselves. In other words, we seek to generate a self-imposed suffering in wrongdoers, through which they reform themselves and repair the harms by undertaking some burdensome tasks or hardships. Inherent in our blame is the commitment to the principle that wrongdoers should be morally awakened and make apologetic reparation to their victims. Once blame is successfully communicated, 'the original condition of security or trust, of good reputation, of friendship', once lost or damaged, is regained or retrieved. *The status quo ante* is restored or reinstated.[33]

Here is where we can identify ethical restoration in Duff's account. In the constructive guise of blame, perpetrators are taken as being separated from the good or moral relationships that make up their identity. When they violate others, they are seen as being alienated from others and themselves, as they break the ties that bind them to others and themselves. In other words, the moral wound is twofold. Perpetrators are not only expected to change their attitudes and actions (self-reform). But they are also asked to make amends for the harms done to victims (reparation and reconciliation). Self-reform is to do with the idea of moral growth and maturation, in which individuals improve the way they look at the world – whereas the ideas of reparation and reconciliation are concerned with re-commitment to the foundational values that they share with others. To sum up, when being blamed, perpetrators are

30 Duff, *Trials and Punishments* p.41.

31 Duff, 'Punishment, communication and community' p.50.; Antony Duff and Zachary Hoskins, 'Legal punishment' in Edward N. Zalta (ed), *The Stanford Encyclopedia of Philosophy* (2021).

32 Antony Duff, 'Penance, punishment and the limits of community' (2003) 5 *Punishment & Society* 295, 299.

33 Antony Duff, 'Restorative punishment and punitive restoration' in Lode Walgrave (ed), *Restorative Justice and the Law* (Routledge 2002) p.84.

invited to suffer the remorse of having done something wrong and repair the harms caused by that wrong, both to others and themselves. This is ideally done in a non-coercive way, as they are given the opportunity to reflect soberly on their behaviour without an external sanction.

Ethically promising though this account of blame may be, little has been said about legal punishment and the restoration of offenders. In our daily life, we can call others to account for their wrong in a communicative dialogue, usually without any harm inflicted upon them. We can also ask them to apologise for their misconduct and demand them to repair the harms without punishing them. But how can we do this at a public level, where wrongs are more serious, concerning not only individuals but also 'the public' – all citizens, by virtue of their shared membership of the political community?[34] To reiterate, blame at a public level is transformed into legal punishment. In other words, when we blame publicly, we impose certain kinds of losses or deprivations on offenders, and it is not clear how punishment provides restoration, either at ethical or legal levels. This question is addressed in the following section.

5. Legal punishment as public blame

For Duff, 'the trial is a formal, legal analogue of the informal, moral process of calling another to answer for an alleged wrong and blaming her for it if she cannot offer a suitably exculpatory answer'.[35] In a similar way to interpersonal blame, the aim of public blame consists in our commitment to take crimes seriously and cause offenders to face up to and recognise the wrongs they have done. Accordingly, Duff thinks, we should see the process of trial, conviction and punishment as 'related to, or continuous with, our moral responses to wrongdoing'.[36] Punishment as a communicative enterprise, in this approach, is a sort of replication or better; the institutionalisation of blame at a social and political level while holding ethical similarities with them in various respects:

> To indict someone for a criminal offence is to offer a particular criticism of his conduct; to try him is to seek to determine the justice of that criticism; to convict him is to blame him publicly for that offence; and the punishment which he may then receive must be imposed.[37]

In a criminal trial, like a two-way communication, offenders are seen as active participants, having an opportunity to answer charges of criminal wrongdoing. When convicted, Duff claims, they are officially condemned for public wrongs. As with blame, formal conviction communicates to offenders the censure that

34 Duff, 'Responsibility, restoration and retribution' p.70.
35 Duff, 'Blame, moral standing and the legitimacy of the criminal trial' p.130.
36 Duff, *Punishment, Communication, and Community* p.25.
37 Duff, *Trials and Punishments* p.39.

they deserve, aiming to make them repent crimes, reform themselves and reconcile with those whom they wronged. In other words, as a communicative enterprise, legal blame is both backward-looking and forward-looking, seeking to induce a specific sort of suffering in offenders in a way that persuades them of the error of their ways and asks them to repair the injuries done by their crimes to their victims and societal relationships.[38]

While an appropriate response to moral breaches in our personal life is usually an apology, Duff says, the response of offenders in serious wrongs should be something *more* than an apology. A mere apology cannot heal the moral wounds done by crimes.[39] This does not mean that this 'more' should include a separate penal measure or sanction, alongside the apology. Instead, Duff argues, it must be 'an apology of a kind that takes and addresses crimes seriously'.[40] In this sense, the undertaking of a reparative work is also a kind of apology, but of a concrete kind. Such a 'material' expression of apology indicates that offenders take their wrongs more seriously, as it adds some depth to their repentant feelings and gives weight to their apology. Because of the burden that it places on offenders, it also helps them to 'focus their attention' on what has been done and provides a setting within which they ponder carefully the nature and consequences of their crime.[41]

There are two arguments here. The first is that offenders owe an apologetic debt that would recognise the character and seriousness of their wrong, by offering a kind of reparative work for the benefit of victims or their fellow citizens. The second is that the moral debt that offenders are required to pay should be burdensome, and go deep with them, occupying their attention, thoughts, and emotions for some considerable time.[42] While the former explains how punishment as a public apology includes attempts to make up to victims and the community and reconcile with them, the latter seems to be concerned more with the question of how offenders are reformed by the suffering inherent in the forced apology.

There is little worry with the idea that offenders reconcile with their victims, and repair the damaged relationships with their victims or fellow citizens by undoing or repairing the harmful effects of their crime. When they redress the harm that they have caused with an appropriate reparative work, their previous status is somehow given back. They are restored to the position they held prior to their harmful wrongdoing: legal restoration. But reparation as something owed to victims and the community is not a form of punishment. It is, at best, a burdensome act that one is required to undergo. Why or how is punishment as an infliction of suffering related to the ideas of reparation and restoration?

38 Duff, 'Responsibility, restoration and retribution' p.80.
39 Duff, *Punishment, Communication, and Community* p.95.
40 Duff, *Punishment, Communication, and Community*.
41 Duff, 'Restorative punishment and punitive restoration' p.94.
42 Duff, *Punishment, Communication, and Community* p.108.

The second idea, however, seems more difficult to defend than the first. It is based on the assumption that offenders can only be restored by having to endure something burdensome that is imposed upon them. Offenders may sometimes suffer the pain of having been separated from others and voluntarily undertake a burdensome work to recover their place in their relationships. This can also go hand in hand with the process of changing or transforming themselves: ethical restoration. Nevertheless, where offenders are unwilling to undertake such a burden and become subject to something painful, however reparative it is said to be, how can this lead to self-reform, reparation and reconciliation or ethical restoration in my own terms?

Two questions have now been raised: the first, how is reparation (in Duff's theory) to do with the idea of punishment; the second, how may the imposition of 'reparation' bring offenders to repent their crimes and reform themselves? Here is where Duff's theory takes its distinctive image, as he maps the sources and principles of retribution on restorative justice in a rather subtle way.

6. On equivalence between retributive punishment and restorative sanction

Like other sorts of reparative sanctions, punishment, says Duff, is 'a species of required apology: offenders are required to go through the motions of apology, even if they do not mean it'.[43] Underlying his conception of punishment is the idea that, by contrast to the widespread and deeply ingrained dichotomy, restorative sanctions are equivalent to punishments. Like retributive practices, restorative measures address the past wrong as well as the harm caused by that wrong; they are burdensome in that they make offenders suffer by imposing some sort of obligation. In a restorative framework, offenders deserve to suffer the censure of offenders, and their own remorse, since censure and remorse are taken as appropriate responses to their crimes.[44] They also deserve to suffer the burden of making moral reparation for what they have done, since it was their own wrong, and it is just and proper that they should bear that burden.[45]

In this light, 'restoration is not only compatible with retribution', says Duff, 'it requires retribution, in that the kind of restoration that crime makes necessary can (given certain deep features of our social lives) be brought about only through retributive punishment'.[46] If this line of thought is right, restorative sanctions are 'not alternatives to punitive "pain delivery": they are themselves ways of trying to induce the appropriate kind of pain'. In other

43 Duff, 'Responsibility, restoration and retribution' p.79.

44 Theo Gavrielides, 'Restorative pain: A new vision of punishment' in Vasso Artinopoulou and Theo Gavrielides (eds), *Reconstructing Restorative Justice Philosophy* (Routledge 2016) p.322.

45 Duff, 'Restoration and retribution' p.49.

46 Duff, 'Restoration and retribution' p.43.

words, they are not *alternative to punishments* but 'alternative punishments'.[47] For these reasons, Duff concludes, the long-established division between restorative and retributive justice is a false one.

This is a false dichotomy not only because restorative justice shares the common ground with retributive ethics but also because retributivism is more complicated than the crude idea that the guilty deserve to be punished. A more nuanced account of retributivism attends not only to whether offenders deserve punishment but also to the meaning and type of suffering that offenders are made to undertake.[48] In Duff's formulation, offenders 'should come to suffer the appropriate kind of pain or burden – of being censured, of remorse, of making reparation; and that appropriate pain is in part at least, insofar as it involves the remorseful recognition of wrongdoing, to be self-imposed'.[49] In this sense, retributive suffering is not simply deserved and imposed on offenders, having only to do with a payback response to the past crime. It is, also, something that offenders impose upon themselves when they come to terms with and restore the harms they have caused.[50] Marked by a kind of moral burden that offenders are obligated to serve, retributive punishment, therefore, seeks to repair damaged relationships and reconcile offenders with those who have been wronged. As such, Duff concludes, our moral response to crimes should be 'neither restoration rather than retribution, nor retribution rather than restoration, but restoration through retribution'.[51]

It is worth noticing that Duff views the conflict between 'the punishment paradigm' and 'the restorative paradigm' as philosophically unsound.[52] It is also worth emphasising that his conceptions of crime and punishment move beyond the classical formulation of the punishment paradigm. In Duff's view, crimes are more than the breaches of laws; they are the ruptures or destruction of social relationships that connect individuals. In a similar vein, punishments are not merely the inflictions of pain for violations of law, but they are penal responses that are designed to repair the harms caused to relationships and reconcile offenders with those who have been violated. Certainly, this 'ethical' or 'restorative' shift in the way we look at legal punishment engenders a wide theoretical space where penal sanctions are more closely linked to the ideas of reparation and restoration.

Understood in this way, in many respects retributive punishments are identical to restorative sanctions. Like requirements decided under criminal

47 Duff, 'Alternatives to punishment–or alternative punishments?'; for a similar view, see: Kathleen Daly, *Restorative Justice and Punishment: The Views of Young People* (1999)

48 Duff, 'Retrieving retributivism' p.22.

49 Duff, 'Restorative punishment and punitive restoration' p.97.

50 Duff, 'Restorative punishment and punitive restoration' p.97.

51 Duff, 'Restorative punishment and punitive restoration' p.98.

52 See for similar views: Kathleen Daly, 'Revisiting the relationship between retributive and restorative justice' in H Strang and J Braithwaite (eds), *Restorative Justice: From Philosophy to Practice* (2000); Garvey, 'Restorative justice, punishment, and atonement'

mediation, community service or probation orders, punishments are morally acceptable forms of obligations, where offenders are asked to apologise and make up to victims or the community. 'Apologies' within a retributive ethics, which are usually concretised by punishment, writes Duff, are 'made, not just suffered':

> Although we naturally talk of punishment as imposed, most punishments are actually requirements rather than mere impositions: the offender must not simply passively undergo something, but do something (undertake some specified unpaid work, take part in a programme that aims to address his wrongdoing, fulfil the requirements of a probation order).[53]

What all the retributive punishments have in common, both in their standard and restorative forms, is that they are deserved sanctions that offenders undertake actively, even though they are not willing to do so. They are forced apologies to make up to victims and the community, within a process where offenders are expected to come to terms with their wrong remorsefully.[54]

Having captured a diversity of values within a single framework, like desert, reform, reparation and reconciliation, Duff's conception of retributivism is theoretically subtle and complicated. It stresses the peculiar sort of suffering that punishment may induce, and substantially enriches and transforms the way the principle of retribution is understood. It also attempts to bridge the gulf between legal punishment and the ideas of ethical restoration and reconciliation. It does so particularly by conceiving of punishment as a requirement or burden, and thereby lending itself easily to a restorative interpretation. In accordance with the arguments proposed in this work, Duff's theory of retributivism seems to set up a basis by which to provide both legal and ethical restoration. It both reaffirms the status of offenders within the community (reconciliation) and restores them in a way that paves the way for their moral progress or re-awakening (reform).

Nevertheless, there is still an incongruence between retributive and restorative justice, especially given that some of the retributive punishments, most notably imprisonment, can be thought of as simply deserved and imposed on offenders. They are neither actively undertaken nor related to the ideas of reparation and restoration. We should, therefore, ask again how separable are the kinds of force, obligations or requirements involved in restorative sanctions from the other retributive punishments. But perhaps more significantly, we should also inquire into a deeper and more foundational question: what is it that makes a penal response restorative? Once these questions are addressed,

53 Anthony Duff, 'Punishment as communication' in Jesper Ryberg (ed), *Oxford Handbook of Punishment Theory and Philosophy* (2022) p.11.

54 Duff, *Punishment, Communication, and Community* p.107.

we will be better able to gain insights into whether retributivism is both legally and ethically restorative.

7. Restorative burden versus retributive punishment

Thinking about the quality of suffering (if it is restorative or retributive) from a restorative justice perspective, one response might be that there are two modes of delivering hardships or burdens to offenders. While retributive punishment is inflicted *deliberately* on offenders, the suffering of restorative interventions is *coincidental* and subordinated to the aims of reparation and healing.[55] Put simply, intention matters. It is the intention of those who administer sanctions on offenders that would give them a retributive or restorative character.[56] If the aim is not merely to have offenders suffer but to heal the wounds caused by crime, then we can see that sanction as restorative. This argument, however, is 'disingenuous':

> If pain is an inevitable, or even highly probable, consequence of restorative interventions, then (unless one adopts a perversely narrow interpretation of the term 'deliberately') somebody who purposely puts an offender through a restorative process, thereby causing them pain, deliberately inflicts pain on them. Whether causing pain is their primary intention, or something they desire, is immaterial.[57]

As Johnstone points out in this passage, the intention does not matter as much as Walgrave assumes. If that were so, we would accept all sorts of hard treatment as restorative, providing that they are imposed with an intention to restore rather than a desire to inflict suffering.

Gavrielides accepts that Walgrave is right when he views suffering in restorative justice not as an end in itself. But, for him, what is distinctive about the sort of suffering that restorative justice seeks to entail is 'personal and specific' to each human being, in the sense that everyone comes to see it as the consequence of their actions, through self-observation and self-reflection.[58] It is, therefore, not something that can be imposed by the state and top-down punishment but 'nurtured' and 'triggered' by a bottom-up process, ideally within 'voluntary agreement reached by the parties with the help of the state'.[59]

55 Lode Walgrave, 'Restorative justice and the republican theory of criminal justice: An exercise in normative theorising on restorative justice' in Heather Strang and John Braithwaite (eds), *Restorative Justice: Philosophy to Practice* (Ashgate 2000) p.166–167; Walgrave, *Restorative Justice, Self-Interest and Responsible Citizenship* p.153.

56 M Wright, *Justice for Victims and Offenders: A Restorative Response to Crime* (Waterside Press 1996) p.15.

57 Gerry Johnstone, *Restorative Justice: Ideas, Values, Debates* (Routledge 2007) p.91.

58 Gavrielides, 'Restorative pain: A new vision of punishment' p.321.

59 Gavrielides, 'Restorative pain: A new vision of punishment' p.322.

Gavrielides describe this as 'restorative catharsis', a term denoting substantial change in the lives of offenders after a period of serious self-examination. Restorative catharsis, Gavrielides thinks, should not be seen as 'a must but as a gift of restorative justice'. 'It is not a moment', he continues, 'but a process', which may be life-long for some. He provides a caveat: though restorative and constructive, the gift of catharsis is also 'painful, retributive, and dangerous'.[60]

It is not entirely clear why Gavrielides's comes to view restorative suffering as dangerous at the end of his analysis, but what he has described as catharsis is at odds with the fundamental tenets of Duff's retributivism in two respects. First, although they may both seem to generate more or less the same process of remorse, moral growth and restoration, Gavrielides's notion of catharsis suggests a non-state-centric and bottom-up approach. It proposes, in his own words, 'a new ethos, or novel way of approach to interpersonal relationships and a way of prioritizing what is important in the process of learning how to coexist'.[61] Second, in contrast to the retributive insistence that punishment must be burdensome, the theory of catharsis takes suffering not as a necessary element of restoration but as a 'natural by-product' of a constructive engagement with offenders.[62] In other words, whilst retributivism assumes that punishment is restorative precisely because it involves a *painful penitential burden placed upon offenders*, the process of catharsis is restorative because it arises out of *a natural process of moral self-inspection*.

To be sure, not all scholars take restorative suffering this way. In fact, as Wilson rightly comments, restorative justice has generally pursued an ethics of suffering that does not 'adequately capture the complex moral and psychological phenomena' that are central to violation and punishment.[63] Restorative justice, she writes, 'has not settled its basic ethical terms' and 'failed to develop the concepts of guilt and shame that it needs' for a better, deeper understanding of restorative suffering.[64] For Wilson, the moral psychologies of guilt and shame as an integrated whole provide a strong basis for offenders to take responsibility, while also prompting reparative action and 'orienting the person towards repairing both the damage they have done and shortcomings in themselves'.[65]

It is not possible within the scope of this work to do justice to this constructive critical reflection on restorative justice; it should also be noted that there is much debate about the philosophical foundations and contours of

60 Gavrielides, 'Restorative pain: A new vision of punishment' p.313.

61 Theo Gavrielides, *Restorative Justice Theory and Practice: Addressing the Discrepancy* (HEUNI 2007) p.129; Theo Gavrielides and Vasso Artinopoulou, 'Prolegomena: Restorative justice philosophy through a value-based methodology' in Theo Gavrielides and Vasso Artinopoulou (eds), *Reconstructing Restorative Justice Philosophy* (Routledge 2016).

62 Gavrielides, 'Restorative pain: A new vision of punishment' p.313.

63 Wilson, 'What a shame! Restorative justice's guilty secret' p.39.

64 Wilson, 'What a shame! Restorative justice's guilty secret' p.40.

65 Wilson, 'What a shame! Restorative justice's guilty secret' p.48.

restorative justice and its distinctive features. Leaving aside these controversies, it seems not unreasonable to think that retributivism is marked out from restorative justice, at least in terms of the pressing demand that punishment must be a burdensome practice. Because of this moral demand, the penitential burden in retributivism seems to involve a kind of suffering that is hardly in the service of offenders' moral self-inspection. Unlike restorative sanctions, where offenders are obliged to do a reparative work that can remind them of the responsibilities towards others and themselves, retributive punishments are disposed to include sufferings that go beyond the burden of reparative or restorative work.

Consider, for example, the way we differentiate certain punishments, like imprisonment, from the other forms of penal response to criminal behaviour, such as community service orders and mediation. At first glance, one reason for our doing so is based on the severity or degree of suffering involved in these punishments. But an underlying reason lies in the thought that, by contrast to others, some forms of punishment (most clearly manifest in the practice of imprisonment) cause suffering that is purely and simply retributive. Pace Duff, these punishments, unlike others, appear to be less concerned with the reparative function that they are supposed to serve. In fact, the basic desert function of punishment is so ingrained in every penal system that it is very hard to reject it. In turn, its strong institutional presence makes Duff's restorative vision either unrealistic or seriously in error in identifying the main tenets of retributivism.

In response, Duff may argue that not all forms of penal burdens, especially imprisonment, are the paradigm of punishment, so we cannot say that any acceptable theory must justify the penal *status quo*. In fact, for Duff, it might be 'a merit rather than a flaw' in a normative theory that it makes these sorts of punishment problematic.[66] Nevertheless, Duff is still at pains to claim that imprisonment can be viewed as an attempted dialogue in which offenders are expected to undertake a kind of 'moral reparation' or of 'seclusion' within the community, rather than outright exclusion from it.[67] For him, if reformed in ways that make it more of a self-punishment venue for offenders, imprisonment may provide a structure within which they can think about the nature and implications of their crime and face up to it more adequately than they might otherwise do.[68] In other words, a prison term, like other restorative sanctions, can be undertaken 'actively' by offenders, says Duff, 'if the prison is minimally decent'. By this, he means a reformed penitential environment, where offenders

66 Duff, 'Punishment as communication' p.6.

67 Antony Duff, 'Offenders as citizens' in Elizabeth Shaw Farah Focquaert and Bruce N. Waller (eds), *The Routledge Handbook of the Philosophy and Science of Punishment* (Routledge 2020) p.34.

68 Anthony Duff and Sandra Marshall, 'Civic punishment' in Richard Sparks and Ian Loader (eds), *Democratic Theory and Mass Incarceration* (Oxford University Press 2016) p.49–51.

can 'make the prison regime their own, rather than merely an alien order that they must obey; to engage in productive work, and in educational programs'.[69] Yet, however reformative a place the prison can be, Duff comes to conclude disappointedly 'the brute fact of prison walls remains'.[70]

The argument here is not concerned particularly with the normative justification of imprisonment; neither is it engaged with the question of whether prisons are places that are reformable.[71] Instead, the aim is to highlight that Duff's ambivalent position regarding imprisonment is instructive, particularly in terms of understanding how the retributive suffering of punishment is linked to the notion of restoration. On the one hand, Duff proposes a peculiar image of imprisonment, where he talks of it as a kind of moral reparation. In this sense, for him, prisons can be seen as places of reform and redemption, i.e., restorative in both ethical and legal senses: they reconcile offenders with their fellow beings by restoring formal relationships, while also providing them with the opportunity to examine their moral self. On the other hand, however, Duff seriously doubts if imprisonment as a form of punishment that is crudely retributive can in any way be reformative or restorative.[72] Thus, he comes to accept that punishment may not always be restorative. My suggestion is that Duff's conception of punishment can still be seen as restorative, and yet in a legalistic sense. The following section unpacks this, and concludes this work's thoughts about Duff's ambivalent position with regards to retributivism and restoration.

8. Between legal and ethical restoration

No doubt, at first sight, it may seem very unusual to view carceral punishment as a reparative work, as it is commonly understood. Offenders are punished in a submissive way, without having to restore the injuries inflicted on their victims. In a way, punishment here looks much like a pointless piling of one harm on another, doing no good to either victim or offender. But, as argued in the previous chapter, the suffering of offenders can provide a symbolic reparation, or an abstract kind of restoration for victims, where their *injured* status is reaffirmed by the legal apparatus. Even so, this does not tell us how offenders are restored by enduring the suffering of confinement, in particular in the face of sternly standing prison walls. Instead, it seems a sheer passive

69 Duff, 'Offenders as citizens' p.34.

70 Duff and Marshall, 'Civic punishment' p.51.

71 Allegra M McLeod, 'Prison abolition and grounded justice' (2015) 62 *UCLA Law Review* 1156.

72 Having seriously engaged with the question of whether seeking a purely non-deterrent rationale is 'quixotic' in his latest work, Duff comes to accept that the deterrent aspect of imprisonment can have a secondary message inherent in the communicative dialogue between offenders and the state. For the purpose of this work, I will not discuss if this makes him a 'mixed' theorist. Duff, 'Punishment as communication' p.16.

suffering at the hands of a punisher that has nothing to do with the reform of offenders.

By drawing on the term 'penance', as Duff suggests, we may think that, just as performing a penance is necessary to release or untie one from the chains of a sin, having to endure something for a crime may signify a renewal to the commitment that is expected from offenders within a political community, and promote a positive individual-level change in them. That is, just as penitential suffering brings about the remission of sin and reconciles the sinner with God or other members of a religious community, punishment – at least formally – can be thought to restore ruptured civic relationships. It *must* be burdensome, because it should focus the attention of the offender on what has been done, and help them arrive at a more authentic repentance, thereby accepting their suffering as a duty to their victims and other fellow citizens.[73] It is questionable whether using force would direct offenders' attention towards their crime or divert it towards the suffering that has been imposed upon them.[74] But what is crucial in this approach is the idea that, even though the initial attempt to get into dialogue with offenders might seem top-down and one-sided, it is practised within a bottom-up and participatory process through which punishment is internalised and self-imposed.

Interestingly, caught between the ideas of 'passive exposure' and 'active engagement', the term penance etymologically reflects a sort of tension and ambiguity, possessing a double meaning about the relationship between 'suffering' and 'sufferer'. While the first meaning is a voluntary 'self-punishment', inflicted as an outward expression of repentance for having done wrong, particularly in a religious context, the second in common parlance means something that one has to do even though he does not like doing it. For Duff, the first crucial point in secular penance is to make the wrongdoer endure something that does not lie within his control, while the other point is *in part* to allow the wrongdoer to accept voluntarily what he has done. Ideally, as Duff notes, 'what began as a punishment inflicted on him in order to induce repentance [should] become a punishment (a fully-fledged penance) that he accepts or wills for himself as an expression of that repentance'.[75]

To actualise such an ideal (transformation of punishment into a self-imposed burden) is a process in which the voluntary aspect of penance is brought about. If successful, punishment would constitute a voluntary apologetic payment to victims and the community. Since it becomes a self-imposed burden that offenders undertake for the benefit of victims and themselves, punishment can

73 Anthony Duff, *The Realm of Criminal Law* (Oxford University Press 2018) p.224.

74 Fergus McNeill, 'The fuel in the tank or the hole in the boat? Can sanctions support desistance?' in Shapland Joanna, Stephen Farrall and Anthony Bottoms (eds), *Global Perspectives on Desistance: Renewing What We Know and Looking to the Future* (Routledge 2016) p.265.

75 Duff, *Punishment, Communication, and Community* p.111.

be seen as restorative in a substantial sense. We may perhaps call this an ethical kind of restoration, from the perspective of offenders.

Yet punishment as a practice having such an ethical project is likely to fail. In Duff's theory however, when it fails, it does not undermine the legitimacy of punishment as secular penance. What ultimately matters for him is not the outcome of restoration but a communicative enterprise in which offenders are required to undergo the formal ritual of apology. To require offenders to take part in that ritual is a duty to offenders as much as to victims and the public. It brings about a formal 'absolution' of offenders through which they are released from the stain that their crime carries and restored to a pre-crime status. In other words, even where some kinds of burden are imposed on offenders with no apologetic response, there might still be some room for the idea of restoration.

For example, consider the metaphor of debt in a new light. When offenders commit crime, they fail to display commitment to their civic relationships and put their formal status into doubt within the political community. By doing so, they become indebted to others because they are seen as those who have failed to do what is expected of them as citizens and who have not done enough to remain part of the community. Punishment then can be seen as a kind of payment that offenders pay to their victims and fellow citizens.

Though dangerously metaphorical as this might seem, there is something to the idea that offenders owe their fellow citizens something to remedy the flaw or rupture in the reciprocal communal relationships, and recover their normative place that has been shaken because of their violative conduct. Ideally, an apology concretised by a reparative action, as Duff suggests, seems the most satisfactory form of payment through which they can also 'turn their lives around'.[76] But even where 'ethical' restoration is not achieved for some reason, we should treat offenders, Duff says, 'as if the debt has been paid'.[77] For they fulfill their duty by engaging in the public ritual of apology and undergoing a penitential burden in response for their crime.[78] If we do so, we can see punishment 'as a mode of moral reparation', though a formal one.[79]

To say that the debt has been 'extracted' or 'paid' would equally be to say that offenders can 'trade up to a restored position as citizens of good character', even though they are not deeply reformed.[80] In other words, when they serve their punishment and take part in the ritual of apology and penance,

76 'One of the best ways for offenders', penned in the Scottish Prison Commission report, 'to pay back is by turning their lives around.' The Scottish Prisons Commission, *Scotland's Choice* (Scottish Prisons Commission 2008).

77 Duff, *Punishment, Communication, and Community* p.124.

78 Duff, *The Realm of Criminal Law* p.224.

79 Duff, 'Retrieving retributivism' p.18.

80 Fergus McNeill, 'Four forms of 'offender'rehabilitation: Towards an interdisciplinary perspective' (2012) 17 *Legal and Criminological Psychology* 18, 15.

even if it is done insincerely, offenders are requalified as full citizens.[81] Their legal status is somehow renewed by punishment, repairing the normative damage that their crime has done to them and others. This is to say that punishment settles the putative debt that crime creates and provides a formal or juridical 'de-labelling' or 'uplifting', where the status and rights of offenders are reinstated. In other words, punishment dissolves the burden of being guilty and sets the legal ground for reintegration, resettlement and re-entry. By having back their rights and status, offenders redeem themselves in the eyes of other fellow citizens and embark on a new life to correct their personality and desist from criminal behaviour.

Clearly, when punishment is imposed without equipping offenders for a new life, it is much more likely to be a source of suffering and struggle than a trigger for change and growth.[82] Indeed, this is often how punishment looks in practice. In this sense, it is perilous to be incognisant of the deep harms of punishment and instead view it as restorative. Nevertheless, formal restoration ensures that no further harm is inflicted on offenders other than the one inherent in legal punishment. It secures the *restored* position of offenders, setting the scene for giving them the rights that have been curtailed because of their being punished. Formal restoration also gives us a normative ground on which to challenge the collateral damage of punishment, mostly vividly its stigmatising and exclusionary effects on society. It may not be as expansive and compelling as ethical restoration, but it is the sort of restoration that needs to be considered.

To conclude, Duff's communicative theory of retributivism seeks to explore a shared and fertile ground between legal punishment as deserved pain, and internal suffering as a moral source for reform, with an emphasis on the idea that punishment can set the scene for ethical restoration. But the theoretical rigidity of retributivism occludes the possibility for a deeper engagement with the ideas of reform or rehabilitation. In other words, Duff's theory is notably stunted by the persistent retributive themes of desert, payback or moral debt. As pointed out in this section, Duff's conception of punishment may certainly still be seen as valuable in terms of providing formal restoration. But it is as much enhancement in retributive thought as limitation: retributivism is in impasse, in its developmental pursuit.

Conclusion

Examining a range of sentencing remarks in the first section, this chapter started with an exploration of different kinds of blaming, from which were

81 This is not to say that offenders forfeit their citizenship when they commit a crime. It is just to say that their status as citizens has been damaged.

82 Fergus McNeill and Marguerite Schinkel, 'Prisons and desistance' in Yvonne Jewkes (ed), *Handbook on Prisons* (Routledge 2016) p.167.

presented two forms of restorative blaming. The first one is a moral practice that seeks to reaffirm the community's values by reminding the transgressor of their status (that has been put into question by violation), while the second one is a reformative engagement that is concerned with the way the blamed relates to themselves and others. Having addressed the suspicions around the connection between blame and legal punishment, I argued that contemporary practices of criminal justice could be linked to the practice of blaming. In the public sphere, we blame offenders and hold them responsible for their past violations of law by punishing them. We blame them because we think our attitude towards them shifts appropriately, precisely because of their past misconduct. That is, punishment as public blame is at root retributive. Nonetheless, as Duff's account of moral psychology of blame indicates, our penal blaming has also a future-oriented function, in the sense that it seeks to shift the way offenders stand in relation to themselves and others. This means that when punishing, we could also ask offenders to change their behaviour and restore the harm done to both themselves and others. In other words, Duff's conception of punishment claims to be both reformative and reconciliatory.

Against this argument, some doubts were raised, in particular questioning the peculiar nature of blame at an institutional level: legal punishment involves more than the practice of blame, moving beyond an expression of disapproval or condemnation of offenders' actions. It comes with some kinds of deprivation, loss and pain. The central question was then of how the infliction of suffering can bring about moral reform or rehabilitation alongside formal restoration and reconciliation? For Duff, the additional burden that comes with blaming is a suitable vehicle through which to enable offenders to apologise effectively for their misconduct and to achieve 'moral cleansing'. In his view, the kind of suffering that punishment involves can still be seen as restorative and reformative, in that it brings offenders' attention towards their wrongdoing, and moves them to restore their relationships with victims and other fellow citizens. In fact, punishment for Duff *should* be painful in order that it is restorative in both legal and ethical senses.

The work acknowledged that, within the idea of inflicting penal suffering, there may be some room for the idea of legal restoration, in that it helps offenders to redeem themselves in the eyes of society. That is, punishment may at least be seen as a debt paid to the society, providing a basis for offenders to regain the trust that they have lost – even if the strict legalistic approach does not allow them to make amends to those they have harmed: earned redemption.[83] Nevertheless, it is not clear if the infliction of suffering is justified and ethically restorative. Certainly, forceful legal intervention may sometimes bring about some kind of internal suffering (the pain at another being pained) which is perhaps an undeniable part of the process of coming to terms with

83 Gordon Bazemore, 'Restorative justice and earned redemption: Communities, victims, and offender reintegration' (1998) 41 *American Behavioral Scientist* 768.

violation. But why this should be done in a coercive manner remains a thorny question that is at the heart of legalistic retributivism.

To summarise, from the perspective of offenders, restoration is double-faced: one is legal, the other ethical. While the legal is concerned with the damaged status of offenders within society, the ethical is more about how they deal with crime to restore a breached sense of wholeness. Duff's revisionist approach suggests that both kinds of restoration are achievable through a conception of retributivism that marries remorse with legal punishment. But, as this chapter made clear, the chasm between the legal and ethical approaches is wider and more difficult to bridge than Duff proposes. Neo-classical retributivism has advanced and broadened the field, in particular in terms of understanding how deserved suffering ties in with the ideas of reform and reconciliation. But it has also reached its 'natural boundaries' that define its limits and scope.

Bibliography

Baker BM, 'Penance as a model for punishment' (1992) 18 *Social Theory and Practice* 311

Bazemore G, 'Restorative justice and earned redemption: Communities, victims, and offender reintegration' (1998) 41 *American Behavioral Scientist* 768

Beade GA, 'Who can blame whom? Moral standing to blame and punish deprived citizens' (2019) 13 *Criminal Law and Philosophy* 271

Bennett C, *The Apology Ritual: A Philosophical Theory of Punishment* (Cambridge University Press 2008)

Bennett, C, 'The varieties of retributive experience' (2002) 52 (247) *The Philosophical Quarterly* 145–163

Carvalho H and Chamberlen A, 'Why punishment pleases: punitive feelings in a world of hostile solidarity' (2018) 20 *Punishment & Society* 217

Daly K, 'Restorative justice and punishment: the views of young people' (Paper presented to the American Society of Criminology Annual Meeting, Toronto 1999)

Duff A, 'Alternatives to punishment–or alternative punishments?' in Cragg W (ed), *Retributivism and Its Critics* (Franz Steiner Verlag 1992)

Duff A, 'Blame, moral standing and the legitimacy of the criminal trial' (2010) 23 *Ratio* 123

Duff A, 'Offenders as citizens' in Farah Focquaert ES and Waller BN (eds), *The Routledge Handbook of the Philosophy and Science of Punishment* (Routledge 2020)

Duff A, 'Penal communications: recent work in the philosophy of punishment' (1996) 20 *Crime and Justice* 1

Duff A, 'Penance, punishment and the limits of community' (2003) 5 *Punishment & Society* 295

Duff A, 'Punishment as communication' in Ryberg J (ed), *The Oxford Handbook of the Philosophy of Punishment* (Oxford University Press 2025)

Duff A, *Punishment, Communication, and Community* (OUP 2001)

Duff A, 'Punishment, communication and community' in Matravers M (ed), *Punishment and Political Theory* (Hart Publishing 1998)

Duff A, *The Realm of Criminal Law* (OUP 2018)

Duff A, 'Restoration and retribution' in Andreas von Hirsch JVR, Bottoms AE, Roach K and Schiff M (eds), *Restorative Justice and Criminal Justice: Competing or Reconcilable Paradigms* (Bloomsbury Publishing 2003)
Duff A, 'Responsibility, restoration and retribution' in Tonry M (ed), *Retributivism Has a Past: Has It a Future?* (OUP 2011)
Duff A, 'Restorative punishment and punitive restoration' in Walgrave L (ed), *Restorative Justice and the Law* (Routledge 2002)
Duff A, 'Retrieving retributivism' in White MD (ed), *Retributivism: Essays on Theory and Policy* (OUP 2011)
Duff A, *Trials and Punishments* (Cambridge University Press 1991)
Duff RA, 'Criminal law and the constitution of civil order' (2020) 70 *University of Toronto Law Journal* 4
Duff A and Hoskins Z,'Legal Punishment' in Zalta EN and Nodelman U (eds), The Stanford Encyclopedia of Philosophy (Spring 2024), https://plato.stanford.edu/entries/legal-punishment/
Duff A and Marshall S, 'Civic punishment' in Sparks R and Loader I (eds), *Democratic Theory and Mass Incarceration* (OUP 2016)
Duff RA, 'Review essay/justice, mercy, and forgiveness' (1990) 9 *Criminal Justice Ethics* 51
Garvey SP, 'Restorative justice, punishment, and atonement' (2003) 1 *Utah Law Review* 303
Gavrielides T, *Restorative Justice Theory and Practice: Addressing the Discrepancy* (HEUNI 2007)
Gavrielides T, 'Restorative pain: a new vision of punishment' in Artinopoulou V and Gavrielides T (eds), *Reconstructing Restorative Justice Philosophy* (Routledge 2016)
Gavrielides T and Artinopoulou V, 'Prolegomena: restorative justice philosophy through a value-based methodology' in Gavrielides T and Artinopoulou V (eds), *Reconstructing Restorative Justice Philosophy* (Routledge 2016)
Hieronymi P, 'The force and fairness of blame' (2004) 18 *Philosophical Perspectives* 115
https://www.birminghammail.co.uk/news/local-news/judge-sent-solihull-neighbour-from-hell-159952
https://www.nottinghampost.com/news/drug-addict-mums-criminal-record-294028
https://www.nottinghampost.com/news/nottingham-news/former-royal-marine-given-another-342607
Johnstone G, *Restorative Justice: Ideas, Values, Debates* (Routledge 2007) 91
Kathleen Daly K, 'Revisiting the relationship between retributive and restorative justice' in Strang H and Braithwaite J (ed), *Restorative Justice: From Philosophy to Practice* (Routledge 2000)
Kelly EI, *The Limits of Blame* (Harvard University Press 2018)
Lacey N and Pickard H, 'From the consulting room to the court room? Taking the clinical model of responsibility without blame into the legal realm' (2013) 33 *Oxford Journal of Legal Studies* 1
Lacey N and Pickard H, 'Why standing to blame may be lost but authority to hold accountable retained: criminal law as a regulative public institution' (2021) 104 *The Monist* 265
Matravers M, 'De-moralising retributivism: agency, blame, and humanity in criminal law theory and practice' in Jackson J and Jacobs J (eds), *The Routledge Handbook of Criminal Justice Ethics* (Routledge 2016)

McGeer V, 'Civilizing blame' in Tognazzini NA and Coates DJ (eds), *Blame: Its Nature and Norms* (2013)

McLeod AM, 'Prison abolition and grounded justice' (2015) 62 *UCLA Law Review* 1156

McNeill F, 'Four forms of 'offender'rehabilitation: towards an interdisciplinary perspective' (2012) 17 *Legal and Criminological Psychology* 18

McNeill F, 'The fuel in the tank or the hole in the boat? Can sanctions support desistance?' in Joanna S, Farrall S and Bottoms A (eds), *Global Perspectives on Desistance: Renewing What We Know and Looking to the Future* (Routledge 2016)

McNeill F and Schinkel M, 'Prisons and desistance' in Jewkes Y (ed), *Handbook on Prisons* (Routledge 2016)

Norrie A, *Justice and the Slaughter Bench: Essays on Law's Broken Dialectic* (Routledge 2016)

Pickard H, 'Irrational blame' (2013) 73 *Analysis* 613

Ramsay P, 'The dialogic community at dusk' (2014) 1 *Critical Analysis of Law* .2291–9732

Regina -v- TEEKO LE <https://www.judiciary.uk/judgments/r-v-le-sentencing-remarks/>

Scambler G, *A Sociology of Shame and Blame: Insiders Versus Outsiders* (Springer 2019)

Sher G, *In Praise of Blame* (OUP 2005)

Shoemaker D, 'Blame and punishment' in Tognazzini NA and Coates DJ (eds), *Blame: Its Nature and Norms* (OUP 2013)

Stafford Regina v Notman <https://www.judiciary.uk/judgments/r-v-notman-sentencing-remarks/>

The Scottish Prisons Commission, Scotland's Choice: Report of the Scottish Prisons Commission 2008

Walgrave L, 'Restorative justice and the republican theory of criminal justice: an exercise in normative theorising on restorative justice' in Strang H and Braithwaite J (eds), *Restorative Justice: Philosophy to Practice* (Ashgate 2000)

Walgrave L, *Restorative Justice, Self-interest and Responsible Citizenship* (Willan 2008)

Wilson A, 'What a shame! Restorative justice's guilty secret' (2022) 61 *The Howard Journal of Crime and Justice* 39

Wright M, *Justice for Victims and Offenders: A Restorative Response to Crime* (Waterside Press 1996)

'You are undoubtedly a dangerous young man - what the judge told murderer Kai Nazir' <https://www.cambridge-news.co.uk/news/cambridge-news/kai-nazir-murder-sentence-west-15133047>

Zimmerman MJ, *An Essay on Moral Responsibility* (NJ: Rowman & Littlefield 1988)

6 Punishment as recognition

Introduction

In the last two chapters, we have seen that retributive punishment can be linked with the restoration of the victim and offender at both legal and ethical levels. At stake in this analysis was the moral psychology of resentment, grief, blame and suffering and how they relate to punishment. In this chapter, though it will pursue the same route in relation to the twofold nature of restoration, the focus will shift to the public or political dimension of punishment. Thus, this chapter will be engaged with punishment as a socio-political enterprise in its foundation, an institution that is mainly concerned with the power or coercion of the state over its individuals.

Central to the focus of this chapter is the claim that punishment is essentially a form of state action that seeks to restore the normative harm caused by the breach of the legal order.[1] In this approach, punishment reasserts the state's challenged authority and repairs the damaged civic relationships that make the common life of citizens possible. Cast in political terms, with the emphasis on the state as a public authority setting up the terms under which individuals interact with others, punishment upholds the freedom of all and reaffirms the values of mutual trust and respect. In other words, punishment vindicates the rule of law and restores the normative regime of rights. I take this function of punishment as legal restoration, the sort of restoration that is achieved by repairing what we may call 'legal relations of mutual recognition'.

At the heart of the political conception of punishment lies the idea that we must ensure that the state as a public authority governs normative relations between individuals as fellow citizens. The normative relationships in question,

1 Thorburn, 'Punishment and public authority'; Chiao, *Criminal Law in the Age of the Administrative State*; Dubber, 'A political theory of criminal law: Autonomy and the legitimacy of state punishment'; Chad Flanders, 'Political philosophy and punishment' in Larry Alexander and Kimberly Kessler Ferzan (eds), *The Palgrave Handbook of Applied Ethics and the Criminal Law* (Springer 2019); Fletcher, 'Political theory and criminal law'; Lacey and Pickard, 'Why standing to blame may be lost but authority to hold accountable retained: Criminal law as a regulative public institution'; Ramsay, 'A democratic theory of imprisonment'

DOI: 10.4324/9781003563150-10

however, are detached and abstract while also being framed within a vertical governance model. What is not addressed and restored by legal punishment is the horizontal intersubjective bonds that have been shattered by criminal violation. After all, crime is not only a challenge to the sovereign's authority but is also violative of ethical ties between individuals as fellow citizens. Punishment in fluid social interactions should not only be concerned with the re-assertion of a public authority. Instead, it should also be oriented towards the healing of the intersubjective wounds that have been created by violation: ethical retribution. This is what we may term ethical restoration – the sort of restoration that can only be achieved by paying due regard to the values that underpin the affective bonds that hold human beings together and vindicating ethical relations of mutual recognition.

This chapter will seek to spell out the dichotomy between these two approaches by drawing on Brudner's political theory of punishment. It will proceed as follows: the first part will shed light on the idea of consent as a normative key to the justification of the state's coercive power. Under examination is, in particular, the claim that punishment is compatible with the freedom of citizens if it is consensual. The discussion will take Brudner's conception of consent as having two dimensions within the context of punishment: one the political and the other ethical. The political dimension of consent is concerned with the question of whether individuals accept the state's authority and thereby largely with an issue about political theory, while its ethical dimension inquires whether the intersubjective facet of legal punishment relates to the inner moral world of offenders. This work will claim that the ethical function of consent in Brudner's account is dominated by its political function. Thus, a consensual punishment can only provide legal restoration.

This is followed in the second part by an analysis of Brudner's conception of punishment in relation to mutual recognition. In response to crime as a form of misrecognition, punishment in Brudner's account vindicates the legal structure of mutual recognition where individuals are required to treat each other in a certain formally specified way and respect the freedom of others. But there is an ethical kind of mutual recognition that is not addressed and buttressed by legal punishment in which individuals have connection with others via solidaristic bonds on a horizontal level. In Brudner's account, restorative justice as 'ethical recognition' takes a vital and yet secondary role by complementing retributivism as 'legal recognition', with a particular focus on reparation, reconciliation and forgiveness. But it fails to redress the defects of legal retributivism, in that the ethical harms remain unrepaired. What is noteworthy is that this is acknowledged by Brudner not as an impasse of retributivism – which makes punishment bereft of moral or political explanation – but as a necessary, natural result of having a complex unified criminal justice system that respects the formal freedom of offenders. Here lies the crux of the matter: neo-classical retributivism defends a conception of punishment that is legally restorative and yet ethically impoverished.

1. Punishment, freedom and consent

Punishment is a paradoxical institution of contemporary democratic societies. It applies force to human beings and does to them what in ordinary circumstances would amount to a criminal wrong. Then, it seeks to claim that it vindicates the freedom of all, including those who are punished. But how can it uphold the freedom of offenders when it does exactly the opposite? For Brudner, it is only when punishment is 'conceived as self-imposed by the sufferer' that this paradox is resolved and that 'penal force by public officials is just punishment rather than wrongful violence'.[2] In other words, punishment is a legitimate state coercion only if offenders 'authorise their moral fate' and it becomes 'something they bring on themselves'.[3] For that to happen, Brudner thinks, there is a need for offenders to consent to what would otherwise be a violation of their rights. Thus, the only way to reconcile punishment with freedom for Brudner is to construct it as 'consensual coercion', in the sense that offenders acknowledge it as a consequence of their own will.

Resonating with other 'public law' conceptions of punishment, Brudner's theory begins in political theory.[4] It views penal sanctions as one of the central problems of state force and addresses the question of whether or how the state has a right to punish its citizens. In parallel with some of the contractual theories, it draws on the normative power of consent through which punishment is rendered a legitimate practice of the state.[5] Underlying this approach is the idea that consent is a transformative interlocutor, rendering permissible what is otherwise impermissible and wrong.[6] But Brudner's conception of consent seems to do something more. It changes the *author* of coercive treatment, in that offenders do not only grant permission to the state to punish them in cases of law violations but also somehow participate in the very act of their being punished.[7] In other words, when consented, legal punishment appears to go deep into the ethical lives of offenders, engaging with them in a such way that it becomes self-inflicted. It seems, therefore, that the function of consent in Brudner's theory is twofold: political and ethical.

2 Brudner, *Punishment and Freedom* p.2.

3 Brudner, *Punishment and Freedom* p.321.

4 See for example: Thorburn, 'Punishment and public authority'; Dubber, 'A political theory of criminal law: Autonomy and the legitimacy of state punishment'; Chiao, *Criminal Law in the Age of the Administrative State*; Ramsay, 'A democratic theory of imprisonment'.

5 Miroslav Imbrisevic, 'The consent solution to punishment and the explicit denial objection' (2010) 25 *Theoria Revista de Teoría, Historia y Fundamentos de la Ciencia* 211; Brettschneider, 'The rights of the guilty: Punishment and political legitimacy'.

6 This is in fact the fundamental feature of any type of consent, either political or moral. see for example: Heidi M Hurd, 'The normative force of consent' in Peter Schaber and Andreas Müller (eds), *The Routledge Handbook of the Ethics of Consent* (Routledge 2008).

7 A piece of etymological note: consent comes from the Latin *consentire*, literally, 'to feel together', 'the act or result of reaching an accord', and 'a concurrence of minds'. https://www.etymonline.com/word/consent.

In its political function, consent at first stroke can be understood as a principle that binds human beings to the state and establishes its legitimate authority. From this approach, punishment as a state force is compatible with freedom mainly because consent produces a political obligation to abide by the legal rules of a social agreement. By willing the sovereign into existence through a social contract, citizens have also willed to receive punishment if they break its law. In this sense, punishment is not a limitation on freedom but a kind of manifestation of it, as regulated in the original social contract.[8] Despite coming to a similar conclusion, however, this is not the route that Brudner takes.

As may be expected from one who portrays himself as a 'Hegelian through and through',[9] for Brudner, consent is not produced by an agreement by self-standing atomistic individuals in a pre-political situation. Rather, within an already established structure of social and intersubjective relations, for Brudner, consent is a moment of *political* action that is revealed and logically found in the very act of crime. In his view, crime as a denial of rights involves a normative claim that one is allowed to breach the bounds of mutual respect, somehow setting up a law that everyone is free to do whatever they want. Accordingly, crime comes with a binding self-legislated law that permits others to strike back at offenders. This means that by committing crime, offenders make themselves vulnerable to an external coercion and give the state a license to punish.[10] In other words, having left offenders in an insecure or unsafe position, the act of crime is constituted by a choice that contradicts or undermines their own freedom. In turn, Brudner argues, punishment resolves the contradiction that exists in the will of offenders and does what is implied by their crime. Punishment is, therefore, a consensual practice that derives its political ground directly from the moral meaning of criminal violation.

Strikingly, when cast this way, the political dimension of consent in Brudner's account becomes intertwined with its ethical dimension. This is to say that the normative basis for justifying state coercion (consent as a socio-political action) also sets up the ethical ground that links punishment to the moral world of offenders (consent as an ethical action). So being, consent accounts for both how punishment is permissible in a politico-juridical sense and how it preserves the moral and rational integrity of offenders in an ethical sense. Put differently, consent consists in both the achievement of personal or interpersonal freedom at the ethical level and the establishment of the political authority to punish.

8 For the contractual reading of the concept of consent in Brudner's work see: Mariana Valverde, 'Comment on Alan Brudner's punishment and freedom' (2011) 14 *New Criminal Law Review* 486, 490–491.

9 Alan Brudner, 'A reply to critics of punishment and freedom' (2011) 14 *New Criminal Law Review* 495, 501.

10 For a similar, and yet non-Hegelian version of this view see: Carlos S Nino, 'A consensual theory of punishment' (1983) 12 (4) *Philosophy & Public Affairs* 289–306.

Brudner may not agree with the term 'ethical' when describing the consent of offenders, in that he is mainly concerned with whether or not their behaviour is rationally contradictory, especially in terms of its moral and normative implications or consequences. But there is ample room to think otherwise. For what criminal violation means morally is essentially a question of ethics and moral psychology, which is concerned with how offenders come to terms with their past wrongful behaviour in a process and whether suffering is part of that process. Therefore, the work will continue to use the term 'ethical' in the following sections, arguing that Brudner's account of punishment consists of an insufficiently developed conception of consent in an ethical sense. The next section will be engaged with the question of how Brudner brings the ethical and political dimensions of consent together.

2. What does consent do?

In Brudner's account, at the core of the interface between the ethical and political dimensions of consent lies the idea of freedom. In other words, when linking the justifiability of state coercion to its ethical relation to individuals, through the idea of consent, Brudner draws on the notion of freedom. Freedom here is as much fundamental to the state's authority as to the moral and rational integrity of individuals. In this sense, it may not seem unreasonable to view the challenge to the state's authority (crime) as a self-destroying act from the perspective of offenders. It is not only an attack against the freedom of others but also the very conception of freedom that offenders enjoy and share with others within an institutionalised framework. In other words, crime can be understood as separating offenders from others with whom they are joined or rupturing the union formed by the shared value of freedom.[11]

From this conception of crime, it may also follow that punishment is a practice that is designed to restore the union shaped by mutual respect and care and actualise the freedom of all – including offenders. As such, it derives its justificatory power and origin from the moral meaning and consequence of criminal violation. Put otherwise, punishment is nothing but a manifestation of the principle that the crime is both – morally and politically – turned back on offenders. For this reason, it is a self-imposed deprivation and loss.

Instead, Brudner takes consensual punishment or self-punishment as relevant or intelligible only insofar as it derives from the logical or rational order of things in the objective normative world. Because crime is inherently self-contradictory and self-destructive in terms of placing offenders in a juridically defenceless position, it necessarily antecedes punishment in the socio-political sphere. In other words, punishment is self-triggered or self-inflicted solely in the sense that it is the logical (and political) – not moral

11 See for this political version of punishment theory: Morris, 'Guilt and suffering'.

psychological – consequence of crime.[12] Understood this way, punishment as a self-imposed injury is not the result of a sense of diremption from the social fabric or the ethical whole of which offenders are a part. It is, rather, the logical and political result of having attacked a public authority which enables the exercise of rights and freedoms for all – including the very offenders who made the attack.[13]

From this perspective, the punishing authority actualises the freedom of offenders *when it engages in punishment* because it seeks to uphold formal law under which offenders are acknowledged as free and equal. Within legalistic relations, offenders do not recognise the punishing authority as morally identical to themselves and consent to it by extension. It is, rather, sufficient that they recognise it as a political power that lays down legal-institutional preconditions for the enjoyment of their basic freedoms.[14] Accordingly, in Brudner's theory, legal punishment does not have to go deep into the ethical lives of offenders; consent remains a conceptual means that justifies the state's coercion.

Therefore, this conception of punishment may be viewed as restorative in a legal sense. It seeks to restore the normative harm done to the rule of law under which human beings are obliged to respect each other's rights reciprocally. Legal restoration is mainly engaged with the reaffirmation of a public authority which has been challenged by violations of law. It ensures that any infringement of freedom is followed by penal coercion, vindicating the state's authority. In this approach, legal punishment remedies the violation of freedom entailed by the crime and restores what Brudner calls the structure of mutual recognition. Consent seems to do the work of upholding formal relations of mutual recognition between the public authority and offenders, where the former preserves the latter's freedom, while the latter acknowledges the former as a legitimate sovereign.

The following sections will discuss the limits of Brudner's conception of recognition, but first, there is a significant point to be addressed in Brudner's account. As argued earlier, consent in Brudner establishes the basis on which legitimate mutual recognition acts as a mode of governance. But his conception of consent is not actual but hypothetical, hinging on a kind of thought experiment in which we are invited to imagine a representative of real offenders who could consent to punishment on their behalf. The representative in Brudner's theory is not an abstract rational subject but a concrete being, acting in the interests of nothing but human freedom in the social world. The next section will examine Brudner's reliance on this hypothetical agent and how it links punishment to the freedom of offenders.

12 Brudner, *Punishment and Freedom* p.318.
13 Brudner, *Punishment and Freedom* p.313.
14 Alan Brudner, *Constitutional Goods* (Oxford University Press 2007) p.20–21.

3. Consent but hypothetical

Brudner argues that almost no offenders choose to have their liberty curtailed. Even if they do (though very rarely), he claims there is no absolute leeway left to them in terms of the content and scope of their consent. In this regard, Brudner says, human beings 'cannot (normatively speaking) do anything or consent to anything inconsistent with their freedom'.[15] In other words, there is always a limit to someone's liberty to give consent. Thus, Brudner continues, 'we must put out of mind any image of a real individual empirically consenting to punishment after persuading himself of the good reasons for it'.[16] Instead, we must find a representative, what Brudner calls the 'Thinking Agent', an agent who could be accepted by the empirical individual and act on their behalf.

There must be 'a thoroughgoing identity of interests between representative and principal' so that there can be no doubt about the moral validity of the consent.[17] The representative should share the principal's human condition of finitude while being situated in the same place and time with them. But like Rawls's citizens in the original position,[18] the representative should not be aware of the principal's subjective ends and desires in a veil of ignorance. Neither should it have any particular goals or needs for itself. It should only possess an interest in freedom and 'act only for the sake of its principle's freedom', and do so without being influenced by 'the idiosyncratic frailties of the principle'.[19]

If we can imagine such a representative, Brudner thinks, we can place it in a position to consent to the punishment imposed on the actual individual irrespective of whether they consent explicitly or tacitly. In other words, whether real lawbreakers give consent to punishment is ultimately immaterial for Brudner. The fictitious self knows better the moral consequences of its consent than the actual offender while having the normative power to authorise their punishment. The assumption here is that there is a certain conception of the self that is common for all, promoting their freedom even where it appears to do the opposite. Moreover, no one in Brudner's account would object to a punishment that has been authorised by a self which can represent them and preserve their freedom. This is perhaps what we may call the 'Kantian moment' in Brudner's line of thinking: the moment where there is a split between the noumenal (the universal) and phenomenal (the actual) selves.

I doubt whether it is possible to imagine an individual stepping outside themselves, giving up the values and convictions which are part of who they are. Perhaps the very idea of abstracting from the personal characteristics of real

15 Brudner, *Punishment and Freedom* p.3.
16 Brudner, *Punishment and Freedom*.
17 Brudner, *Punishment and Freedom* p.3.
18 Rawls, *A Theory of Justice*.
19 Brudner, *Punishment and Freedom* p.4.

individuals is in itself problematic, as it requires us to ignore their needs and aspirations that are often deeply influenced by the social conditions in which they live. Even if we can imagine such a being, Ristroph argues, that person would be so abstract that it 'can do little other than think', having 'no body and hence no physical needs' and lacking 'any interest in self-preservation'.[20] It acts 'only for reasons', like an abstract ideal being in the German idealist sense. Indeed, it would never break the law in the first instance, so by its very definition, it is incapable of committing crime.[21]

There is some truth in this set of objections in terms of the gap between the actual and the ideal. But that gap, at least to a certain degree, seems to be filled by the thought that the actual and ideal agents should share 'a thoroughgoing identity of interests'. Nevertheless, it is not clear which interests the ideal person should share with the actual person for genuine representation. Brudner maintains that 'the representative possesses no interest other than an interest in independence that all agents qua agents possess and choose'.[22] This, however, does not tell us what sorts of interest independence encompasses.

It seems that what Brudner tries to frame is an actualised version of the ideal representative or an idealised version of the empirical individual. It is finite, like the empirical, and so is capable of making mistakes and criminal wrongdoing. But it cannot commit the crime that the empirical individual commits, as it is not subject to the same forms of moral weakness. This looks like a complete contradiction.

It may arguably be more desirable to have an imaginary being that can be as concrete as possible when acting for actual individuals. That said, the more concrete the imaginary agent, the less comprehensively it covers different sorts of actual people. Every person has their own fragility and so should be represented by a being who avoids a fall into that particular fragility. But because the imaginary person should be a proxy for all, it should not lean into any sort of weakness. To represent all, in other words, Brudner's imaginary being must overcome any human flaws or imperfections and necessarily become an ideal person who makes no mistake or does no wrong. On the other hand, to represent particular individuals or become their 'reasonable' versions, it must have the same interests as them.

Put differently, the imaginary person must be so abstract and ideal that it never wrongs, and at the same time it must be concrete and actual enough that it can represent real human beings. Both features may be desired and necessary for a normative theory of punishment, but they inhabit ontologically distinct worlds, and never the twain shall meet. As a result, all of this moves us to suspect that Brudner's thinking agent either can never exist or is theoretically

20 Alice Ristroph, 'Just violence' (2014) 56 *Arizona Law Review* 1017, 1046.

21 For the same criticism against similar sort of idealistic retributive theory of Kant see: Norrie, *Law, Ideology and Punishment.*

22 Brudner, *Punishment and Freedom* p.4.

unfit for purpose. In either case, it does not stand in a position to give consent to state coercion on behalf of actual individuals.

To conclude, I am dubious whether Brudner needs to draw on a hypothetical or representative agent to 'extract' consent from actual individuals. After all, consent in his theory seems already given under the structure of mutual recognition, a reciprocally formed socio-political organisation of which individuals are necessarily a part. That is, punishment is consensual because the normative regime in which it is exercised is consensual or because mutually recognised laws are consensual. The discussion will now move to the idea of punishment as legal recognition, an idea that is necessary and yet ethically insufficient and which often blocks us from exploring the limits of legal intervention and better structures of recognition in the socio-political realm.

4. Punishment as recognition: legal and ethical restoration

As stated earlier, punishment in Brudner's theory can be seen as a legitimate public practice that is designed to uphold the normative framework of legal and citizen relations. It affirms the institutionalised structure of recognition, under which everyone is respected as legal persons having certain rights and freedoms. This function of punishment is restorative in a formal sense, where the violation of legal relationship of recognition is addressed and redressed with an emphasis on the idea that the shared value of freedom should be upheld.

Yet punishment in legal relations of recognition is vindicative and restorative only of a formal and an abstract kind of freedom, the kind of freedom defined in terms of whether individuals possess rights and civic duties. In this light, one's freedom is backed up by punishment only insofar as it is understood as having an ability to live a 'juridical' life, shaped by rights and obligations. With its exclusive focus on the idea of individuals as responsible legal subjects, punishment is indifferent to the question of whether existing social interactions engender freedom equally for everyone. It adopts a single lens that is concerned only with whether someone's behaviour is a violation of due recognition that occurs in the legal realm. The presumption is that there is an already established structure of human relations based on reciprocal respect, in which everyone is treated as equal free beings.

There is, however, a more substantial kind of freedom that is not backed up by legal punishment, one that is enjoyed by individuals within ethically satisfactory relationships, shaped by an affective and solidaristic form of mutual recognition. In this type of recognition, what is at work is a conception of freedom enabled by a social world in which individuals are sufficiently recognised such that they are unified with others in a flourishing manner. Here the legality of freedom is replaced by a more robust conception, where individuals are taken as free only when they can equally contribute to both the economic and legal-political reproduction of the social world, or when they live in a world shaped by social cooperation and reciprocal care and love.

That is, ethical recognition demands more than the formal legal kind, seeing individuals as those being dependent on others, bound not by formal ties but by intersubjective ethical ties.

Thus, derived from two distinct forms of mutual recognition, there are two kinds of freedom that need to be upheld when dealing with violations of law. The first kind of freedom is concerned with individuals as legal subjects having certain rights and duties under the governance of a political sovereign, while the second kind views individuals as socio-ethical beings existing in connection and solidarity with others within the horizontal space of intersubjective relations.[23] In his overall theory of criminal justice, Brudner identifies the limitations of the formal approach while also complementing it with a more demanding form of mutual recognition, which he associates with the restorative justice paradigm. But, unlike my dual approach, Brudner locates it within a tripartite model, where the notion of freedom is at the centre, being developed in a progressive way at three phases, in each of which a different conception of punishment is produced. Broadly speaking, his first two conceptions of freedom (formal freedom and real autonomy) are protected by what might be considered legal relations of mutual recognition, while the third conception (freedom as communal solidarity) is supported by ethical relations of recognition. What follows is an elaboration of how Brudner develops his conceptions of freedom and punishment under the threefold structure of mutual recognition.

5. Three shades of freedom and punishment

Brudner starts his analysis of freedom with its common parlance. Freedom in everyday discourse is usually associated with an absence of obstacles, barriers, constraints or interference from others. In this sense, it is often characterized as a 'freedom *from*' something, rather than a 'freedom *to*' do something. Simply put, one is free to the extent that one's choices to act are not limited by others. Behind this 'common sense' and 'the most basic liberal' understanding lies the idea that individuals should be able to make choices freely, and pursue their desires and goals without interference from external coercion. In other words, they should have the right to act as they choose so long as they do not infringe on the freedom of others. In contemporary political philosophy, this kind of freedom is typically identified with a libertarian approach, where individuals are conceived as self-supporting and detached from all the social relationships in which they find themselves.[24] Because of the emphasis on the principle of non-interference, it is usually termed as 'negative freedom' or

23 The second kind of freedom I propose is similar to what Axel Honneth calls social freedom, the sort of freedom that overcomes legal freedom and can only be found in intersubjective relations of mutual recognition. Axel Honneth, *Three, Not Two, Concepts of Liberty* (Dewey Lectures 2014).

24 Nozick, *Anarchy, State and Utopia*; Friedrich August Hayek, *The Constitution of Liberty: The Definitive Edition* (Routledge 2020).

'negative liberty'.[25] In Brudner's account, it is described as *formal freedom* or *the libertarian paradigm*.[26]

Formal freedom provides a fundamental basis for individuals to pursue their own goals and interests. Without it, individuals are prone to the coercion of others. In turn, according to the formalist paradigm, the law should primarily be adjusted to protect individuals from 'pre-emption, interference, or destruction by the action of another'.[27] Where one intentionally intervenes with another's liberty (by committing crime), one negates the most basic form of freedom another enjoys. For this reason, Brudner thinks, we should negate this negation of freedom by punishing the offender. In other words, if there is a clear right denial and challenge to the order that guarantees formal freedom, we should deny that denial with punishment. Expressed in a retributive logic, punishment in the formal paradigm is portrayed as a reactive practice following the criminal's choice to violate another, and one that upholds freedom.[28] When Brudner argues that punishment upholds freedom, by that he means formal freedom.

Brudner continues his analysis to argue that freedom in the formalist paradigm is provided in a very thin sense, concerned only with whether atomistic individuals are not free from external interferences. It is, thus, inherently abstract and incomplete. It should be completed by a richer conception of freedom that is concerned not only with whether individuals' choices are set back but with whether they have the power to lead their life without being shaped by those other than their own rational faculty. Individuals are free, in this conception, only if they act from self-authored ends while also being sheltered from an unlimited vulnerability to external forces. In order to realise their freedom more effectively, individuals should be provided not only with free choices but also with agency goods, such as physical health, bodily integrity, property or in general 'laws and public services ordered to health, safety and insurance against misfortune'.[29] This is the kind of freedom that is commonly associated with egalitarianism, where individuals are portrayed as equals, having the same rights and opportunities, irrespective of their gender, race, religion, social class or any other characteristic.[30] Favouring the equal treatment of all citizens and emphasising the (positive) duty of the state to promote equality, it is usually

25 Isaiah Berlin, 'Two concepts of liberty' in I. Berlin (ed), *Four Essays on Liberty* (Oxford University Press 1969).

26 Brudner, *Punishment and Freedom*; Brudner, *Constitutional Goods*; Alan Brudner, 'The evolution of authority' in Patrick Capps and Henrik Palmer Olsen (eds), *Legal Authority Beyond the State* (Cambridge University Press 2018).

27 Brudner, *Punishment and Freedom* p.3.

28 Brudner, *Punishment and Freedom*.

29 Brudner, *Punishment and Freedom* p.138.

30 Ronald Dworkin, *Sovereign Virtue: The Theory and Practice of Equality* (Harvard University Press 2000); John Rawls, *Political Liberalism* (Columbia University Press 2005).

termed positive freedom' or 'positive liberty'.[31] In Brudner's account, it is termed as 'real autonomy' or the 'egalitarian paradigm'.[32]

The autonomy paradigm sets up its own constraints on state coercion. It is concerned with protecting the welfare of others with a less strict set of conditions on the justifiability of penal force than pure retributivism. Punishment is compatible with freedom as real autonomy, 'only if it is a fate within the agent's power to avoid and only if it is tied to outcomes of its action the reasonable agent could have foreseen'.[33] Within the sphere of public welfare offences, where crime is seen as setting back others' welfare, the legitimacy of penal sanctions consists in a consequentialist philosophy. 'Their purpose', Brudner says, is 'to deter with threats of disadvantage breaches of statutes that regulate the pursuit of satisfactions or that protect an agency good'.[34]

This does not mean, however, that desert plays no role in the justification of penal sanctions. The autonomy paradigm incorporates 'all the protections against coercion generated by the formalist paradigm within its more expansive guarantees', including desert and proportionality.[35] The principle of desert is, therefore, intertwined with the goal of protecting public welfare. This is what is usually called in the literature 'negative retributivism', where the main idea is that it is impermissible to punish offenders who do not deserve it.[36] Desert does not provide a positive reason for punishment in negative retributivism, but it only sets a limit to it.[37] Notice that retributivism takes a more complex form, with its emphasis on the protection of welfare. But there comes a contradiction between the idea of giving just deserts and the aim of preserving public welfare, one being retributivist and the other consequentialist.

The first two conceptions of freedom and punishment are based on what may be termed 'legal relations of mutual recognition', which carry within themselves an internal tension. In the third phase, this tension is resolved by a conception of freedom defined by the principle of intersubjective solidarity.[38] In this communal solidarity paradigm, human beings as citizens willingly act in accordance with the moral norms of the community, the norms they choose for themselves for the sake of a good life. The freedom of human beings in this conception is provided and reinforced by a sense of unity between themselves

31 Berlin, 'Two concepts of liberty'.

32 Brudner, *Punishment and Freedom*; Brudner, *Constitutional Goods.*

33 Brudner, *Punishment and Freedom* p.6.

34 Brudner, *Punishment and Freedom* p.317.

35 Brudner, *Punishment and Freedom* p.301.

36 Richard L Lippke, 'Some surprising implications of negative retributivism' (2014) 31 *Journal of Applied Philosophy* 49.

37 For some, it is not unlikely that the desert element in public welfare offences can be so strong that they can be punished from a retributive perspective, see: Dudley Knowles, 'Alan Brudner, punishment and freedom' (2012) 3 *Jurisprudence* 229 and Douglas Husak, *Punishment and Freedom: A Liberal Theory of Penal Justice,* trans. by A. Brudner, vol. 120, no. 4 (The University of Chicago Press 2010).

38 Brudner, 'The evolution of authority' p.45; Brudner, *Punishment and Freedom* p.307.

and the community: social freedom. In various roles they occupy, such as parent, job holder and citizen, they accept political authority without loss to their independence by synthesising the common good with their individual agency. Punishment in this framework becomes a coercion that is good not only for the state as a political authority but also for the stakeholders who have been affected by crime – including those who are punished. They benefit, in particular, from the possibility of reinterpreting and actualising the solidarity of the community.[39]

This conception of freedom generates what we call today 'restorative justice', where the aim of punishment is to repair the harms caused by criminal violation in a setting where individuals are given the opportunity for repentance, restitution and forgiveness. Punishment in freedom as communal solidarity is geared towards reintegrating offenders into intersubjective relations and reconciliation with their victims and the political community.[40] With a specific focus on the bonds that glue together the community, restorative punishment also seeks to repair the community's integrity as a moral unit. It does not simply give a deserved response to criminal violation (retribution); neither does it only aim to minimise crime (utilitarianism). It does both by reconciling offenders with the victim and community so that a wholeness reappears in the community's holistic existence. In this sense, it is more constructive and comprehensive than the other conceptions of punishment.

6. Dialogic community: a synthesis of legal and ethical recognition

From this picture, we realise that the conceptions of freedom and punishment become increasingly complicated, progressing from formal agency to communal solidarity. Within restorative justice, freedom becomes the successor of the previous two conceptions, while being richer and more concrete than the others. It redresses the defects of formal recognition and provides an ethical kind of recognition in which individuals feel 'at home' with themselves in the other.

It is noteworthy that ethical recognition as proposed in this work – as opposed to legal recognition – has much in common with the sort of ethical recognition Brudner's restorative justice proposes, in terms of the emphasis placed upon the ideas of solidarity and intersubjective relations, and the need for a more substantial kind of restoration. Nevertheless, this work's conception of ethical recognition differs from Brudner's restorative justice in that it draws

39 Brudner, *Punishment and Freedom* p.308.

40 Brudner, *Punishment and Freedom* p.307–313. Brudner is notoriously vague about whether restorative justice advocates punishment. At some places in *Punishment and Freedom*, he draws on the term 'penal force' when describing restorative justice while at another point, he claims that 'the central institution of restorative justice is not punishment but the meeting.'

a distinction between mutual intersubjectivity and the community. Although it acknowledges that the community may provide an ethical foundation for intersubjective freedom, it presents it as a dynamic set of social interactions that are prone to producing unbalanced power relations, as well as horizontal, equal relationships between individuals. In other words, this work's conception of ethical recognition does not rely on an understanding of community that necessarily leads to satisfactory forms of intersubjectivity. In this sense, the addressing of a criminal wrong in ethical recognition is not simply a process that is oriented to restore the ruptured unity of a community. Rather, it involves an attempt to *reconstruct* or *renew* the broken ties of intersubjectivity by paying due justice to the structural deficiencies in communal relations.

That said, with the central values of constructive cooperation and solidarity, restorative justice in Brudner's theory can still be seen as providing an ethical form of recognition in which the freedom of individuals takes its most developed form. Does this mean that restorative justice provides the highest and most complete form of freedom and that the ethical form of recognition should overcome the formal one, even though it may not always actually be reachable in current socio-political conditions?

Surprisingly, Brudner thinks that no conception of freedom is superior to another. Each conception is on the same level, supporting one another where the other lacks something significant. Formal agency, for example, protects human beings against interferences with their freedom, but it does not protect them against vulnerability to causal chains, initiated by a culpable wrong, which are beyond their power to foresee and control. In Brudner's view, there is a need for the real autonomy framework. But this does not mean that the autonomy paradigm replaces formal agency as a higher framework, since it cannot 'provide on its own what formalism contributes: an immovable desert-based constraint on punishment for crimes'.[41] Certainly, the autonomy paradigm in Brudner also involves the idea of desert, but it plays a marginal role. More significantly, because desert does not figure in the justification of punishment, the autonomy paradigm for Brudner is prone to treat human beings as a means to the end of public protection. Thus, the idea of desert is key to any understanding of punishment that respects individual freedom.

In a similar vein, the formalist paradigm would justify punishment only in a metaphysical sense, not in a real sense, if those who are punished do not actually reconcile with their victim and community. It should integrate restorative institutions so that real offenders can be educated to the standpoint of their representative who gives consent to punishment. But in Brudner's account, this does not lead us to think that communal solidarity provides an adequate conception of punishment. 'Where justice is exclusively restorative',

41 Brudner, *Punishment and Freedom* p.58; Here is perhaps where Brudner's account shares the very same solid ground as Duff's communicative theory, in which desert is an irreducible element in establishing the justification of punishment.

says Brudner, 'there are no justice constraints on the term or manner of expulsion when restoration fails. Within restorative justice, punishment is constrained by what is necessary to restore. Outside that process, there are no limits'.[42] Punishment reflects either the victim's input or is imposed by the offended community, rather than by an impartial judge.

On the other hand, the principle to restore in the communal solidarity paradigm is so central and overwhelming that there is no room left for offenders to disagree with the punishment that has been given as a burden to reconcile with their fellow members. In other words, the penal system would not respect recalcitrant or unrepentant offenders as having an independent agency if it is exclusively driven by restorative justice. Offenders are 'expected to confess guilt' from their heart in supplication of acceptance or else suffer penal coercion. In Brudner's words, 'the subject recognizes the civic body as an end, but the civic body does not recognize the discrete person as an end'.[43] Accordingly, the free agency of offenders as outsiders is completely effaced in the restorative justice in contrast to the formal paradigm (legal retributivism) where punishment respects at least a basic kind of freedom.[44]

For Brudner, all of this suggests that no paradigm on its own can provide conditions sufficient to distinguish official force from arbitrary violence. Each leaves a normative gap that can only be supplemented by the other paradigms. Forming a 'federation' together, they draw a consistent and holistic picture of what he calls 'dialogic community'. Despite the misleading connotations it arouses, 'dialogic community' is a term used for the state. It is clearly separated from the notion of community that is shaped by communal solidarity. Dialogic community may involve or subsume the idea of community, but it is more than that, giving us an ideal image of the state mediating and organising the contrasting demands of each conception of freedom.

Accordingly, in Brudner's view, the state provides an internally differentiated and multivocal ethical order, an order shaped by both relations of legal and ethical recognition. In that order, every conception of freedom has a certain role to play while being followed by a certain theory of punishment. Where formal freedom is infringed, for example, retributive punishment comes into play to restore the normative legal harm caused by crime and reaffirm formal relations of mutual recognition. But where the requirements of ethical recognition are not met and there are unrepaired harms left, restorative justice must supplement legal retributivism. Similarly, where freedom as communal solidarity is violated, restorative justice functions to bring about reconciliation and unity in the community. But without retributive principles of legal recognition (desert and proportionality), restorative justice is perilously close to becoming an unjust intrusive criminal justice paradigm. Every theory of

42 Brudner, *Punishment and Freedom* p.310.
43 Brudner, 'The evolution of authority' p.45.
44 Brudner, *Punishment and Freedom* p.311.

punishment has, therefore, something valuable to preserve the complex fusion of legal and ethical mutual recognition when violated by harmful wrongs.

7. Caught between legal restoration and ethical restoration: revised retributivism

Be that as it may, there remain serious doubts about whether the conjunction of the legal and ethical approaches provide a consistent and coherent unity or synthesis. Different conceptions of freedom and punishment are often in a competition both theoretically and practically, trying to overtake each other.[45] In practice, from the second half of the twentieth century, for example, punishment took an instrumentalist role in light of crime prevention objectives in the Anglo-American world, while after 1970 it became influenced largely by retributivism.[46] In that period, the values and principles of restorative justice were hardly recognised, let alone understood and implemented. Within the same world, criminal justice policies at present seem to be made up of a tangled mixture of retributive, utilitarian and restorative conceptions of punishment where the idea of unity seems to be the last thing to characterise penal practices of the states in question.

This is not because criminal justice systems are constructed in a disorderly way, being an insufficient implementation of what Brudner calls 'dialogic community'. In other words, the disunity or contradictions in the principles of penal systems do not exist because one theoretical position takes a much more dominant position than it should be. Rather, these contradictions are because there has been a somehow constantly changing weight placed upon different conceptions of punishment, depending on the historical and socio-political contexts. Every period comes with its own moral demands while being supported by a particular political outlook. This shows that the relationship between different conceptions of freedom and punishment is historical and quite contingent and far from giving us a unified and ideal picture of criminal justice.[47]

On the other hand, there is also an inherent theoretical conflict between different conceptions of punishment that undermine each other's place within the criminal justice complex. While retributive justice views desert and the reaffirmation of legal freedom as sufficient for the legitimacy of state punishment, restorative justice with its emphasis on solidarity stands against it by seeking reparation, reconciliation, and forgiveness. Within this antagonistic

45 This is most visible in the history of human rights, from civil rights to social rights. See: Ramsay, 'The dialogic community at dusk'.

46 Adnan Sattar, 'Neo-retributivism in the embrace of human rights' (2016) 30 *Socialism and Democracy* 55.

47 Shai Lavi, 'Justice, plurality, and criminal law: A review of Alan Brudner's punishment and freedom: A liberal theory of penal law' (2011) 14 *New Criminal Law Review: An International and Interdisciplinary Journal* 439, 445.

relationship, retributive punishment is generally prioritised and seen as justified, as it restores legal harm caused by criminal behaviour, regardless of whether it achieves restoration in an ethical sense. In fact, as Brudner acknowledges, when not supported by a restorative approach, retributive justice 'leaves physical people with little solace'.[48] So being, punishment remains peculiarly 'metaphysical'. Yet, he also argues, 'this is not an argument for dismantling the system justified by metaphysics, but for educating real criminals to the social basis of the worth they seek in isolation'.[49]

Inherent in this claim is the acknowledgement that offenders feel 'isolated from' their fellow citizens and the socio-political system in which they live. They feel worthless and seek recognition and respect. There is, thus, at least, a 'felt' sense of social injustice that befalls many offenders who resist seeing any justice done by legal punishment. In fact, Brudner goes further than this, accepting that 'it is very probably true that social injustice engenders crime'.[50] Confronting the old and notorious problem of 'doing justice in an unjust society', he comes to admit that this problem remains unresolved within a retributive paradigm, and needs to be addressed and redressed by restorative justice.

That said, despite identifying the criminogenic effects of structural injustices or vulnerabilities, Brudner does not think of social injustice as a 'wrong' that justifies or excuses legal wrong (crime), or as a form of misrecognition that calls into question the idea of punishment as legal recognition. In other words, for him, social injustice cannot be seen as an element that absolves offenders of criminal liability or deserved punishment. The denial of rights in crime, unlike systemic injustices, is universal or absolute, attacking the very idea of freedom that sets the basis for all freedoms. Thus, retributive justice as a means of protecting 'formal freedom', that is, the most basic kind of freedom, must precede restorative justice, the sort of justice that seeks to uphold 'social freedom'.

Restorative justice as a form of 'criminal justice' would seem extremely unsuited to addressing the root causes of social inequalities or injustices that generate crime. Additionally, a deeper problem with this hierarchical mode of thinking is that retributive justice demands offenders to respect the freedom of others in a social context, in which their own freedom is hardly realised. In other words, offenders are held responsible and punished under the terms of legal relations of mutual recognition, where normative guarantees are provided. But this is done in the absence of reciprocal recognition at an intersubjective level, where social guarantees are insufficiently available. Understood this way, punishment may lead to legal restoration, in the sense that it reasserts the inalienable priority of formal freedom. But, by causing

48 Brudner, *Punishment and Freedom* p.324.
49 Brudner, *Punishment and Freedom* p.323.
50 Brudner, *Punishment and Freedom* p.324.

stigma, family break-ups or social isolation, any penal intervention is also likely to come with new injustices, vulnerabilities or forms of misrecognition that not only exacerbate already broken ties of intersubjectivity but also undermine legal relations of recognition.

To sum up, what is most crucial for Brudner is to restore the normative harm inflicted on legal relations in cases of criminal violation. In other words, punishment should, first and foremost, address the harm that undermines the legal base on which individuals realise their most basic kinds of freedom. Without a vertically structured type of legal ordering, in which punishment is appointed as a gatekeeper, freedom as solidarity or social freedom cannot be achieved, and it is rightly deemed to be secondary or subordinate to the mainstream justice paradigm.

The tenability of Brudner's hierarchical model has been discussed throughout this work; to conclude, this section will briefly rehearse what this means in terms of the two modes of restoration. From a political point of view, retributive punishment is restorative of formal legal relations in which individuals are linked to each other by the normative regime of mutual recognition. As is made clear by Brudner's account of criminal justice, it is also likely that punishment is restorative of intersubjective ethical relations (restorative justice), where individuals are connected to each other by the affective solidaristic bonds of mutual recognition. Indeed, the abstraction of the legal model demands it to be supplemented by the terms of an ethical approach. In other words, there has to be a space for ethical retribution that arises from within legal relations of mutual recognition. Nevertheless, being firmly rooted in a normative realm in which legal freedom is taken to be the exclusive value, retributive punishment is considerably limited and impoverished, while its restorative supplement is both necessary and marginal.

Conclusion

By visiting Brudner's complex account of criminal justice, this chapter took seriously the idea of punishment as 'state coercion'. It looked at the political conception of punishment in particular in light of the claim that penal power can be reconciled with the moral inviolability of individuals if it is consented by them. Having examined Brudner's concept of consent in its ethical and political dimensions, it presented legal punishment as a practice that is mainly to do with a relationship between the state and its citizens. In this sense, punishment in Brudner's account is portrayed as a response that restores the normative political order that makes collective life possible. At the centre of his account lies the premise that judicial sanctions can reassert both legal and ethical relations of mutual recognition.

At the legalistic level, retributive punishment is a consensual public practice that reaffirms the sovereign's right to rule in face of its denial. At stake here is the restoration of the vertical organisation of political relations that has been breached by crime. But, as discussed throughout the chapter, it is not clear whether retributive punishment as public force can attend to the harms inflicted on the horizontal relations of intersubjectivity. In fact, it may even aggravate the ruptures in the already fragile social relationships.

In his account, Brudner seeks to make up the moral defects of legal retributivism by drawing on restorative justice, where crime and its correction are driven by the principle of solidarity, oriented towards the identification of moral injuries done to ethical intersubjectivity. But Brudner thinks that restorative justice can only fill in the gaps that retributivism leaves and cannot take a central role in the construction of criminal justice. This is to mean that legal retributivism is open to being revised and developed by a conception of penal justice that is to be in service of ethical relations of recognition – in other words, lacking in attention to the goals of substantial reconciliation and ethical restoration, retributivism acknowledges its moral incompleteness. Nevertheless, it finds itself legally sufficient and remains located in the formal approach.

By employing the idea of restoration as both an interpretative and a reconstructive tool, so far this work has given a dichotomous view of retributivism in relation to the three stakeholders: the victim, offender and state. It has provided an extensive analysis of neo-retributive theories, in particular around the question of how they are framed by the synthetic approach. It has not, however, addressed the question of whether neo-retributivism is intrinsically poorly suited to provide ethical restoration. In the next chapter, through an analysis of Murphy's works, this work's position in relation to neo-classical retributivism will be clarified in order to convey the tension between legal justice and loving ethics. Engaging with recent critical criminal justice scholarship, it will then be followed by the question of whether it is possible to reconcile legal and ethical approaches.

Bibliography

Berlin I, 'Two concepts of liberty' in Berlin I (ed), *Four Essays on Liberty* (OUP 1969)

Brudner A, *Constitutional Goods* (OUP 2007)

Brudner A, 'The contraction of crime in hegel's rechtsphilosophie' in Dubber MD (ed), *Foundational Texts in Modern Criminal Law* (OUP 2014)

Brudner A, 'The evolution of authority' in Capps P and Olsen HP (eds), *Legal Authority Beyond the State* (Cambridge University Press 2018)

Brudner A, *Punishment and Freedom* (OUP 2009)

Brudner A, 'A reply to critics of punishment and freedom' (2011) 14 *New Criminal Law Review* 495

Chiao V, *Criminal Law in the Age of the Administrative State* (OUP 2018)

Dubber MD, 'A political theory of criminal law: autonomy and the legitimacy of state punishment' (2004) <https://ssrncom/abstract=529522 or http://dxdoiorg/102139/ssrn529522>

Dworkin R, *Sovereign Virtue: The Theory and Practice of Equality* (Harvard University Press 2000)

Flanders C, 'Political philosophy and punishment' in Ferzan LAK (ed), *The Palgrave Handbook of Applied Ethics and the Criminal Law* (Springer 2019)

Fletcher GP, 'Political theory and criminal law' (2006) 25(1) *Criminal Justice Ethics* 18
Honneth A, *Three, Not Two, Concepts of Liberty* (Dewey Lectures 2014)
Hurd HM, 'The normative force of consent' in Schaber P and Müller A (eds), *The Routledge Handbook of the Ethics of Consent* (Routledge 2008)
Husak D, *Punishment and Freedom: A Liberal Theory of Penal Justice.* Translate by Brudner A, vol. 120, no. 4 (University of Chicago Press 2010)
Imbrisevic M, 'The consent solution to punishment and the explicit denial objection' (2010) 25 *Theoria Revista de Teoría, Historia y Fundamentos de la Ciencia* 211 Brettschneider, 'The rights of the guilty: punishment and political legitimacy'
Knowles D, 'Alan Brudner, punishment and freedom' (2012) 3 *Jurisprudence* 229
Lacey N and Pickard H, 'Why standing to blame may be lost but authority to hold accountable retained: criminal law as a regulative public institution' (2021) 104 *The Monist* 265
Lavi S, 'Justice, plurality, and criminal law: a review of alan brudner's punishment and freedom: a liberal theory of penal law' (2011) 14 *New Criminal Law Review: An International and Interdisciplinary Journal* 439
Lippke R L, 'Some surprising implications of negative retributivism' (2014) 31 *Journal of Applied Philosophy* 49
Morris H, 'Guilt and suffering' (1971) 21 *Philosophy East and West* 419
Nino CS, 'A consensual theory of punishment' (1983) 12(4) *Philosophy & Public Affairs* 289–306
Norrie A, *Law, Ideology and Punishment* (Springer 1991)
Nozick R, *Anarchy, State and Utopia; Friedrich August Hayek, The Constitution of Liberty: The Definitive Edition* (Routledge 2020)
Ramsay P, 'A democratic theory of imprisonment' in Dzur AW, Loader I and Sparks R (eds), *Democratic Theory and Mass Incarceration* (OUP 2016)
Ramsay P, 'The dialogic community at dusk' (2014) 1 *Critical Analysis of Law* 2291–9732
Rawls J, *Political Liberalism* (Columbia University Press 2005)
Rawls J, *A Theory of Justice* (Harvard University Press 2009)
Ristroph A, 'Just violence' (2014) 56 *Arizona Law Review* 1017, 1046
Sattar A, 'Neo-retributivism in the embrace of human rights' (2016) 30 *Socialism and Democracy* 55
Thorburn M, 'Punishment and public authority' in Antje du Bois-Pedain MUaPA (ed), *Criminal Law and the Authority of the State* (Hart Publishing 2017)
Valverde M, 'Comment on Alan Brudner's punishment and freedom' (2011) 14 *New Criminal Law Review* 486

Part IV

Beyond impasse

7 Seeking a shared ground

Between loving ethics and legal justice

Introduction

Bringing to light the origins of contemporary retributive thoughts through Hegel, and analysing them from the perspectives of the victim, offender and state, this book has so far addressed the question of how punishment is restorative in two senses: the legal and the ethical. It has provided a framework for a critical approach to an important strand in modern punishment theory, by exploring an ethical terrain that hitherto has not been sufficiently brought out. It has argued that neo-classical retributivism is rightly and yet incompletely informed by a restorative perspective, that places the ethical experiences of human beings at its centre. In other words, this book has shown that the legalistic paradigm in neo-classical retributivism is enriched by the ethical paradigm and yet not fully reconciled with it. This is, as discussed in detail in Part III, due to the ongoing contradiction between the two paradigms – a theoretical impasse.

In this chapter, exploring Lacey and Pickard's therapeutic theory of punishment, and Norrie's account of mature retributivism, I will argue that there are two ways to overcome that impasse. The first, as articulated by Lacey and Pickard, is 'radical reformism', a strategy that suggests a way forward beyond the old themes of desert and pay-back, without abandoning the core idea of free individual agency. Radical reformism does not debunk the (legalistic) punishment paradigm; it seeks to radically change it. For them, we could create penal practices that punish and forgive offenders at the same time, while also providing healing for victims through a dual-track system designed to meet their distinct needs. The second, as developed by Alan Norrie, is a 'radical reconstructive' strategy that introduces a moral psychological account, and develops an ethic to transform the standard criminal justice thinking. Keeping its distance from law in a distinctive way, radical reconstruction, unlike radical reformism, is sharper in its critical tone. It is ultimately in favour of penal abolition though it does not necessarily entail the immediate shutdown of prisons.

In this first two sections, I will argue that both critical accounts of Lacey and Pickard, and Norrie are based on a framework of 'loving justice' through

DOI: 10.4324/9781003563150-12

which we could overcome the impasse in neo-retributivism. However, there is also a tension—though not a contradiction—within the idea of loving justice, between penal reform and abolition, a tension that may not be resolvable. I will address this tension in the last section, concluding that we should maintain it and adopt an ambivalent position between penal reform and abolition in particular to gain a better understanding of current carceral reforms.

1. Radical reformism: therapeutic theory of punishment

Nicola Lacey, in collaboration with Hanna Pickard, recently produced a series of articles that take seriously the fundamental tenets of legal retributivism, with the emphasis on the offender's capacity for responsible agency, and offer a non-desert model that detaches punishment from the components of hard treatment and stigma, and attaches it to a compassionate legal intervention. At the core of the proposed model lies a clinical or therapeutic vision that punishment can be practiced in a way that holds offenders accountable in response to blameworthiness for criminal conduct, while also imposing 'negative consequences' on them with 'an attitude of concern, respect and compassion'.[1] As with the clinical practice's caring ethos, where we demand of patients to 'change patterns of actions and omissions' in order to improve or recover without losing sight of the adverse circumstances that stand in the way of change, punishment can be practised in a therapeutic manner.[2] That is, we can marry the goals of rehabilitation and reform to the interests of justice, by designing institutions and practices that hold offenders responsible in a restorative way, without sliding back into punitiveness.

When understood this way, according to this new model, punishment can also be viewed as an institutionalised form of forgiving, not blaming. In this approach, we can punish and forgive offenders at the same time, 'not on behalf or in place of victims, but in its own right'.[3] By visiting negative and yet constructive consequences upon offenders without vengeance and affective blame, we can move away from unacceptably harsh retributive practices and towards legal interventions that 'embody reparative and corresponding risk-reduction strategies'.[4] Note, however, that even if the idea of punishing with forgiveness is 'allied with' restorative justice in general terms, it is more pragmatic and realistic, 'suggesting how we can potentially shift cultural attitudes and reconfigure elements of existing criminal justice theory and

1 Lacey and Pickard, 'From the consulting room to the court room? Taking the clinical model of responsibility without blame into the legal realm' p.10.

2 Lacey and Pickard, 'From the consulting room to the court room? Taking the clinical model of responsibility without blame into the legal realm' p.16.

3 Lacey and Pickard, 'To blame or to forgive? Reconciling punishment and forgiveness in criminal justice' p.677 fn.38

4 Lacey and Pickard, 'To blame or to forgive? Reconciling punishment and forgiveness in criminal justice' p.668.

practice, broadly speaking within the confines of the current system'.[5] By doing so, it not only preserves the ongoing relationship between offenders and the community; it also re-establishes 'the perceived value of that relationship' to them.[6]

Lacey and Pickard suggest that where punishment is practiced within a single offender-oriented process, justice for victims might wrongly be equated with the idea of infliction of suffering or placing demands on offenders for their criminal wrongdoing. Yet, there are a wide variety of needs that victims have, moving beyond the desire to see the conviction and punishment of offenders, or their being held accountable.[7] Some of them, like compensation, assistance in testifying, or offering opinions on sentencing, are directly justice related, concerning the way victims relate to the world in a normative sense. Others, however, such as having an opportunity to have a voice and to give expression, are more to do with the welfare and emotional recovery of victims. Because of the complex and distinct needs of victims, therefore, we need to create 'a victim-oriented track that runs separately from but parallel to the track for offenders'.[8] The victim-oriented process, alongside the offender-centric procedure, stands to address the wrongs done to victims within a validating and caring environment that is safe and supportive, in order to make 'a genuine difference to their wellbeing'.[9]

With its dual process approach, the therapeutic model offers a more regulatory and non-moralistic enterprise of criminal justice, in which the state's welfarist image is recognisably visible in practices of penal sanctions and services dedicated to supporting victims of crime.[10] In this sense, the justice system in this model is a 'horizontally constructed' public institution that communicates with both direct stakeholders (the victim and offender) out of compassion and love. Its central function is not to condemn those who do moral wrongs from top to down, and show solidarity with victims by inflicting pain on offenders. Rather, it is to hold offenders responsible with a forgiving disposition and do justice to victims – without conflating their interests and needs.[11] Behind the welfarist aspirations of the state in legal interventions also lies a more central

5 Lacey and Pickard, 'To blame or to forgive? Reconciling punishment and forgiveness in criminal justice'.

6 Lacey and Pickard, 'To blame or to forgive? Reconciling punishment and forgiveness in criminal justice' p.681.

7 Lacey and Pickard, 'A dual-process approach to criminal law: Victims and the clinical model of responsibility without blame'.

8 Lacey and Pickard, 'A dual-process approach to criminal law: Victims and the clinical model of responsibility without blame'.

9 Lacey and Pickard, 'A dual-process approach to criminal law: Victims and the clinical model of responsibility without blame' p.15.

10 Lacey and Pickard, 'Why standing to blame may be lost but authority to hold accountable retained: criminal law as a regulative public institution'.

11 Nicola Lacey, 'Institutionalising forgiveness in criminal justice' LSE Law, Society and Economy Working Papers 1/2024 p.8.

and pervasive aim of 'reducing harm and upholding approved legal standards protecting the public against harm'.[12] Understood this way, punishment is at bottom a political practice that reaffirms the authority's right to preserve civil order and sustain social cooperation, as well as to set the conditions for the flourishing of individual members.

It is significant to note that the therapeutic model does not advocate the abolition of legal punishment. Rather, it suggests reconceptualising it in different terms, with an understanding of criminal responsibility that involves the imposition of 'reparative consequences.' That is, it acknowledges that the state can provide better legal responses when responding to harm and violence. It does so by drawing attention to the limitations of traditional state responses to crime, and proposes a separate process designed to serve the various needs of victims and offenders.

There is insufficient capacity in this work to discuss the relative merits and shortcomings of this model in much detail. Yet, it is worth emphasising that there is a ground, as suggested by Lacey and Pickard, on which to develop a conception of punishment that is attuned to the ethical form of retributivism without slipping back into punitiveness. And the ethical strength of legal therapeutic intervention lies particularly in the stress placed on the idea of free responsible agency, alongside the circumstances that bear on its limitations. Accordingly, the therapeutic model rightly draws our attention to the possible practices that require offenders to change behaviour that is damaging to them, while also taking into account the structural violence inflicted upon them.

Nonetheless, what is unclear and contentious in this account is the definition and contours of punishment, which are suggested to be reconceptualised as 'the imposition of consequences – typically negative but occasionally not, so long as they are serious and appropriate to the crime and the context- in response to blameworthiness for wrongdoing or harm'.[13] Significant is the fact that an ethical terrain is explored, in which legal response is linked to a past crime in somehow a retributive logic, without having recourse to the infliction of pain and desert. But it is unclear what kinds of negative consequences punishment includes, and how these consequences differ from what we understand from a typical conception of punishment that is associated with hard treatment. This model, for example, does not regard imprisonment as categorically unjustified, suggesting that prisons can be sites of 'invitation' to offenders to acknowledge their crime, 'creating the opportunity to move forward in their lives'.[14] In this

12 Nicola Lacey, 'Criminalisation as regulation: The role of criminal law' in Christine Parker and others (eds), *Regulating Law* (OUP 2004).

13 Lacey and Pickard, 'From the consulting room to the court room? Taking the clinical model of responsibility without blame into the legal realm' p.3.

14 Lacey and Pickard, 'To blame or to forgive? Reconciling punishment and forgiveness in criminal justice' p.695.

sense, Lacey and Pickard's model advocates, like perhaps many other revisionist theories, a reformist strategy that seeks to transform the way we punish.

That said, it seems that the therapeutic model eludes the discussion around whether imprisonment, even in its reformed fashion, is always a form of 'invitation', rather than of 'coercion', especially given that prisons are consisted of non-porous walls that set a clear and uncrossable boundary between offenders and others. They are ultimately designed to produce a community which is also supposed to protect the main community in Lacey and Pickard's framework, whatever the reparative aims we may want to pursue within them. For sure, the therapeutic model raises the possibility of reforming prisons in a manner that changes the way we relate to offenders, by expressing our concern, respect, and compassion for them. That is, prisons can be the types of communities that are built by a larger, more humane, and democratic community. Put differently, it may be possible to embrace the institution of punishment without slipping into a punitive logic. Yet, as discussed in my analysis of Duff's conception of punishment, prisons or any 'walled' institution in contemporary liberal societies are very prone to creating a coercive border that can be predominantly punitive and exclusionary. We should, therefore, always be cautious about the intrinsic unreformable nature of imprisonment in societies, standing in the way of ethical restoration and substantial reconciliation.

In her latest article, in which she engages with the question of how we could institutionalise forgiveness in practical terms, Lacey explicitly acknowledges that it is unrealistic to expect modern states to 'entirely dispense with more coercive, less dialogic' sanctions, in particular where offenders resist to take responsibility and reject reconciliation.[15] Nevertheless, she argues that this should not simply lead us to accept that imprisonment or other forms of punitive measures are legitimate or acceptable. Instead, she warns that we should view more coercive measure as 'second best -even imposed with a sense of failure.' What follows from this is the idea that even non-therapeutic punishments should be buttressed by 'mechanisms that leave the door to forgiveness and reconciliation open.'[16]

At first instance, Lacey and Pickard's radical reformist approach might be seen as another not fully developed theory of neo-retributivism, where what I call legal justice and ethical love are not totally reconciled. In very broad terms, their model can also be associated with Duff's communicative theory, in particular because both appear to fail to build up a reformed conception of punishment out of values and principles of interpersonal relations. There are, however, substantial differences between the two, one of which I want to highlight for the purpose of this work is their endgame, so to speak. Duff does not view imprisonment as intrinsically problematic while Lacey and Pickard

15 Lacey, 'Institutionalising forgiveness in criminal justice' p.13.
16 Lacey, 'Institutionalising forgiveness in criminal justice'.

do. For the latter, imprisonment is ultimately a failure of criminal justice systems and should be abandoned whenever possible, even though they do not openly speak out about it.

Another equally important difference between the two is perhaps their level of sensitivity to the ongoing problem of doing justice in an unjust world. With the ideas of forgiveness and non-moralistic judgement, Lacey and Pickard seek ways to ease the problem that background injustice causes for criminal justice. For sure, the therapeutic model, like my own utopian ethically retributivist framework, operates within criminal justice, which means that it does not provide a clear roadmap to address structural violence and inequality. Nevertheless, that is a problem, one might argue, which can only be "eased" or "alleviated", not fully solved without real social and political transformations. In this sense, the therapeutic model's proponents, I assume, may sympathise with the values and aspirations of transformative justice even though they may ultimately diverge from each other in particular about the complaint that the state and law are at the root of all forms of harm, abuse, and assault.

There is some ground to believe that the state and its laws are evil or have a kind of "evil disposition" at least in its practices of criminal justice. Nevertheless, I am not sure whether this necessarily requires us to dispose of the sources of evil. Perhaps quite the opposite. We need a radically reformed way of thinking, like the therapeutic model offers, which can pay due regard to the ethical sensitivity that the transformative justice advocates demand. After all, the therapeutic model proposes 'a project, which sets out to begin creating the institutions of a new society within the shell of the old" while also "exposing", "subverting" and "undermining" structures of domination.[17] Because it is a project that tries to change the world within a specific terrain, the terrain where state power is most visible, it must be less ambitious and more realistic to fulfil its purpose.

Of course, we may sometimes want the radical reformists more utopian thinking where we think they compromise some of the values and principles we should follow. With its dual process approach, for example, the therapeutic model convincingly challenges the so-called link between punishment of offenders and recovery of victims. It argues that the suffering of the former and what is required of them are not inherently to do with how they come to terms with criminal violation. According to this model, it seems that the worlds of offenders and victims are in a way fundamentally different from each other. That said, we could challenge this way of dismantling the connection between the two parties, arguing that there is another way of linking their pains and sufferings to each other.

Underlying our challenge might be the idea that their worlds are the same, and – perhaps more strongly than normal – tied to one another by an unpleasant event, while dialectically coexisting and reciprocally penetrating

17 David Graeber, *Fragments of an Anarchist Anthropology* (Prickly Paradigm Press 2004) p.5.

into one another. This is to say that there is an undeniable interaction or transaction between how both parties deal with the same event. A victim's (internal) suffering can potentially be transformed into a source of wholeness for both the perpetrator and the victim, when one observes and participates in the other's suffering. For example, the feelings of guilt and remorse in offenders (or lack of them, for any reason) may profoundly affect whether victims are in a mental position to be liberated from the hurt of violation, or from revenge, anger, and vindictiveness, or filled with compassion and forgiveness. Likewise, the suffering and grief of victims can provide perhaps the best ethical moment, in which a dialogue can be unfolded between offenders and victims.

This does not mean that there is no other way than a moral transaction between victims and offenders for a substantial kind of restoration. Neither does this suggest that we should bring both parties together at all costs. After all, despite our best efforts to achieve a fully restored moral world, especially in the dual reciprocal space of victims and offenders, some relationships will never be the same; some debts will never be repaid; some negative feelings will never be fully purged. The fact that crime has occurred will remain, looming in the background for all. That said, we should insist that we share the same world that has been ruptured by criminal violation, and that we can live in that world in a peaceful way.

In this regard, the suffering of victims may almost always be seen as a good starting point for offenders to take responsibility. In a way, it is the suffering of victims which can hold a kind of ethical power and make an unconditional demand on offenders to make things right.[18] It is not simply the fact that their legal rights have been violated. In fact, once both *meet in* the suffering of victims, it may become easier for both to address the suffering of offenders too and recognise how vulnerable they are or they have been. There is therefore perhaps much more room Lacey and Pickard allowed in the shared world of both offenders and victims that we should work more on reconciliation and healing.

To conclude this reflection, the therapeutic theory of punishment introduces an ethically loaded legal vision that seeks to avoid the potential pitfalls of legal retributivism. If we speak in Hegelian terms, it is an attempt to cancel, preserve, and transcend (*Aufhebung*) recent neo-classical retributivism, by pointing to a way-out of the theoretical deadlock that this work has illustrated. It does so by debunking the idea of deserved pain, and placing reform, reconciliation, and forgiveness at the centre of its penal vision. Within 'the legal', it explores and stresses 'the ethical', by building up the former from the materials of the latter. In other words, it opens the door towards a more ambitious reconciliation of legal and ethical retributivism. In many ways, it is realistic in its critically-oriented theoretical project, as it draws on the idea of reforming existing penal

18 Emmanuel Levinas, *Totality and Infinity: An Essay on Exteriority*, trans. A. Lingis (Pittsburgh, PA: Dusquesne University Press 2007) p.199.

practices. Moreover, it does this by evading the punitive implications of the current punishment paradigm.

The only caveat might be that the reformist framework, however radical it can be, may not sufficiently address the question of whether there is something 'incorrigible' in current practices that would always remain punitive and coercive. That said, this may not always be a failure of theoretical thinking, but of modern societies – that are too reliant on caging people as a typical penal response to criminal violations, a response that is so firmly, deeply seated that any disengagement with the orthodoxy can only result in unrealistic utopian fantasies. I now want to turn my attention to a much more radical, or better "abolitionist" approach to criminal justice, in which the law and punishment discourse is completely abandoned.

2. Radical reconstruction: mature retributivism

Norrie's moral psychological account is parallel to the therapeutic theory of punishment, in terms of penal aims and aspirations, and yet dissimilar to it in terms of its 'reconstructive' strategy. As noted above, while the therapeutic model draws on non-legal, ethical sources to transform retributivism by *remaining within law*, the moral psychological account does so by *keeping its distance from law*. Although both try to find ways to radically reconstruct an account of criminal justice that declines to think of crime and punishment in standard legal terms, Norrie's 'alternative' account, unlike Lacey and Pickard's, does not develop *from within* the state-centred approach in order to be *against* it, but develops from *within the ethical* in order to be *against* the legal. Accordingly, Norrie's account takes a more radical approach than Lacey and Pickard, with his emphasis on the problems of formal legal justice and the need for 'deep tendential abolition'.

In his words, Norrie's moral psychological account is based on an 'ontology'. It understands human beings as "metaphysical animals', animals who think and love, a species with animal needs and roots capable of feeling the pull of the universe'.[19] In his view, we need 'a different way of thinking about how human beings live together and deal with each other' and 'address wrongdoing in ways that are open to individual and social change'.[20] Much in parallel with ethical retributivism, the moral psychological account Norrie defends stands sharply against the orthodox retributive paradigm. He argues that we should understand law and punishment in broader terms without dismissing its ethical promise, and by developing a better understanding of what legal retributive punishment 'claims to do, but does badly'.[21]

19 Norrie, *Criminal Justice and Moral Psychology* p.19.
20 Norrie, *Criminal Justice and Moral Psychology* p.3.
21 Norrie, *Criminal Justice and Moral Psychology* p.3.

Retributive punishment in its orthodox legal form seeks to restore the balance of an order that has been upset by the crime. Occurring in a unilateral, one-sided manner, it is 'carried out by the state' as an institutional blaming mechanism which is 'directed at the criminal'. Moreover, as Norrie writes,

> *As the criminal's own act returning to him [by the state], it tends to ignore the victim. It easily becomes seen as the vindicated allocation of a just amount of pain on a criminal, without a further progressive outcome either for the criminal, the victim, or society as a whole. It easily becomes seen, in other words, as punitive, persecutory, pain for its own sake.*[22]

With its emphasis on the idea of imbalance in human relationships, retributive punishment may start from the right place, but by tying 'responsibility' to 'the infliction of pain', it goes in the wrong direction. Missing in this formal ordering of crime and punishment is 'the relationship that remains most central to what happened, that between the perpetrator and the victim'.[23] The suffering of offenders, even if it is sometimes said to be meaningful (particularly when it leads to moral growth), goes past victims when it is administered from the top down. At the heart of legal retributivism, thus, lies an institutional barrier that stands in the way of more substantial reconciliation and moral resolution.

There is, however, another way of understanding this 'retributive cycle', which is not 'abstracted from real moral psychological processes' that give rise to better moral outcomes. In what Norrie calls mature retributivism, 'the abstract rebalancing of right and wrong can take on a real, human, form', in which punishment is produced 'from within the individual towards the victim'.[24] What triggers the operation of retribution in this reciprocal progressive cycle is not the criminal's desert and his moral debt to society. Neither is it an abstract sense of justice that demands punishment in cases of law violations. Rather, it is the sense of disunity within the criminal that places him 'at odds with the world' which he shares with the victim and others.

In mature retributivism, the penal vocabulary is substantially shifted and renewed, such that it is no longer understood as a punitive payback; but as 'a restorative giving back'.[25] Under this renovated form of retributivism, we can stop speaking of crime and punishment, and start talking of 'violation and of making amends'. This would take place in 'a process in which the state and law may or may not play a part. If they do, it could only be a limited one'.[26] When revamped this way, retributivism can be recalibrated into both the agendas of penal reform and abolitionism.

22 Norrie, 'Taking guilt seriously: Towards mature retributivism' p.141.
23 Norrie, *Criminal Justice and Moral Psychology* Cp.8 p.29.
24 Norrie, *Criminal Justice and Moral Psychology* Cp.8 p.26.
25 Norrie, 'Taking guilt seriously: Towards mature retributivism' p.141.
26 Norrie, 'Taking guilt seriously: Towards mature retributivism' p.141.

Norrie provides greater depth and insight into his mature retributivist account, by analysing a now almost-forgotten practice of imprisonment in the early 1970's in Glasgow, Scotland, called The Barlinnie Special Unit. 'Drawing upon ideas of a therapeutic community', Norrie argues, this form of imprisonment shows how it is possible to actualise 'an alternative that [is] both a logical corollary of prison reform and a radical challenge to the existing system'.[27] In its design and practices, the Barlinnie prison is geared towards the building of a community that develops freedom 'from the inside' both institutionally and psychologically. It produces 'creative citizens out of troubled, violent and angry young men' by freeing them from the negative, destructive feelings of anger and hatred within an environment that is built on democratic and civic values.[28]

The Barlinnie Unit is a restorative prison project that embraces a radically different kind of penal philosophy. It produced a caring and supportive space that allowed prisoners 'to retrieve and develop essential human elements enabling them to flourish' by placing 'love, solidarity, democratic action, individual respect and responsibility, and human creativity at the heart of the prison'.[29] It gave offenders an opportunity to reflect on their personality and identity, enabling them to see the prison as a setting for 'a moral and emotional coming to terms with' what they were, how they would like to be, should relate to others, change and grow.[30] Norrie argues that in fact, the Barlinnie Unit did something that abolitionists have never imagined of prisons: rehabilitation, moral growth, healing, and reconciliation, albeit in a very limited setting. Thus, in its radical image lie facets of both a reformist and an abolitionist, seeking both to improve the way prisons are administered, and to deconstruct them from within. It is what Norrie calls 'a concrete utopian practice of the loving prison'.[31]

The loving prison project reveals how prisons can become an engine of change for both themselves and the external world, in that the model not only criticises prisons in their current form, but also reveals the underlying problems of the society that 'spawned' them. That said, perhaps just because of the punitive social culture within which it emerges, it is said to be doomed to be marginalised and to fail. It is 'concrete' with its realistic aims which can be actualised within an existing penal system, but it is also 'utopian' in the sense that it seeks to cultivate a nurturing, supportive, and compassionate mode of penal communication within a hostile, fear-inducive society. Indeed, the project was eventually shut down in the early 1990s.

27 Norrie, *Criminal Justice and Moral Psychology* Cp.11 p.29.

28 Norrie, *Criminal Justice and Moral Psychology* Cp.11 p.3.

29 Alan Norrie, 'Restoration, abolition and the loving prison: Jimmy Boyle and Barlinnie Special Unit' (2022) 61 *The Howard Journal of Crime and Justice* 103, 105.

30 Norrie, 'Restoration, abolition and the loving prison' p.112.

31 Norrie, 'Restoration, abolition and the loving prison' p.114.

Such a project, Thomas Mathiesen warns, may be seen as 'a new form of diversion against a developing counter-organisation as a way of absorbing its forces'.[32] After all, by opening doors to a better version of itself, the loving prison does not only 'operate as an immanent critique of the system that houses them' and 'reveal its inner tendency towards its own abolition'.[33] It may also be viewed as confirming or condoning some of the inherent problems of current penal regimes, and thus potentially shoring up the dominant punishment paradigm and established penal order. As stated above, prisons are ultimately made up of walls separating offenders from the rest of society, within which the former are kept for a certain period of time in response to their transgressive behaviour. Most of the time, they are inevitably taken as 'buffers' against future harm, and natural consequence of having committed a crime. They are not only a physical barrier that is imposed by an external force, but also a metaphor that divides the community, while being a constant reminder of the rupture caused by criminal violation between offenders and others. As such, they further perpetuate the idea that the rupture between offenders and others is originated in the 'violation' – thereby putting the responsibility solely or predominantly in the hands of offenders, instead of recognising a collective responsibility for justice.

I do not want to talk more about the caution Thomas Mathiesen points out as I believe that radical reforms are more likely to undermine the current prison regimes than it reinforces them. Ultimately, "tendential abolition" provides a strategy that can potentially reveal the repeated failures and flaws of the system in a way that calls into questions all the principles on which it rests. It also teaches a lesson to be learned by all policymakers, reminding the idea that another world is possible.

Nevertheless, we may ask how radical penal reforms relate to Norrie's mature retributivism, a model of what I call ethical love which is mainly defined by the retributive cycle between the victim and offender, not between the state and offender. Remember that Norrie suggests another way of thinking about the principle of pay-back by linking it to the notions of restorative giving back and making amends. He also adds that the state plays at best a secondary or limited role in our moral engagement with violation. I do think, as I said earlier, the loving prison is a kind of radical reform which may challenge the penal status quo. But I suspect whether the loving prison could be seen as an example of restorative pay-back. How are the victims of Jimmy Boyle, for example, restored when he goes out of the prison and becomes another man? What was "given back" to those victims when their offender becomes a fully rehabilitated and socially productive citizen? Does the state play a minimum role here? How can we see the loving prison as a form of moral transaction between victims and offenders?

32 Thomas Mathiesen, *The politics of abolition revisited* (Routledge 1974/2015) p.153.

33 Norrie, *Criminal Justice and Moral Psychology* Cp.8 p.30.

Norrie does not frankly argue that the loving prison is a concrete example of mature retributivism. Neither does he explain his intersubjective loving ethics further with concrete examples, like the Barlianne Special Unit either. I would expect him to develop his mature retributivism with concrete "non-carceral" examples which links the suffering of offenders to that of victims without the state's direct involvement. It seems that almost all the penal reforms, however radical we would want them to be, are in some way or another state-centred and necessarily imposed from top down. Perhaps the reason why mature retributivism is not readily seen in the real penal practices is because the state is necessarily the main actor that does not give up being part of the retributive cycle. It is the one which acts as if it gets hurt and wants to hurt back. In Chapter 3, for example, we saw that the practice of confronting sexual offenders with what they did to their victims can be seen as a mature retributive suffering. But we also raised questions whether that sort of retributive suffering can be fully restorative in a broadly state-oriented setting.

The question is thus whether it is realistic to create practices of mature retributivism that the state plays no or a minimal role. After all, the state's juridical machine always *deforms* or *distorts* the real human conflicts and translates them into a formal language while being far from creating a medium through which to mobilise loving dynamics of interpersonal life.[34] For this reason, some may think this leaves us a rather bleak picture about state-oriented reformist approaches, pushing us necessarily towards an absolute abolitionist position. It may also mean that what I call legal and ethical retributivism cannot be totally reconciled in particular where the state takes a dominant role. To put it differently, the chasm between the abolitionist framework and the punishment paradigm is sometimes so wide, like perhaps in most of the prison reforms, that 'to plant the ethical within the legal' may not be as fertile an environment as expected. This is perhaps one of the central messages given by this book: 'do not underestimate how much the mainstream punishment paradigm has taken root in modern legal thought and practices.'

3. Loving justice: between prison reform and abolition

Let me now give you a sharper picture of the point at which we arrive by linking it to the broad discourse around the recent criminal justice paradigm, the discourse often framed in terms of two broad positions: penal reform and abolition. Penal reforms frequently address overcrowding and unsafe conditions in prisons alongside the lack of resources to prepare prisoners for life after incarceration. They stress the necessity of remaking the prison environment in a way that meets the essential needs of prisoners and provides them with rehabilitative and educational programs. Reformism relies on the premise that offenders are sent to prison as punishment, not for punishment.

34 Lacey, 'Institutionalising forgiveness in criminal justice' p.8.

On this view, imprisonment as punishment can be justifiable only if it is made humane and reformed in a way that respects the dignity, rights, and welfare of prisoners.[35]

There is, however, also a more radical vision, as should now be clear, which rejects the reformist agenda: penal abolition. Abolitionism is animated by the idea that prisons are by their nature places of pain, coercion and punitive social control. They are, therefore, fundamentally flawed and indefensible in all their forms. Rejecting the gradual approach of penal reform, abolitionism seeks to challenge 'the stultifying idea that nothing lies beyond the prison.'[36] On this approach, the fundamental aim should not be to improve prisons, but rather to transform societies so that prisons are no longer deemed necessary.[37]

The discourses of penal abolition and reform seem to be irreconcilably opposed. The abolitionist approach is frequently debunked as utopian, having no feasible alternatives to offer in place of prisons, while the reformist approach is accused of being complicit in the violence perpetrated by the carceral system.[38] Unsurprisingly, then, the holy grail of recent criminal justice literature is the identification of a third path between the two approaches.[39]

It is in this transitional moment that the critical accounts of Lacey and Pickard, as well as Norrie, take shape. Both avoid falling entirely into either reformism or abolitionism. They criticise the current penal system for resting on unjustified assumptions, bringing them close to abolitionism. But they do not completely lose hope in the potential for meaningful change within criminal justice systems. In the final analysis, Norrie's account leans more toward abolitionism whereas Lacey and Pickard's offers a more reformist approach. Yet, in my own terms, both embody what I would describe as loving justice—the kind of justice I position between reform and abolition.

What underpins the vision of loving justice is the belief that penal reforms can take us into abolition. They can be so radical that even the most progressive abolitionists can be pleased with them as a plausible strategy for ultimate penal abolition. In this sense, radical reform can transform into an incremental abolitionist framework.[40] We may call this "strategy" "non-reformist reforms",

35 Richard Lippke, *Rethinking Imprisonment* (Oxford University Press 2007); Michael H Tonry, *The Future of Imprisonment* (Oxford University Press 2004).

36 Angela Y Davis, *Are Prisons Obsolete?* (Seven Stories Press 2011).

37 Mick Ryan and Joe Sim, 'Campaigning for and campaigning against prisons: Excavating and reaffirming the case for prison abolition' in Yvonne Jewkes (ed), *Handbook on Prisons* (Routledge 2012).

38 Tommie Shelby, *The Idea of Prison Abolition* (Princeton University Press 2022) p.15.

39 Marina Bell, 'Abolition: A new paradigm for reform' (2021) 46 *Law & Social Inquiry* 32; Liat Ben-Moshe, 'The tension between abolition and reform' in ME Nagel and AJ Nocella (eds), *The End of Prisons: Reflections from the Decarceration Movement* (Brill 2013) p.83–92.

40 Joe Sim, *Punishment and Prisons: Power and the Carceral State* (Sage 2009).

as done in the recent literature, which refer to measures that diminish the carceral state without legitimising it.[41]

Illuminating the state's inability to solve the problems it creates, non-reformist reforms are thought to facilitate transformational change in the broader society. While these changes may be gradual, their final goal is not correction of the system, but rather abolition. The reduction of the incarcerated population through a variety of means (decarceration), reducing policing, creating voluntary, accessible, community-run services, and finally rejecting government spending on prison renovation, are the primary measures suggested as steps to be taken.[42] There is, however, a robust debate about the wisdom of defunding prisons. While some welcome "revolutionary" reforms in current carceral practices as radical alternatives that could unveil the failures of the system, others are of the view that they stand in the way of investment in local infrastructures that support people and prevent further incarceration.[43]

This debate defies easy resolution—and perhaps it does not need one. In fact, keeping the debate alive is essential for navigating the nuanced and fertile line between reform and abolition, in that it reveals how these two approaches, often seen as oppositional, can be understood as deeply intertwined, coexisting in a dynamic or symbiotic relationship and enriching each other. Within this ongoing debate, "non-reformist" reforms invite us to reimagine imprisonment, transforming it from a punitive measure into something closer to what Norrie calls a restorative *giving back*. When offenders are rehabilitated or significantly change their lives within the prison system, their transformation can be seen as a form of restitution—a way to address the harm done to society. After serving their sentence, they can be reintegrated into society as fully absolved of both their debt and fault. In other words, prisons can become places of change, self-growth, and hope, not places of pain, violence, and despair.

One might caution us here that intersubjective forms of penal measures are also not free from power relations. In its exclusive reliance on the idea of moral correction, an intersubjective response can also intervene in the lives of offenders to have 'rulership over their souls' even if it presents itself as a constructive alternative to legal sanctions. In other words, although it is derived from an ethics of love –along with compassion, benevolence and caring– it may, in essence, turn into an exercise of sovereignty towards offenders, albeit in a hidden way. Thus, we should keep in mind that the state is inherently inclined to produce a peculiar form of power or dominion over individuals.

41 Eli Salamon-Abrams, 'Remaking public defense in an abolitionist framework: non-reformist reform and the gideon problem' (2021) 49 *Fordham Urban Law Journal* 435; Allegra M McLeod, 'Prison abolition and grounded justice' (2015) 62 *UCLA Law Review* 1156.

42 Shiri Pasternak, Kevin Walby and Abby Stadnyk, *Disarm, Defund, Dismantle: Police Abolition in Canada* (Between the Lines 2022).

43 Joe Sim, *Punishment and Prisons: Power and the Carceral State* (Sage 2009).

At times, "the guardianship over souls" may become more problematic especially when vertical authority diffuses its power and control over all relational practices, such that punitive sanctions appear in the guise of loving penal involvement. What happened in the rehabilitative ideals in the 1960's can perhaps precisely be seen as punitive interventions cloaked under the veil of restoration, reform, and rehabilitation. In that period, the way welfarist states treated individuals shows us how legal techniques and institutions can create the modern penal system of disciplinary power in a horizontal manner. In Foucault's words, punishment at that period is 'not so much that [it] renders docile those who are liable to transgress the law, but that [it] tends to assimilate the transgression of the laws in the general tactics of subjection'.[44] Control in the reformatory framework is exercised over individuals by the guidance and manipulation of their souls and self-directed internal monitoring. To put otherwise, an ethically self-imposed punishment is somehow an externally imposed punishment in another sense, driven largely by an outsider that engages to correct deviant behaviour.[45] The penal power of a sovereign can therefore be more amorphous and perilous than a traditional exercise of coercion, while being covertly embedded in specific cultural conventions and mechanisms.

There is something to this Foucauldian line of critique, in the sense that the intersubjective forms of power are produced in myriad ways within the diverse and intersecting networks of social life. In other words, there are ongoing power dynamics in the society that may undermine loving relations of mutual recognition. In this sense, relational ties can play a constitutive role in shaping or worse manipulating what individuals come to feel and do, when they reflect upon their violation. It is then not unlikely that we may create forms of misrecognition, maintaining the repressive or coercive elements of the current penal status quo.

Yet, there is also the ethical loving emancipatory ties rooted in intersubjective relationships that are not decisively dominated or eaten up by the supreme authority of a political sovereign, with its disseminated power relations. Within those ties, according to the intersubjective character of mutual recognition, lies an ethical terrain in which individuals can be given the opportunity to take responsibility without being judged punitively and intrusively by others. As highlighted in the transformative justice movement, there is also the chance that we could rebuild the state -or better the community- from bottom to top and work with offenders who have harmed to take responsibility for the harm they have done and make amends. After all, it is not simply individual responsibility that matters, but also the collective response to violence that we need in order to prevent cycles of violence: community accountability. Quite appealing in the transformative justice approach is the exploration of

44 Michel Foucault, *Discipline and Punish: The Birth of the Prison* (Penguin Books 1995) p.272.
45 Jacques Derrida, *The Death Penalty, Volume II* (The University of Chicago Press 2017) p.37.

non-state-centred models of responsibility under the idea of collective response that could minimise the risks of manipulative control and domination.

But does this collective response involve imprisonment? For transformative justice advocates, it does not. For reformists, it might. If so, can we conceptualise and implement a prison regime that facilitates healing for both victims and offenders without being deeply entrenched in and driven by the mechanisms of state power? That is not an easy task to be achieved. Also, one might claim that criminal violation ultimately requires an involvement that concerns not only the victim and offender but all members of the public. This brings us to the idea of state as "a moral third" in Jessica Benjamin's sense,[46] which can open a space for constructive dialogue and restoration as well as "the stabilisation of a public sense of justice".[47] In this light, the aim should not merely be to encourage non-state mechanisms for reconciliation and reparations. Rather, it should be to reimagine the state as "an intersubjective third" that enables meaningful interactions and proper mutual recognition among citizens by trying to build a just social order grounded in cooperation. Prisons might be part of this political framework, but their function must be transformed to align with the ethical values of intersubjectivity.

It now becomes clear that prisons pose a special challenge to what I call forms of loving justice, demanding that we may always have to confront the difficult question of whether to support or oppose their existence. Instead of taking a definitive stance, I aim to leave the reader in a position of deliberate ambivalence—one that invites critical examination of prisons without being confined to the binary of endorsement or rejection. I want to do so precisely because I believe this approach allows for a more nuanced grasp of prisons—their role, complexities, and implications, helping us to have a deeper understanding of how they might align with or challenge principles of loving justice and mutual recognition.

Conclusion

I started this chapter with addressing the question of whether it is possible to overcome the impasse that neo-classical retributivism finds itself and resolve the conflict between loving ethics and legal justice. To this end, I identified two paths out of the impasse: radical reformism and radical reconstruction, both of which may be seen as what I call loving justice.

In the first section, I analysed Lacey and Pickard's radical reformist strategy, which replaces desert with a therapeutic model based on love, care, and compassion. For them, there is a loving version of legal justice that has not been

46 Jessica Benjamin, 'Beyond doer and done to: An intersubjective view of thirdness' (2004) 73(1) *Psychoanalytic Quarterly* p.5–46.

47 Vincent Chiao, *Criminal Law in the Age of the Administrative State* (Oxford University Press 2019) p.37.

sufficiently developed, a version that can aim to equip offenders with greater insight into their own behaviour and instil in them a greater sense of responsibility. The therapeutic model they advocate is based on a radically reformist version of penal institutions with a dual-track system separately designed for offenders and victims to address their distinct needs. In other words, forgiveness of offenders and recognition of victims can go hand in hand when they are designed to address the distinct needs of both, enabling healing and justice at the same time.

In the second section, I moved on to Norrie's 'tendential' abolitionist approach, which aims to reconstruct the legal landscape in which violation is poorly understood and addressed. In his view, we should make space for a moral psychological approach in criminal justice to cultivate repair and loving relationships. For him, a retributive form of justice can be radically reconstructed if understood as a response that moves from the victim to the offender, triggering the latter's sense of responsibility. It is the offender's mature retributive suffering that can allow for the creation of new forms of penal practices, such as the loving prison. It remains, however, unclear whether prisons—however loving they might be—can sustain or undermine the current carceral regime.

In the third section, I went on to describe the tension between the ideas of penal reformism and abolitionism especially in relation to imprisonment. I argued that the idea of loving justice may reconcile the legal and ethical approaches in neo-classical retributivism, but it also carries within itself a tension between penal reform and abolition. I then came to conclude that we should have an ambivalent position that leaves us room for a deeper understanding of reformed imprisonment.

Bibliography

Bell M, 'Abolition: a new paradigm for reform' (2021) 46 *Law & Social Inquiry* 32

Benjamin J, 'Beyond doer and done to: an intersubjective view of thirdness' (2004) 73 (1) *Psychoanalytic Quarterly* 73

Ben-Moshe L, 'The tension between abolition and reform' in Nagel ME and Nocella AJ (eds), *The End of Prisons: Reflections from the Decarceration Movement* (Brill 2013) 83–92

Chiao V, *Criminal Law in the Age of the Administrative State* (OUP 2019)

Davis AY, *Are Prisons Obsolete?* (Seven Stories Press 2011)

Derrida J, *The Death Penalty*, vol. II (University of Chicago Press 2017)

Foucault M, *Discipline and Punish: The Birth of the Prison* (Penguin 1995)

Graeber D, *Fragments of an Anarchist Anthropology* (Prickly Paradigm Press, 2004)

Lacey N, 'Criminal justice and social (In)justice' (2022) LSE Law School and International Inequalities Institute Working Paper 84

Lacey N, 'Criminalisation as regulation: the role of criminal law' in Parker C and others (eds), *Regulating Law* (OUP 2004)

Lacey N and Pickard H, 'A dual-process approach to criminal law: victims and the clinical model of responsibility without blame' (2019) 27 *Journal of Political Philosophy* 229

Lacey N and Pickard H, 'From the consulting room to the court room? Taking the clinical model of responsibility without blame into the legal realm' (2013) 33 *Oxford Journal of Legal Studies* 1

Lacey N and Pickard H, 'To blame or to forgive? Reconciling punishment and forgiveness in criminal justice' (2015) 35 *Oxford Journal of Legal Studies* 665

Lacey N and Pickard H, 'Why standing to blame may be lost but authority to hold accountable retained: criminal law as a regulative public institution' (2021) 104 *The Monist* 265

Levinas E, *Totality and Infinity: An Essay on Exteriority*. Translated by Lingis A (Dusquesne University Press 2007)

Lippke R, *Rethinking Imprisonment* (OUP 2007)

Mathiesen T, *The Politics of Abolition Revisited* (Routledge 1974/2015)

McLeod AM, 'Prison abolition and grounded justice' (2015) 62 *UCLA Law Review* 1156

Norrie A, *Criminal Justice and Moral Psychology* (Cambridge University Press 2025)

Norrie A, 'Restoration, abolition and the loving prison: jimmy boyle and barlinnie special unit' (2022) 61 *The Howard Journal of Crime and Justice* 103

Norrie A, 'Taking guilt seriously: towards mature retributivism' in Solanke I (ed), *On Crime, Society, and Responsibility in the Work of Nicola Lacey* (OUP 2021)

Pasternak S, *Kevin Walby and Abby Stadnyk, Disarm, Defund, Dismantle: Police Abolition in Canada* (Between the Lines 2022)

Ryan M and Sim J, 'Campaigning for and campaigning against prisons: excavating and reaffirming the case for prison abolition' in Jewkes Y (ed), *Handbook on Prisons* (Routledge 2012)

Salamon-Abrams E, 'Remaking public defense in an abolitionist framework: non-reformist reform and the gideon problem' (2021) 49 *Fordham Urban Law Journal* 435

Shelby T, *The Idea of Prison Abolition* (Princeton University Press 2022)

Sim J, *Punishment and Prisons: Power and the Carceral State* (Sage 2009)

Tonry MH, *The Future of Imprisonment* (OUP 2004)

Conclusion

Criminal violation brings about a vast variety of harms. It intrudes upon the subjectivity of victims in a manner that causes them to suffer physical, material and psychological loss and puts into question their normative status in the society while also distorting the way they view the world. It also intrudes upon the subjectivity of offenders by rupturing their relationship with the victim(s) and themselves while putting into question their status within the political community. It also damages or threatens society's collective sense of security and trust as well as the values that the political body wants preserved. In the face of such a wide range of harms, the idea of restoration is pressing and stands in need of further defence.

Perhaps for most, retributivism is the last place to look for restoration when coming to terms with crimes. But this book shows that within retributive philosophy there might be a double sense of restoration that addresses both legal/normative and ethical harms. It is, in fact, the recent double vision of neo-retributivism that has triggered the book's central aim. The question from the very beginning is whether or how neo-retributivism can restore the normative/legal and ethical harms caused by crimes.

In Part I, Chapter 1, this book started with an analysis of Murphy's ambivalent approach to legal punishment. On the one hand, he believes that offenders deserve to suffer simply because they commit crimes. For him, this means that state sanctions could provide legal restoration. On the other hand, however, he raises questions about the strict demands of just deserts, searching for more humanistic, loving versions of retributivism. From this he comes to think later that state sanctions should also provide ethical restoration by repairing the deeper harms that have not been addressed by the standard retributive framework. In the final analysis, he finds himself in a deadlock, like other neo-retributivists, between what I call 'legal justice' (moral desert) and 'ethical love' (reconciliation and healing), a deadlock between the two contrasting faces of retributive philosophy.

In Part II, this book gave an analysis of Hegel's moral and legal philosophy as an exemplary domain to account for the two faces of retributivism, examining his different periods of intellectual life, in which he produced two distinct sets of thoughts with regard to law and punishment. It juxtaposed Hegel's

DOI: 10.4324/9781003563150-13

later formal, state-centred theory of retributivism with that of the earlier, broader, ethical theory that invites us to view crime and punishment in moral psychological terms. It judged both theories to have room for restoration at different levels. In other words, both models of retributivism have a sense of restoration in their own terms.

Revisiting the modern classical version of retributivism through Hegel's Philosophy of Right, Chapter 2 explained how punishment restores the normative/legal harm, the sort of harm that disrupts formal relations and patterns of life governed by law. In this approach, punishment is taken to be the restoration of the legal order or of 'the Right', in Hegelian vocabulary. It reconciles the law with itself through the negation of crime, reaffirming the rule of law and the state's political authority. It also reconciles the will of offenders with the law, as internalised by them as their own. In other words, punishment does not only repair the damage done to the law; it also corrects the deflected will of offenders. Hegel's well-known formulation of punishment is adopted, more or less, by various contemporary penal scholars. This book terms such a position 'legal retributivism'.

As stated in Chapter 2, what is less known and relatively undiscovered is the radical critique of this formulation in Hegel's young period, where law's retribution is downplayed and replaced by a non-legal relational retribution. As opposed to the formal logical circuit between the doing of what is forbidden by law and penal coercibility, Hegel's early writings present retribution as a moral psychological experience that occurs in the natural flow of life triggered by love. In this approach, punishment restores the injured sense of life caused by transgressive action, deriving its origin from the irreplaceable bonds of intersubjectivity that move the offender to morally engage with what has happened. It is the offender's own response in his moral world to the wrongful damage he has done to his victim and fellow beings. In this framework, punishment restores the loss caused by ethical harm, the sort of harm that damages the intersubjective bonds of social life. This work terms such a conception of punishment as 'ethical retributivism'.

The second part of this work presented two approaches to retributivism in a dichotomous way, which may be described as a contradiction between legal justice and the ethics of love. While legal retributivism – falling short of the moral depth of violation – leads to a shallow restoration of the socio-political order, ethical retributivism provides a substantially deeper kind of restoration in its subtle engagement with the actual moral psychological experiences of crime and punishment. At one end, there is the formal, institutional face of law and criminal justice that seeks to guarantee basic forms of freedom with a less rigorous engagement with the wrong. At the other end, however, lies an intersubjective, less formal – or even informal – model of justice that aims for a reconciliatory ethical intervention through reconciliation and healing. Are these two approaches to punishment reconcilable?

I partly answered this question in Chapter 1 with a diagnosis that neo-retributivism is at a deadlock. However, further analysis was needed to turn this diagnosis from a rough sketch into a fully drawn map. Drawing on the antinomy between legal justice and ethical love as an interpretative critical tool, Part III provided a more detailed – restorative – analysis of neo-classical retributivism. The underlying idea in that part was that neo-classical retributivism takes seriously the core features of the legal formal approach, with its model of the free responsible subject, and fuses it with the principles of the ethical approach that promote reconciliation, reform and forgiveness. The resulting relational or intersubjective approach enriches neo-classical retributivism, and yet this also stands in tension with its main legalistic approach.

Holding a unique position in the current literature, thus, neo-retributivism is a blend or synthesis – albeit an imperfect one – of various values that occupy criminal justice thinking, such as desert, justice, reparation and reconciliation. To explore the ambivalence of the new retributivism with regard to multiple competing principles, this book sheds light on it through the double sense of restoration. It did so by anchoring it in the tripartite model of stakeholders who are involved in crime and punishment: the victim, offender and state.

By reference to Hampton's theory, Chapter 3 engaged with the victim's soul, moral psychology and particularly their emotional or mental transition in the post-violation process. It argues that at a certain level, resentment is a justified emotion directed at wrongs, setting a sound basis for a retributive response. In this sense, punishment restores the victim in a legalistic or normative sense, expressing the message that the victim is violated and should be 'uplifted'. By not allowing the offender to get away with crime with impunity, it shows solidarity with the victim. It reaffirms and restores the status of the victim by somehow addressing and redressing their sense of injustice and moral vulnerability: legal restoration. Nevertheless, the sense of injustice is different from the sense of loss or grief. That is, even if retributive punishment might be a means of communicating solidarity with the victim in a normative sense, it is doubtful how it provides healing for the losses and injuries left unrepaired. Let alone healing the pains of violation, an offender-centred legal process often reconfigures them into a peculiar juridical language and repeats them in a different tone. The victim needs a therapeutic environment or setting, in which they may come to terms with the ethical pains of violation: ethical restoration.

Reflecting on the links between legal punishment and the offender's world through Duff's works, Chapter 4 focused on the question of what it means to blame others and whether it can be practised in a restorative manner. In its normative, formal dimension, punishment is restorative in the sense that it repairs the damaged position of the offender within the political community. By holding the offender criminally responsible, it releases the debt they owe to the society and makes them entitled to fully regain their rights: legal restoration. There is, however, a deeper sense of restoration that is not always achieved by punishment. The offender needs a legal intervention that paves the way for self-reform and moral growth: ethical restoration. Duff maintains that punishment can also be seen as ethically restorative if it is constructed as a burden placed on the offender within a communicative process that brings about remorse, reparation and reconciliation. Nonetheless, even though this may be the case in ideal circumstances, it is unclear how the coercive nature of punishment is justified or how ethical restoration is possible when it is delivered from top to bottom.

Finally, engaging critically with Brudner's political theory of punishment, Chapter 5 connected legal punishment directly to the authority of the state and freedom of individuals. If crime is a violation of the socio-political order that provides everyone with freedom, punishment is the vindication of the authority that maintains that order. This conception of punishment is accounted for by the reaffirmation of a sovereign's authority in face of its denial. In this approach, punishment is taken to be restorative of legal relations of mutual recognition, in which individuals are required to treat each other in a certain formally specified way and respect the freedom of others: legal restoration. That said, even if punishment addresses the normative harm done to vertically organised relations of political governance, it is indifferent to the ethical harm inflicted on horizontally structured relations of intersubjectivity, shaped by affective solidarity. Thus, equally significant is the need to address the harm done to violated relational bonds and interactions moulded by social cooperation, reciprocal care and love: ethical restoration.

In sum, understanding punishment through the twofold prism of legal and ethical restoration, this book adopted a critical interpretative analysis of recent retributive theories and opened up new ground on which to explore their strengths and limitations. In the construction of these theories, it identified an opposition centred on the conflict between legalistic and ethical approaches where the principles of desert, payback and justice clash with the ideas of reform, reparation and reconciliation. By doing so, it brought to light 'the dissonant chorus of ethical voices' within the boundaries of revised retributive thinking. This book concluded that neo-classical retributivism fails to reconcile the demanding principles of mutual intersubjectivity with those of liberal political theory in a satisfactory way.

In the final chapter, this book moved on to answer the question of whether the requirements of legal justice and ethical love are ever reconcilable and whether the deadlock neo-retributivism finds itself in is surmountable. To this end, it sought ways out of that impasse by visiting two critical accounts of punishment. In other words, it searched for models of what is called 'loving justice'.

The first is a radical reformist framework, in which Lacey and Pickard propose a therapeutic theory that takes individual agency and criminal responsibility seriously without appealing to moral desert. In their model, forgiveness for offenders and healing for victims can go hand in hand within a dual process that seeks to meet the distinct needs of both. Despite their theory's abolitionist potential, it can ultimately be described as reformist, as they aim to radically reform the values underpinning the penal system. The second is a radical reconstructive framework, in which Norrie proposes another mature way of addressing the retributive cycle, one that does not move from the state to the offender but rather from the victim to the offender. He argues that the penal vocabulary – and thus its philosophy – should shift from 'crime and punishment' to 'violation and making amends'. Only through this shift, he contends, can we take meaningful steps towards abolition and a more substantive form of penal justice.

The gist of the final chapter (Part III) was the idea that there is room to reconcile legal and ethical paradigms that can guide us from reform towards abolition and the pursuit of loving justice. However, the ideal of loving justice is not without tension. There is always an overt contradiction and competition between reformism and abolitionism. In this regard, I argued that prisons pose a specific challenge to the concept of loving justice, urging us to continually question whether their existence should be supported or opposed. Rather than offering a conclusive position, I left the reader in a space of intentional ambivalence – one that suggests a critical examination of the institution without being limited to a binary choice of endorsement or rejection.

Nevertheless, throughout this book, I have also challenged, in one way or another, the taken-for-granted assumption that the prison system is necessary to maintain a just social order and public safety. At this stage, I do not want to introduce a new argument into an already concluded work, but I will offer a final thought, drawing inspiration from the influential sociologist Harold Garfinkel's concept of trust.

Garfinkel, the founder of ethnomethodology, argues that much of social life is governed by unspoken, background assumptions that people rely on to make sense of their interactions. Through his famous breaching experiments, Garfinkel demonstrates how fragile these assumptions are: when social norms are disrupted, it becomes evident how much we depend on implicit trust to maintain social order. For example, in one experiment, Garfinkel asked participants to behave as if they were strangers in their own homes, treating family members as guests and interacting with them in a formal, distant manner. The results were striking – family members were confused, disoriented and often upset – as the disruption of everyday expectations revealed how deeply we rely on trust and shared understanding to navigate even the most basic social interactions.[1]

This insight, I believe, can also be applied to the prison system, which, like many other institutions, relies on a trust that its practices are justified. Drawing on Garfinkel's work, we are encouraged to scrutinise this trust by asking whether imprisonment truly maintains social order – or whether it, in fact, erodes the very trust that holds society together.

In this regard, abolitionist or radical reformist practices may be seen as challenges to the trust upon which the prison system is built. Just as Garfinkel's breaching experiments expose the shaky foundations of social norms, we may

1 Harold Garfinkel. *Studies in Ethnomethodology* (Englewood 1967) s.47.

expose the dysfunctions, inequalities and harms embedded in prisons. Rather than seeking to maintain social order through punitive measures, we must shift our focus to practices that rebuild trust within and between communities in more constructive ways. These practices, which are grounded in principles of love and intersubjective mutual recognition, highlight an alternative vision of social trust – one that does not rely on coercion and control but on cooperation, healing and shared responsibility.

In sum, the idea of loving justice may not offer a tensionless penal project that resolves all complexities, but it provides a vision that has the potential to transform not only the penal system but also the social world that produces it. Therefore, we must seek to develop and implement more models of loving justice – approaches that unsettle the taken-for-granted assumption that traditional imprisonment is the only means by which trust can be established and social order maintained.

Bibliography

Garfinkel H, *Studies in Ethnomethodology* (Englewood 1967)

Index

FSC
www.fsc.org
MIX
Papier | Fördert gute Waldnutzung
FSC® C083411

Kolibri 360 GmbH
Ferdinand-Jühlke-Straße 7
99095 Erfurt, Deutschland
produktsicherheit@kolibri360.de